THE ART OF CONDUCTING

Consulting Editor in Music
ALLAN W. SCHINDLER
The Eastman School of Music of the University of Rochester

THE ART OF CONDUCTING

SECOND EDITION

DONALD HUNSBERGER
ROY E. ERNST

The Eastman School of Music of the University of Rochester

McGRAW-HILL, INC.

New York St. Louis San Francisco Auckland Bogotá Caracas Lisbon London Madrid Mexico Milan Montreal New Delhi Paris San Juan Singapore Sydney Tokyo Toronto

THE ART OF CONDUCTING

18 19 QPD/QPD 0 9 8 7 6 5

ISBN 0-07-031326-1

This book was set in Times Roman by Music-Book Associates, Inc.
The editors were Cynthia Ward and Susan Gamer;
the designer was Rafael Hernandez;
the production supervisor was Annette Mayeski.
The permissions editor was Elsa Peterson.

Quebecor Printing/Dubuque was printer and binder.

Library of Congress Cataloging-in-Publication Data

Hunsberger, Donald.
The art of conducting / Donald Hunsberger, Roy E. Ernst. — 2nd ed.
p. cm.
Includes bibliographical references and index.
ISBN 0-07-031326-1
1. Conducting. I. Ernst, Roy. II. Title.
MT85.H92 1992
781.45—dc20 91-721

ABOUT THE AUTHORS

Donald Hunsberger is Conductor of the Eastman Wind Ensemble and Chair of the Conducting and Ensemble Department at the Eastman School of Music of the University of Rochester. Considered one of the leading international authorities on conducting pedagogy, Dr. Hunsberger is also one of the leading American voices in the development of wind band literature and research.

His research into American theater orchestra repertoire and performance practices led to an association with the Film Archives at the International Museum of Photography at George Eastman House in Rochester, New York. He has presented concerts featuring live orchestral accompaniment to classic silent films with major symphony orchestras such as The National, Milwaukee, and Vancouver, among others, as well as with his own Eastman-Dryden Orchestra.

Dr. Hunsberger is active in wind band and theater orchestra recording; his CD of turn-of-the-century cornet solos featuring Wynton Marsalis and the Eastman Wind Ensemble was nominated for a Grammy Award for "Best Solo with Orchestral Accompaniment." Music from his series of theater orchestra music on Arabesque Records with the Eastman-Dryden Orchestra was included in the sound track of the film *Room with a View.* He has recorded on Sony, CBS Masterworks, DGG, Philips, Mercury, Toshiba EMI, Tioch, and others.

Roy E. Ernst is chair and professor of music education at the Eastman School of Music of the University of Rochester. He teaches courses in curriculum, research, and conducting and rehearsal techniques. He is the founding director of both the Aesthetic Education Institute and the Eastman New Horizons Band. Dr. Ernst was awarded a grant from the National Association of Music merchants to develop the New Horizons Band as a model to encourage similar ensembles throughout the United States. He is active as a consultant for music education and is a frequent clinician and adjudicator. Before moving to the Eastman School of Music in 1975, Dr. Ernst taught at Georgia State University in Atlanta, where he taught flute, conducted the wind ensemble, and was a member of the music education faculty. In 1984, he was a visiting professor at the Sydney Conservatorium of Music in Sydney, Australia.

Dr. Ernst began his career in Michigan, where he taught in elementary and secondary schools, free-lanced as a performer, and taught flute at Wayne State University. He received his Ph. D. from the University of Michigan and studied conducting with Harry M. Begian. He has written numerous articles and books on music education and flute performance.

CONTENTS

Excerpts for Chapter 3

Excerpts for Chapter 4

Excerpt for Chapter 5

Excerpts for Chapter 6

Excerpts for Chapter 7

Excerpts for Chapter 8

Excerpts for Chapter 9

Excerpts for Chapter 11

PREFACE

TO THE INSTRUCTOR

The improvement of college conducting classes is a matter of widespread concern, particularly since a large percentage of graduates will use their conducting skills extensively during their careers and many—perhaps most—will receive no additional formal instruction. The number of students who need to receive individual instruction and experience in a limited amount of class time seems inevitably to make accomplishments too limited.

What can be done to increase the effectiveness of conducting classes, given the amount of class time and the number of students? More specifically: How can classes be organized so that each student will receive as much time as possible to actually conduct? What are the best methods and sequences for presenting instruction? How can instrumentalists and vocalists be accommodated in the same conducting class? What musical repertoire can be conducted and performed in class? How can score reading and analysis be integrated with the development of technique? How can the wide array of background knowledge and administrative skills required to become a successful conductor today be included? These were among the questions that we addressed during 10 years of concentrated evaluation and revision of the basic conducting curriculum at the Eastman School of Music. The organization and instructional materials which were developed are presented in this comprehensive text for introductory through advanced conducting classes consisting of vocalists, instrumentalists, or both.

The techniques and information included in most undergraduate conducting courses are thoroughly covered in the first ten chapters of the book (Section One) and classes that progress only to this point will give students an excellent grasp of the fundamentals of conducting technique. Many instructors will find, as we have, however, that the more efficient procedures and instructional sequence reflected in the text will make it possible to include the additional material in Chapters 11 to 14 (Section Two). If this is not the case, owing to the size of the class or the number of hours available per week, these chapters can be included in subsequent courses rather than the introductory course. These chapters, which take up special topics and techniques, will also serve as an important reference resource for students who are not able to study them in other courses.

The main focus of the text is on conducting technique, score reading, score analysis, and general rehearsal procedures. More detailed information on rehearsal procedures and repertoire for each type of ensemble is expected to be covered in subsequent courses. If the class consists of all vocalists or all instrumentalists, however, this specialized information can be easily integrated.

We have found that concise instructions, directly to the point, are most helpful to students, but this should not be mistaken for a dogmatic approach. Alternative procedures are discussed, and teachers and students are encouraged to consider and analyze still additional alternatives.

Every musical concept or physical skill presented in the text is accompanied by musical excerpts (Section Three) for illustration and conducting practice. The excerpts are long enough to establish a musical context for conducting—not just three or four measures to illustrate a point. We have found—not surprisingly—that students prefer to conduct standard repertoire ("real music," as they say) rather than études. This is also an opportunity to learn additional repertoire. Single-pitch exercises are provided where they will be useful for unison conducting in class.

The musical excerpts have been selected from the standard choral, orchestral, and wind repertoire, so that it is possible for classes with vocalists and instrumentalists to function both as an instrumental ensemble and as a choral ensemble. Classes consisting of vocalists only or instrumentalists only will find sufficient repertoire for each type of ensemble. Classes that are not able to perform some of the more difficult excerpts can use those for analysis and the less difficult excerpts for class performance. We recommend that students perform in class on either their major instrument or a secondary instrument on which they are fairly advanced.

Musical excerpts for the earlier chapters are to be sung (with piano accompaniment) and conducted by the class in unison with the instructor. This enables the class to learn and practice each technique before individual students conduct—an efficient procedure that makes it possible for the class to learn the fundamentals of technique very quickly. Instruments can be added to the vocal line when individuals conduct the class.

For the later chapters, instrumental excerpts are included that are arranged for performance by small groups of random instrumentation. Students are expected to transpose, if necessary, when playing easy excerpts. Transposed performance parts are included for more difficult excerpts.

Developing fluency and confidence in score-reading techniques—clefs, transpositions, and orchestration schemes—requires continual practice over a long period of time. Some of the exercises for reading clefs and transpositions, however, can be omitted if this has been adequately covered in other courses and time does not permit additional practice. These can also be grouped and reviewed as a single unit. Score-reading assignments include reading clefs and transpositions working toward a comprehensive analysis of compositions.

The Appendixes (Section Four) include a course description, daily exercises, seating charts, forms for planning and organization, a glossary, and a selection of recommended readings.

ABOUT THE SECOND EDITION

Several changes have been made in the second edition. The content has been reorganized on the basis of evaluations of conducting classes at Eastman and the suggestions of conducting teachers from other universities who have used the first edition. This process has affirmed that there is more than one good way to organize the material; and although we feel that the present organization works very well, we encourage you to make changes in the sequence of topics to suit your own preferences and needs.

New repertoire has been added to this edition. We have selected a broad variety of good repertoire that students will enjoy. It is possible to achieve musical results with almost any combination of singers and instrumentalists by creatively adapting the excerpts for the class. Students should be encouraged to make their own decisions about how to use the performing resources of the class. The excerpts are now presented as an Anthology (Section Three) rather than at the end of each chapter. This should make it more convenient for students to use excerpts from any of the chapters to supplement those for the chapter currently under study.

Aural analysis sections and other exercises have been added to give students more practice in analyzing performance and making musical decisions. We recommend taping the class so that students will be analyzing real performances rather than performances with contrived mistakes. A "designated listener" procedure also gives students more practice in analyzing real performance. New assignments and tests make students more accountable for the aspects of technique that they should be able to accomplish through individual practice. This makes it possible to devote more class time to rehearsal techniques and other aspects of musical leadership.

Chapter 5, on score reading and rehearsal techniques, is entirely new. It provides a systematic approach to score study and a basic repertoire of rehearsal techniques. Both of these are presented so that they will be treated as the beginning of a learning process that can be continued throughout an entire career.

An Instructor's Guide consisting of teaching suggestions for use with this new edition is available from the publisher. It discusses priorities for the use of time, procedures for emphasizing musical leadership, and other objective and subjective factors for consideration in evaluating and improving the teaching of conducting.

ACKNOWLEDGMENTS

We want to express our appreciation to Carl Atkins, John Boyd, Donald Kendrick, Grzegorz Nowak, Michael Ramey, Munro Sherrill, and Rodney Winther, who used the first edition in its early stages of development and assisted with its evaluation. Jeffrey Renshaw, Craig Arnold, Shinik Ham, Peggy Dettwiler, Gerald Floriano, and John Russo provided many helpful suggestions based on their use of a draft of this second edition. The comments and suggestions from the following people, who reviewed the manuscript of the first edition, were extremely helpful in making revisions: John Boyd, Kent State University; Joseph L. Estock, James Madison University; C. Dale Fjerstad, University of the Pacific; Robert C. Fleming, Arizona State University; Craig J. Kirchhoff, Ohio State University; Albert F. Ligotti, University of Georgia; H. Robert Reynolds, University of Michigan; Barry M. Shank, East Carolina University; and Charles H. Webb, Indiana University, Bloomington. We also want to thank the following people, who reviewed the second edition and made many helpful suggestions: Robert Erbes, Michigan State University; Allen Gross, Occidental College; Brian Moore, University of Nebraska, Lincoln; David Nelson, University of New Orleans; Douglas A. Nelson, Keene State College; Carl Topilow, Cleveland Institute of Music; Carlton R. Woods, University of Arkansas.

We are deeply indebted to Susan Gamer, our editing supervisor at McGraw-Hill, for her editorial revisions of this second edition; to our sponsoring editor, Cynthia Ward; to our consulting editor in music, Allan Schindler; and to our designer, Rafael Hernandez.

Finally, we are particularly indebted to the many students with whom we have worked, both at Eastman and throughout the United States, whose enthusiasm and musicianship are a constant source of inspiration to us. We hope that this book will help many of them to have rewarding musical careers.

Donald Hunsberger
Roy E. Ernst

INTRODUCTION

TO THE STUDENT

Conducting is a great privilege—an opportunity to use the vast resources of musical composition and performance for artistic creativity. It also carries with it many responsibilities, particularly to the composer, the members of the ensemble, the audience, and the conductor's own standards of musical and personal integrity.

To become a conductor, scholarship is essential, for in addition to possessing the skills to analyze a score thoroughly before rehearsal, a conductor must be able to draw upon extensive knowledge and long experience to develop the inherent, distinctive characteristics of each composition. Interpretation of any composition requires a knowledge of the composer's other works and of how this composer's style is similar to or different from that of his or her contemporaries, predecessors, and followers. The ability to clearly differentiate compositional and performance styles will result in performances that are distinctive and interesting, while failure to do so usually results in bland and monotonous renditions. Even the experience of many years of conducting will not lead to convincing, stylistically valid interpretations if the conductor's research and analysis habits are superficial rather than thorough.

In addition to possessing a broad knowledge of traditional repertoire, conductors should study the works of contemporary composers—the music of their own time—and develop the special knowledge and skills necessary for analyzing, interpreting, and conducting contemporary compositions. Jazz performance and musical theater are important areas of contemporary composition that should not be ignored.

The conductor must be worthy of leading other musicians, allowing his or her conducting abilities and other accomplishments as a musician to speak for themselves without indulging in pompous self-flattery. Conductors must be able to inspire and challenge musicians to perform at their highest possible level through instructive assistance that is supportive and positive rather than intimidating and destructive. Fortunately, the era has passed when it was common for egotistical or personally insecure conductors to psychologically abuse performers through verbal intimidation. Such actions are usually an attempt to draw attention away from the conductor's own deficiencies. A conductor should never hesitate to display sincere caring for the performers and the music being performed.

In addition to scholarship, a clear, fluent conducting technique is essential. A secure technique enables a conductor to concentrate entirely on the needs of the performers and the music. It also serves to reduce the use of verbal instruction during the rehearsal, since performers will recognize good technique and react positively to it. A polished technique by itself is not sufficient, however, it is only the means through which the conductor expresses knowledge and musicianship. Flamboyant and dramatic gestures made primarily to impress an audience should not be mistaken for good conducting technique.

Conductors frequently must be responsible for administrative details that are essentially nonmusical but can become critical obstructions if neglected. An enormous amount of behind-the-scenes detail work is necessary for the successful operation of a musical ensemble. The conductor's objective is to develop organizational procedures to handle each problem as efficiently as possible.

The subject of right-handed and left-handed conductors is frequently discussed. According to the traditional concept, the right hand is primarily assigned to beating time patterns while the left hand is relegated to indicating sostenuto support, dynamic levels, cuing, and so forth. Today, however, conductors face musical tasks so complex that they must be able to use either hand independently. To perform Renaissance antiphonal choir music, contemporary aleatoric and proportional-notation compositions, or accompaniments of all periods requires a free and independent use of *both* hands for rhythmic pulse, cuing, or dynamics. Thus an *ambidextrous approach* is essential for the beginning conductor.

There are many different styles of conducting. In presenting, for example, a particular style of beat pattern, we do not intend to imply that we consider it superior to other styles, or that you must use one particular style to be a good conductor. We are well aware that many conducting teachers will prefer different styles, and we encourage their inclusion from the beginning. We feel that students will be well served if they learn both the basic style suggested in the text and alternatives that their instructors recommend. Both can then be used as points of reference to evaluate the infinity of alternatives that will be encountered or discovered in the future.

Once the fundamental knowledge and techniques are acquired, each conductor must strive to develop an individual style and personality—avoiding the common tendency to mimic other conductors. Do not hesitate to learn from others, but be selective in what you choose to adapt to your own style. You must be able to analyze the logic and validity of the many dogmatic concepts and myths about conducting. For each new technique you try, ask yourself such questions as these: What are the advantages for my own development? What are the disadvantages? In what type of situation would this work best? Where would an alternative technique work better? Using this analytical approach—rather than attempting to reduce conducting to a set of simple rules—will lead you, as a musically sincere conductor, to continuous intellectual growth and superior conducting capabilities.

THE ART OF CONDUCTING

SECTION ONE

BASIC PRINCIPLES AND TECHNIQUES

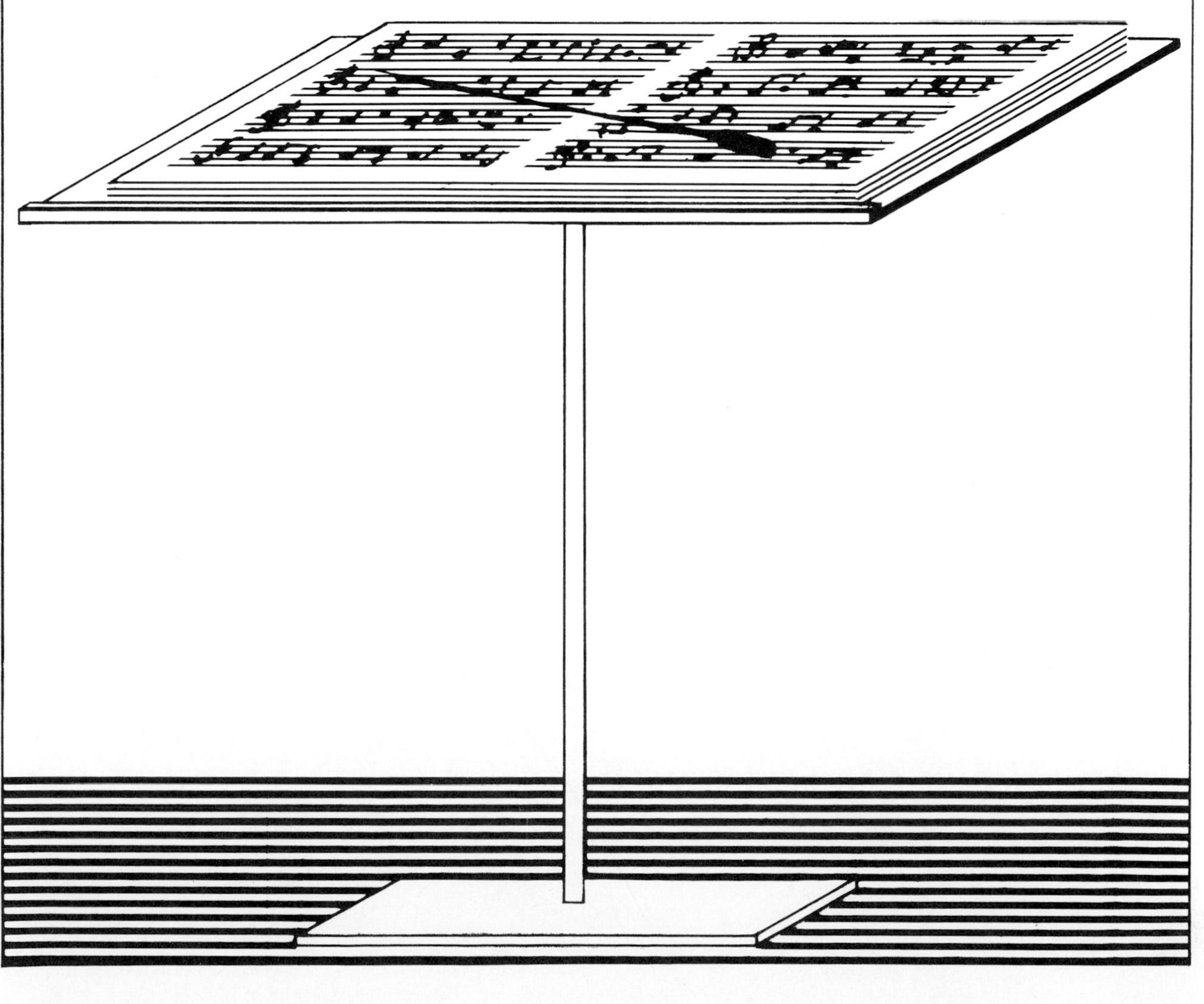

CHAPTER 1

POSTURE

PREPARATORY GESTURES AND DOWNBEATS

RELEASES FOUR- AND THREE-BEAT PATTERNS

STYLE OF ARTICULATION

POSTURE

The foundation of good conducting technique begins with correct posture. A knowledge of how each aspect of posture affects conducting will lead to maximum physical flexibility and will give a general impression of confident leadership and artistic elegance.

Stance

The following stance is recommended for beginning conductors. Slight variations will develop naturally as each person's individual conducting style begins to take form.

- Stand erect with your feet 5 or 6 inches apart, toes pointed slightly outward. This position will provide good balance and allow you to turn comfortably to each side. (Some conductors develop the habit of placing one foot forward, creating a tendency to face one side of the ensemble more than the other. This presents a somewhat lopsided appearance to the audience.)
- Keep your knees straight but not locked. Distribute your weight evenly on both feet.
- Keep your shoulders back, though not uncomfortably stiff or rigid.
- Hold your head high with your neck relaxed. Avoid holding or twisting your head to one side or the other, as this may produce tension in the neck and shoulders and possibly cause you to turn the entire body in that direction.
- When you turn your upper body to face sections of the ensemble, do not give the impression that your feet are immobile or fastened to the floor. Change your foot position for a more decisive turn or move.

Practice this stance and experiment with variations that feel natural to you.

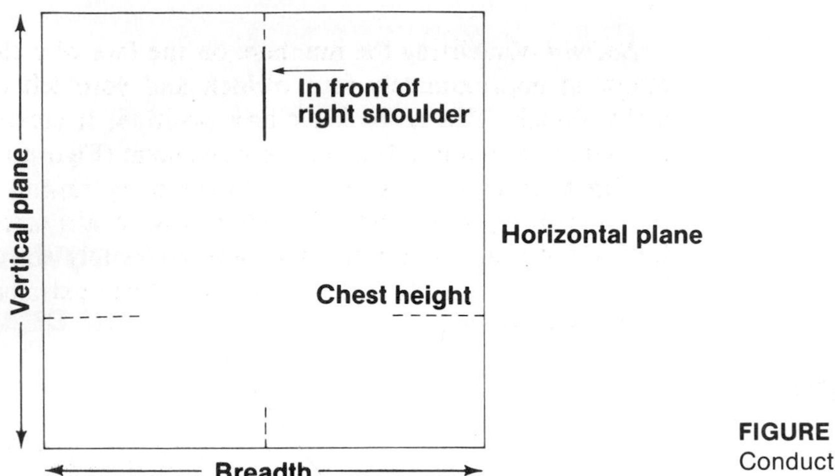

FIGURE 1-1
Conducting area.

Conducting Area

Ordinarily, the conducting area extends from the top of the head to the waist (approximately the height to which a conductor's stand is generally raised) for vertical strokes, and the full reach of the arms to either side for horizontal strokes. The horizontal center of the beat patterns should be approximately at chest height. The vertical beat patterns should be in front of the body slightly to the right of center for the right hand (approximately in front of the right shoulder) and slightly to the left of center for the left hand (again in front of the shoulder area). (See Figure 1-1.)

Arm Position

To develop a basic arm position, do the following (see Figures 1-2 and 1-3):

First, fully extend both arms in front of your body. Retract your hands toward your chest until the bending of the elbows creates an angle of slightly more than 90 degrees between the upper arm and the forearm. Your elbows should be in front of your body, not by your sides. Figure 1-2 illustrates this position.

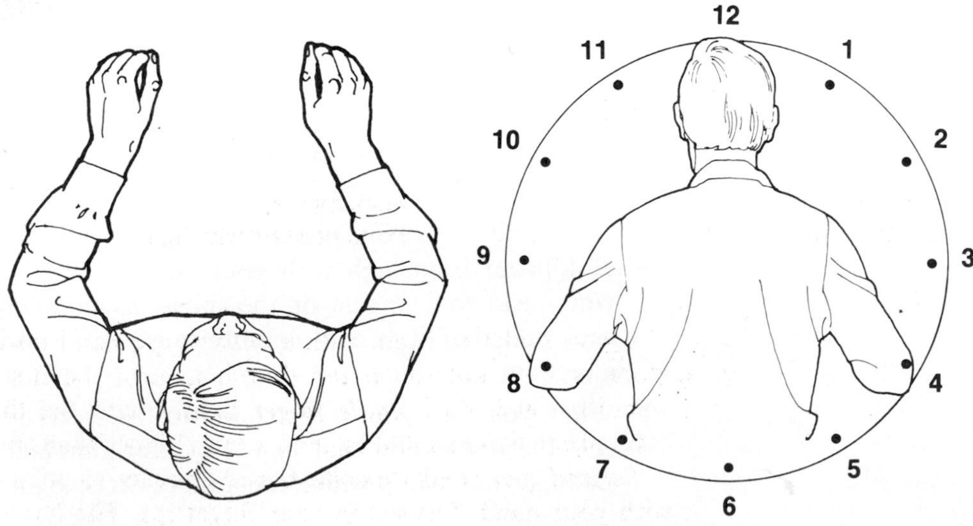

FIGURE 1-2
Conducting arm position viewed from above.

FIGURE 1-3
Conducting arm position viewed from the back.

Second, visualizing the numbers on the face of a clock, position your right elbow at approximately four o'clock and your left elbow at approximately eight o'clock. This is the basic arm position. It creates a natural appearance and allows maximum freedom of movement (Figure 1-3).

Third, practice adjusting this position by raising the right elbow to the three-o'clock position and the left elbow to a nine-o'clock position. Rotate both elbows and lower them to approximately six o'clock, or close to the body. Be aware of the feeling of each of these extreme positions. Now return to the basic position.

Hand Position

It is best to begin learning the basic beat patterns without a baton, because this approach encourages a more relaxed and natural grip when you add the baton later. Also, developing the ability to "feel the pulse" in your hand will assist you when the baton is used. If your instructor prefers to begin the entire process with a baton, however, read "Using the Baton" in Chapter 3 (pages 30–35) before proceeding.

To develop a basic hand position, do the following.

First, turn the palm of the right hand downward with a slight inward roll and lightly touch the thumb against the first finger at the first joint. Curve the remaining fingers inward naturally toward the palm. This will be approximately the same shape as the hand assumes when it is hanging, relaxed, by your side. It is also the same basic shape you will use later with the baton. Positioning the thumb against the first finger will help to control the shape and prepare for the use of a baton. (See Figures 1-4 and 1-5.) This is not, however, a hand position that would be used by most choral conductors.

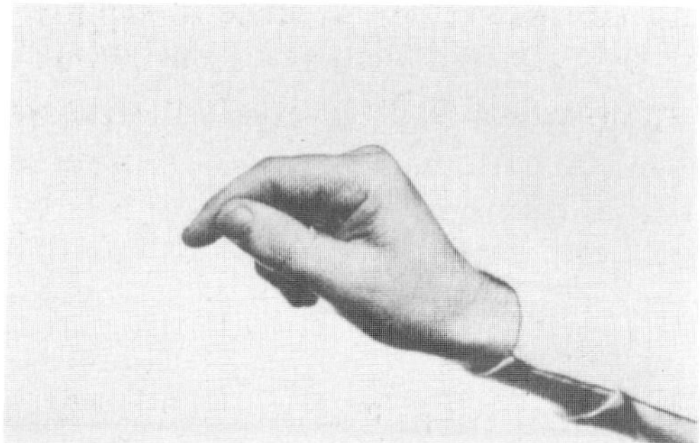

FIGURE 1-4
Hand position without baton.

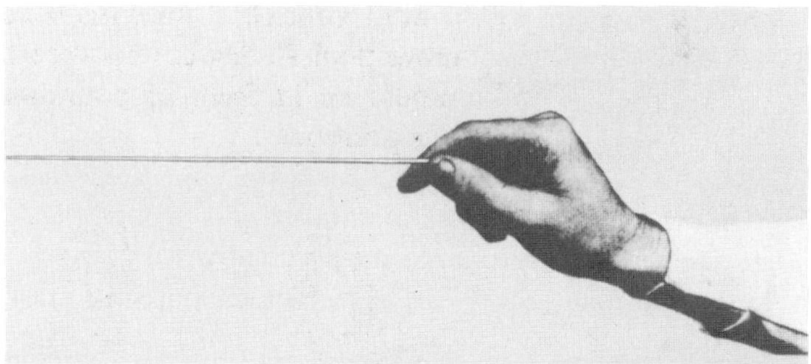

FIGURE 1-5
Hand position with baton.

If you prefer to begin with a *choral-type* hand position, open your fingers more and do not touch the thumb against the first finger. You may also want to touch the *middle finger* lightly with the thumb. In any case, the back of the hand should be held a little higher than the wrist.

Second, give small downbeats and upbeats, in order to feel a rhythmic pulse with your hand, focused in your fingertips. The hand should flex downward slightly at the wrist as downbeats are given, as though you were flicking water from your fingers. Observe the wrist action carefully; too much motion will produce a floppy effect, and too little motion will appear stiff and rigid.

PREPARATORY GESTURES AND DOWNBEATS

It takes a great deal of practice and analysis to produce consistently clear and rhythmical preparatory gestures and downbeats. These introductory motions must convey:

- Exact beginning of the first tone
- Dynamic level
- Articulation style of the opening statement
- Tempo

Practice giving preparatory gestures and downbeats as follows:

1 Assume the basic conducting positions described above. Check the position of your feet, shoulders, and head. Extend your right hand and arm to the position shown in Figures 1-2 and 1-3. Let your left arm hang in a comfortable position by your side.

2 Give a preparatory gesture and downbeat, inhaling slightly as you raise your hand through the preparatory gesture. Breathe quietly—do not make a loud gasp. Breathing along with the preparatory gesture places the conductor in a sympathetic position with regard to the performers, who will usually breathe on the preparatory beat. It will also help to avoid rushing on the preparatory gesture.

3 Bring your hand downward to the same horizontal plane where the preparatory gesture began (see Figure 1-6, opposite page) and sing a syllable such as *tu* or *du*. The tone should begin at the point when the downward motion stops. The hand can either remain in this position or make a slight upward rebound. The precise moment when the metric pulse is felt and the tone begins is called the *ictus*.

When making preparatory gestures and downbeats, always establish eye contact with your performers and pause for a moment until you sense their concentration and readiness. Practice until the breathing motion, the preparatory gesture, and the downbeat are coordinated within an overall feeling of rhythmic flow. Practice the patterns in Figure 1-6.

The various parts of the preparatory gesture and downbeat should be carefully analyzed to see how they indicate specific musical qualities, such as dynamic level, style of articulation, and tempo. For example, the size and intensity of the preparatory gesture and the downbeat gesture can indicate an expected *dynamic level*. You may want to concentrate on the size of the gesture at this point. Intensity is more difficult to convey; it comes from the total effect of posture, facial expression, and muscle tension.

The contour and speed of the preparatory gesture will indicate *articulation style*. An abrupt, angular motion would indicate an accented or *staccato* style; a smooth, curved gesture indicates a more flowing, *legato* style. (These styles are discussed later in the chapter.)

It is particularly important to analyze how the *tempo* is set. In a scientific sense, setting the tempo means defining a unit of time duration that will be repeated exactly to create a steady metric pulse. Just as two specific points in space are needed to define a unit of distance, two specific points in time are needed to define a unit of duration.

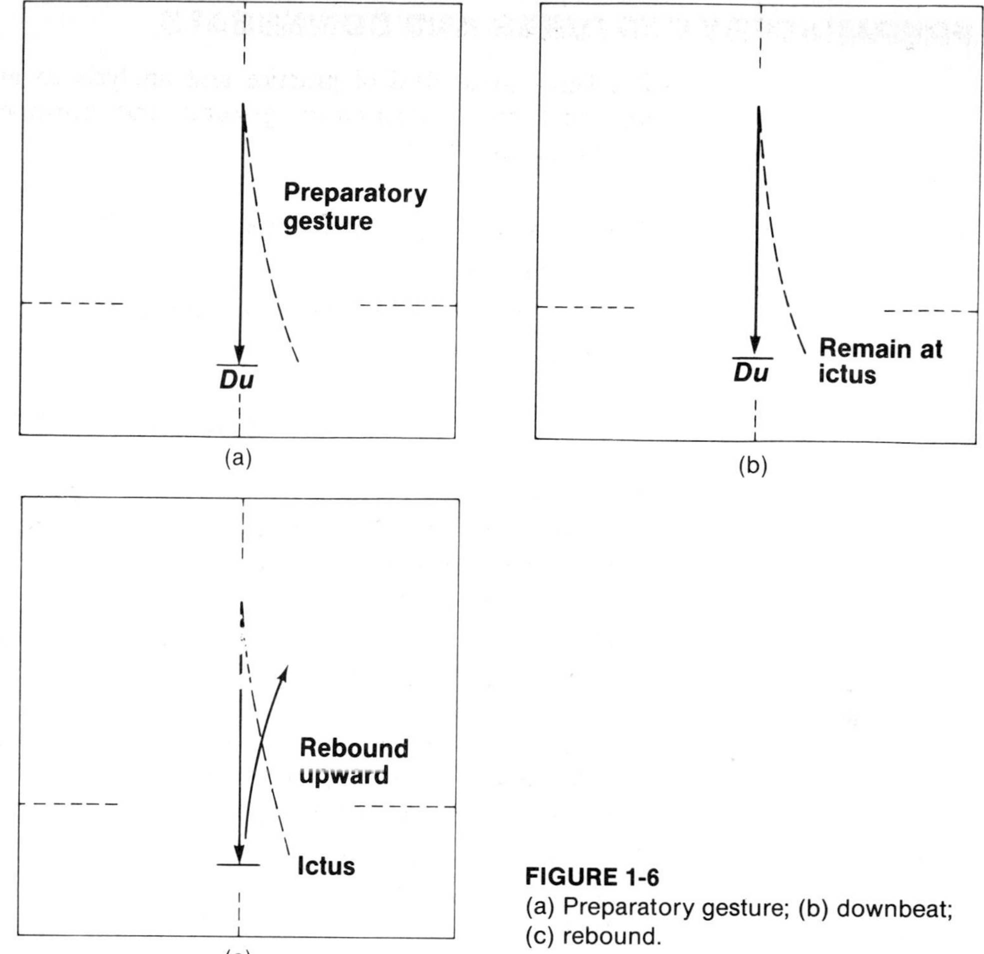

FIGURE 1-6
(a) Preparatory gesture; (b) downbeat; (c) rebound.

The beginning of the preparatory gesture cannot be consistently identified by observers as a specific point in time because it is impossible to recognize the exact moment when motion begins; thus the upward motion from the beginning to the end of the preparatory gesture gives only an approximation of the tempo. The end of the preparatory gesture, which we will now call the *preparatory ictus,* can be observed as a specific point in time. Therefore, the duration of time between the preparatory ictus and the downbeat ictus precisely defines the length of metric unit or pulse. (See Figure 1-7.)

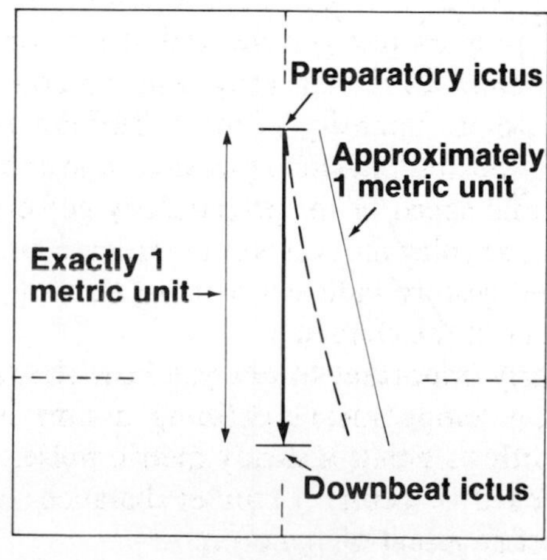

FIGURE 1-7
Defining the tempo.

PRACTICING PREPARATORY GESTURES

Now practice giving preparatory gestures as shown in Figure 1-8. Do not continue conducting after the downbeat, but continue singing *du* on the pulse established by the preparatory ictus and the downbeat ictus. Repeat this at different tempos. Your conducting should enable the class to sing the right dynamic level, articulation style, and tempo consistently and confidently from the information communicated by only the preparatory gesture and downbeat.

FIGURE 1-8
Exercise for preparatory gesture and downbeat. The conductor should try different dynamic levels, articulation styles, and tempos.

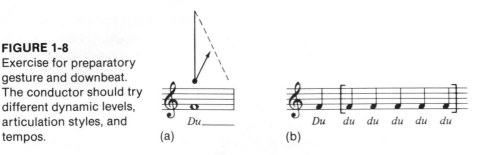

With practice, all the aspects of the preparatory gesture and downbeat described above can interact with each other to produce an infinite range of subtle variations. A clear, secure technique must be developed, as the slightest indecision can produce disastrous and demoralizing results. Performers quickly lose confidence in conductors who do not give consistently clear and confident preparatory gestures and downbeats.

RELEASES

There are an infinite number of ways to release the sound, but only one basic pattern is required at this time. Prepare the release with an upward motion and make an ictus with a downward motion as shown in Figure 1-9. The stopping of the downward motion, with or without rebound, will create an ictus that indicates the precise point at which the sound should end or, in singing, the point at which the final consonant should be articulated. In some situations, you may want to make the up-and-down motion in the shape of a loop. Practice this motion with various speeds and sizes. Stretch out the upward motion if you want to sustain the last note.

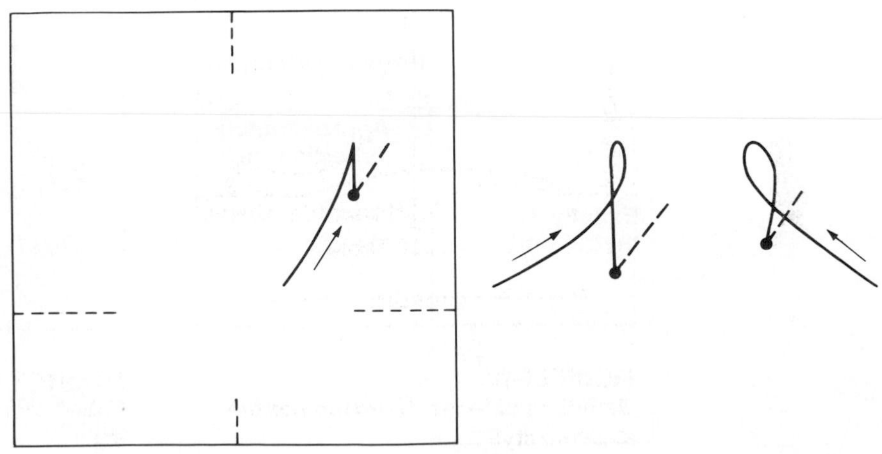

FIGURE 1-9
Release, up-down.

The size of the release motion should be consistent with the dynamic level and style of the music. Avoid the tendency to use a large circular motion constantly, for all styles of music. Practice each type of release along with the preparatory gesture and downbeat exercises described above. Think of how you want the release to sound, and make a visual representation with your gesture.

FOUR- AND THREE-BEAT PATTERNS

Several different styles and shapes of beat patterns can be used. The type of beat pattern recommended at this point, called the *modified classical style,* places the ictus of the downbeat on a slightly lower plane than the ictus of beats to the left or right, making the downbeat ictus more prominent. The ictus for the two sideward beats should occur at the extremities of the pattern: for example, the ictus for beat 2 in a four-beat pattern will be at the extreme left and the ictus for beat 3 at the extreme right. This style of beat pattern is probably the easiest for performers to follow, since the distinctive character of each ictus can be easily seen from any direction.

Later chapters will show patterns in which the location of ictuses can be changed for expressive purposes, generally moving more toward the center of the pattern for legato styles.

Some conductors may want to use other styles of patterns and will choose to modify the patterns shown in the diagrams which follow. Other styles are described in Chapter 2.

Four-Beat Patterns

Figure 1-10 illustrates useful reference points in the conducting area, with the horizontal broken line indicating approximate chest height. The center of the pattern, indicated by the vertical broken line, should be approximately in front of the shoulder. The articulation style shown here for the four-beat pattern is somewhat staccato, with the ictuses at the extremities of each direction in the pattern. Figure 1-11 shows a more rounded pattern for a legato-style four-beat pattern.

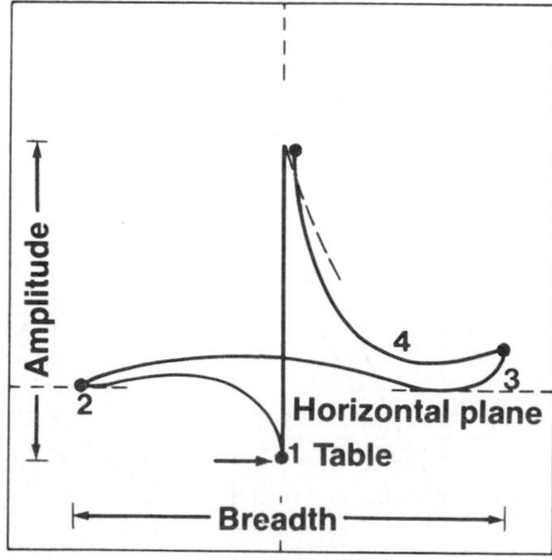

FIGURE 1-10
Definition of terms: four-beat pattern, staccato style.

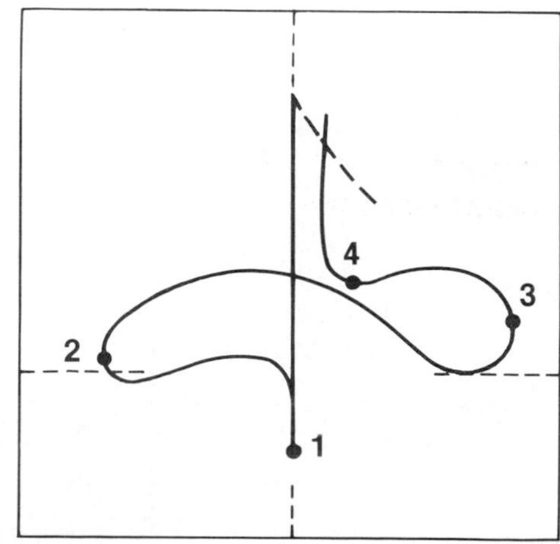

FIGURE 1-11
Four-beat pattern, rounded for legato style.

With a martial air (♩= 120)
f
Let ty - rants shake their i - ron rod,
and slav - 'ry clank her gall - ing chains.

FIGURE 1-12
William Billings, "Chester."

Practice the four-beat pattern in unison with your instructor, varying the size and speed of the movements. At first, stop at the ictus of each beat while your instructor checks your body position, arm position, and hand position. Next, practice singing and conducting the melodic excerpt in Figure 1-12. (Practice singing and conducting all the excerpts in the text as you come to them.)

Three-Beat Patterns

Practice conducting the angular and rounded three-beat patterns shown in Figures 1-13 and 1-14. At first, stop at the ictus of each beat to check hand and arm position; then conduct the pattern without stopping. Sing and practice conducting the melodic excerpt in Figure 1-15.

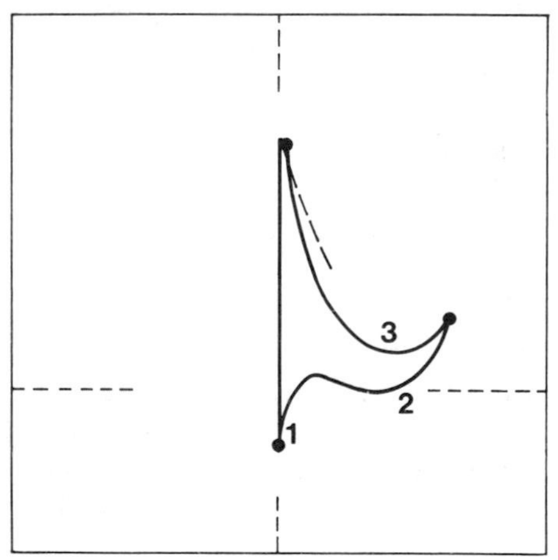
3
2
1

FIGURE 1-13
Three-beat pattern, angular.

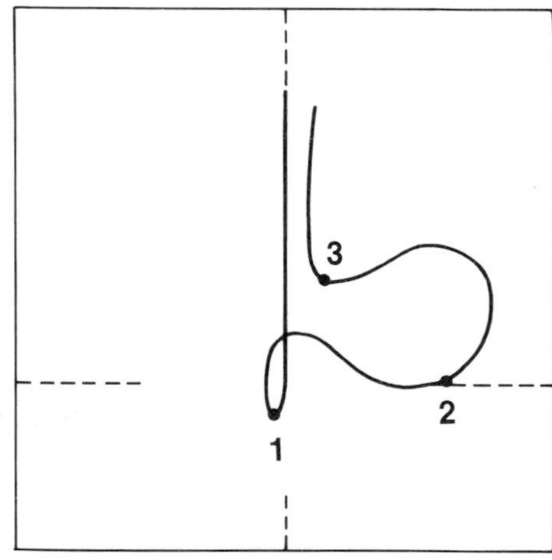
3
2
1

FIGURE 1-14
Three-beat pattern, rounded.

FIGURE 1-15
Traditional, "Aura Lee."
Verse 3.

Moderato ♩= 104
mf
When the mis - tle - toe was green, midst the win - ter snows,
sun - shine in thy face was seen, kiss - ing lips of rose

Pattern Clarity

Two common problems can detract from the clarity of beat patterns—*lack of rebound control* and *insufficient horizontal motion.*

The distance of the *rebound* should be less than half the length of the beat itself. (The one-beat pattern, described in Chapter 3, is an exception.) An overly large rebound tends to make the following beat look like another downbeat, as shown in Figure 1-16. This is probably the most frequent cause of beat patterns that are unclear to performers. Compare this with Figure 1-17, which shows a beat pattern with better control of the rebound. Practice conducting three-beat and four-beat patterns with a small rebound and then an overly large rebound, and study the effect of the size of the rebound on the clarity of the patterns.

Failure to use sufficient *horizontal motion* for beats to the left or right also detracts from the clarity of patterns. Figure 1-18 shows a four-beat pattern that is somewhat unclear because the rightward horizontal motion is not sufficient, placing beat 3 too close to the location of beats 1 and 4. Compare this with Figure 1-19, which is clearer because of the increased horizontal motion.

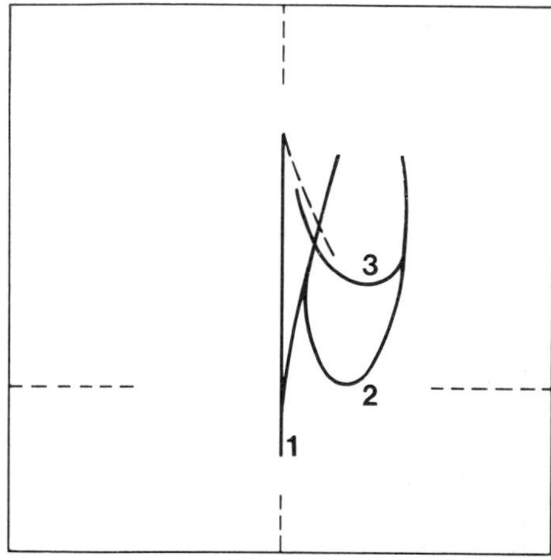

FIGURE 1-16
Three-beat pattern; rebound too large.

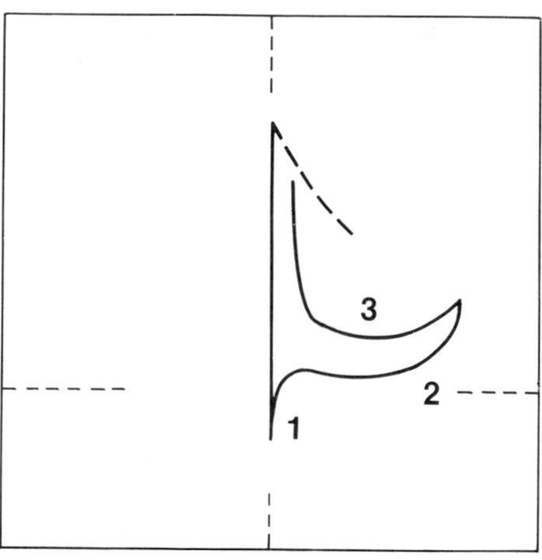

FIGURE 1-17
Three-beat pattern; rebound controlled for greater clarity.

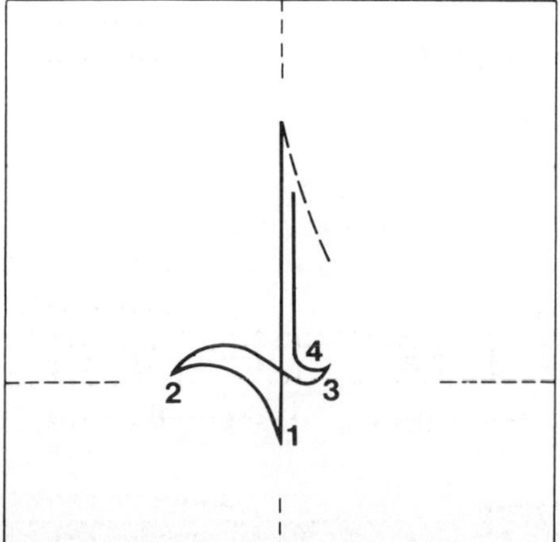

FIGURE 1-18
Four-beat pattern; insufficient horizontal motion.

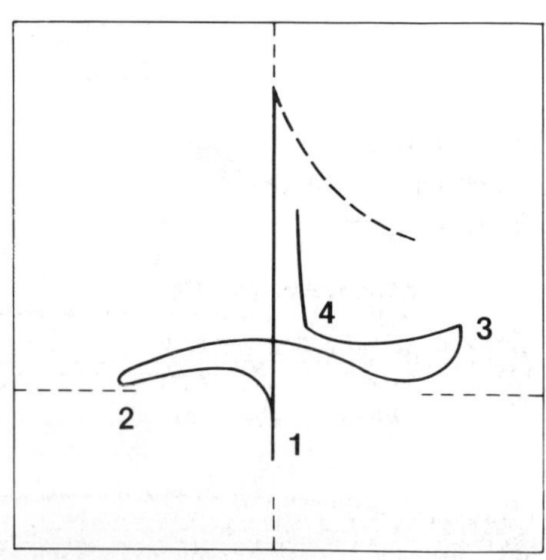

FIGURE 1-19
Four-beat pattern; more horizontal motion for greater clarity.

STYLE OF ARTICULATION

Style of articulation is indicated by the shape of the beat pattern and the speed of the movement from one ictus to the next. The movement from ictus to ictus is called *travel.*

Staccato Style

In a staccato style, the beat pattern is usually angular, as shown in Figure 1-20, and the travel is quick.

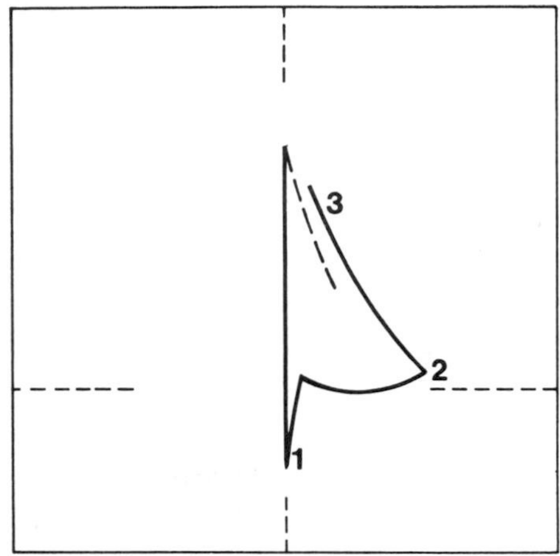

FIGURE 1-20
Three-beat pattern, staccato style.

The travel should make a definite stop either at the ictus or after the rebound from the ictus. Stopping after the rebound is often done with a quick flicking motion of the wrist leading to and rebounding from the ictus. This is commonly called a *click beat* because of the quickness of the wrist motion. The click motion is nearly always used in indicating staccato, but staccato can also be indicated with a motion primarily of the arm for a heavier staccato style. Practice four-beat and three-beat patterns in staccato-style, using a slow tempo at first and carefully analyzing the movements. Then practice conducting and singing the excerpt in Figure 1-21.

FIGURE 1-21
Gioacchino Rossini, *L'Italiana in Algeri* ("The Italian Girl in Algiers").

Legato Style

Legato style is indicated by rounded beat patterns, as shown in Figure 1-22, and by the smooth, even travel from one ictus to the next. Notice also that the ictuses are not at the extreme direction but rather are somewhat closer to the pattern's center, to show a stretching out of the travel after each ictus. In legato-style conducting, the *motion between ictuses* must receive careful attention. This motion should convey the desired breadth of sound and flowing quality.

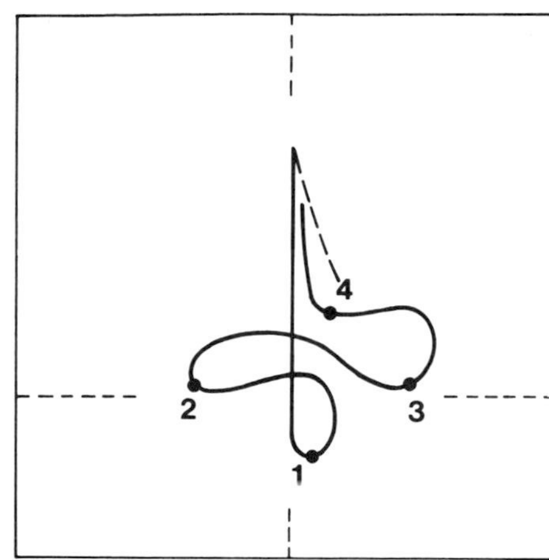

FIGURE 1-22
Four-beat pattern, legato style.

Moving the hands slowly and smoothly in a way that will emphasize the sustained quality of the sound usually requires considerable practice. It may help at first to pretend that you are moving your hand against a resisting force, like what you would feel when stretching a strong elastic cord or when moving your hand through a thick liquid. It may also be helpful to think of slowly painting the pattern with a brush. Practice conducting and singing the excerpt in Figure 1-23. (Four- and three-beat patterns and the excerpt in Figure 1-21 can also be practiced in legato style.)

FIGURE 1-23
Maurice Ravel, *Pavane pour une enfante défunte* ("Pavane for a Dead Princess").

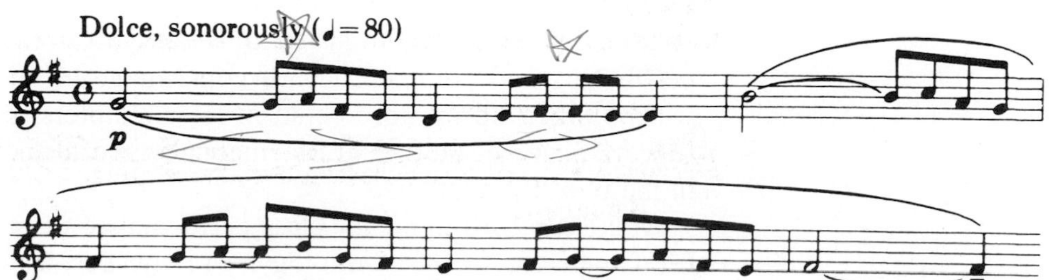

CONDUCTING THE CLASS

When preparing to conduct the class, it is important to set the correct tempo for a composition with the preparatory gesture and the downbeat. Do not make a rough estimation of the tempo in your mind and then change it slightly in the first measure or two. Think through one or more sections of the composition before raising your hand to give the preparatory gesture, keeping in mind that the opening measures may not always provide the most reliable feeling for the correct tempo; often a section in faster note values or a strongly rhythmic section will be a better guide.

Practice conducting the class in two ways, using the musical excerpts in Section Three (pages 163–171). *First,* give only the preparatory gesture and the downbeat for the opening measure to practice setting the tempo and the articulation style. Have the class sing the first few measures on a neutral syllable. The purpose of this procedure is to focus on the preparatory gesture and downbeat and rely entirely on them to determine the character of the performance. Deliberately change one aspect, such as the tempo or the dynamic level, to see if the class can follow.

Next, conduct through the entire excerpt with the class singing the upper-staff melodic line accompanied by a pianist. Check the following points as you practice:

1 Is your posture commanding?

2 Are your hand position and your arm position correct?

3 Are you breathing rhythmically with the preparatory gesture?

4 Are the preparatory gesture and the downbeat a rhythmic motion with no pause or hesitation?

5 Can you feel the ictus with your hand?

6 Can you imagine the sound of the opening notes?

7 Are you communicating the proper articulation style and dynamic level?

8 Is the release gesture clear and of appropriate size?

AURAL ANALYSIS

Developing a good baton technique is the easiest part of conducting. You also need to develop musicianship and learn how to use it as a conductor. First, you must have a vivid image of what you want to hear. This is a result of all your experiences as a musician and your study of the score being conducted. You need to listen to what you are actually hearing from the performers and compare it with your image of what you should hear. This will be taken up in more detail in later chapters, but you should begin now to work on it constantly and systematically. Aural analysis exercises are included in many of the chapters.

Make a recording of the class performance of at least four of the excerpts for Chapter 1 in the Anthology. Use the best equipment available, but do it even if you can only use a portable cassette recorder. You will be surprised at how much you can hear, even on an inexpensive recorder. If the class is being videotaped, you can use the audio portion of the tape. (Try turning off the picture in order to concentrate on the sound. As an optional step, you can then look at the picture after evaluating the sound to discuss how the conducting influenced what was heard.)

AURAL ANALYSIS FORM FOR CHAPTER 1

Name: ____________________ Date: __________

Evaluate each of the recorded excerpts for the following: *precision of entrance; precision of release; expressive quality of release; tempo; style of rhythm and articulation; balance and blend;* and *quality of unison.* You can also list other factors that seem important to you. For each piece, list in priority order two things that are particularly good and the two things that most need improvement.

First excerpt: ____________________

Second excerpt: ____________________

Third excerpt: ____________________

Fourth excerpt: ____________________

After the class has discussed and compared observations, listen to the tape again to try to hear more and to confirm or revise your first observations. List some of the things that others heard and you missed, for your future attention.

You will be asked to listen for specific things in the aural analysis exercises, but we do *not* present them in the form of a checklist for each piece, because you will not use a checklist when you conduct. As you fill out the form, simply list one or two aspects of the performance that are particularly good and one or two aspects that need to be improved.

The aural analysis exercises can be done individually, with the class, or both. Doing the exercises in class is highly recommended because you can compare your own observations with those of your classmates. Don't be intimidated, however, when someone hears something that you did not hear; it is normal for each student to hear different things. You will learn from each other.

ASSIGNMENTS

1 Practice preparatory gestures and downbeats, checking yourself against the list on page 6.

2 Practice conducting the excerpts for this chapter in Section Three, using the following approach:

- Sing the excerpt through to develop a sense of the melodic line, the rhythmic movement of the keyboard accompaniment, and the harmonic movement. *Form a clear mental image of what you want to hear.*
- Make your preparatory gesture reflect the mood or style and tempo of the excerpt.
- Conduct the excerpt in two ways: while singing the melodic line and while hearing it internally without singing.

3 Use a large mirror for practice. Observe your posture, hand movements, and arm movements.

4 Reread the chapter to be sure that you remember all the details that go into a good technical foundation.

ADDITIONAL EXERCISES

The Preparatory Gesture

You can benefit from carefully analyzing each detail of the preparatory gesture, asking yourself, "Does this work? If so, exactly how does it work?" Analyze other concepts of preparatory gestures in the same way, experimenting and using a scientific attitude.

1 Make only the upward gesture to the preparatory ictus and see if it can define a unit of time. Try setting different tempos, and ask other class members to sing a pulse on *du* at what they perceive the tempo to be. There may be some success because this does give an *approximation* of tempo; but the *beginning* of the preparatory gesture cannot be precisely observed.

2 Now have class members sing *du* on both the preparatory ictus and the downbeat ictus and then continue the pulse. Do it again, feeling the upbeat ictus but starting to sing the pulse on the downbeat ictus.

3 Try experimenting with a rounded up-down motion that does not define a preparatory ictus.

Knowing how the various aspects of the preparatory gesture function may seem at first like unnecessary attention to detail, but it will enable you to improve your technique by analyzing exactly what aspect of the gesture needs to be changed to achieve a particular effect.

Metronome Markings

Conductors must often be able to make very close approximations of metronome markings for setting tempos. This ability can be developed through systematic study and practice over a long period of time. Begin with the following steps:

1 Select three compositions from your personal repertoire—one fast, one moderate, and one slow—that you know well and usually perform consistently at the same tempo.

2 Check the tempo of each composition by using a metronome or a watch with a sweep second hand. To check tempo with a watch, sing or play a section to establish the tempo, then count beats for 15 seconds, starting the count with zero. Multiply the number of beats in 15 seconds by 4 to give the metronome marking. For example: 18 counts in 15 seconds equals 18 × 4 = ♩ = 72MM. This is a convenient and accurate procedure which should be practiced frequently.

3 Use these three compositions as points of reference for estimating other tempos. Add more compositions at other tempos to your repertoire over a period of time.

Muscle Conditioning

Many beginning conductors are surprised to discover that some muscles become tired and sore after even a relatively short period of conducting. This is usually a temporary problem, but poor posture and unnecessary tension, if uncorrected, can cause continual soreness and sometimes bursitis.

Good posture and a general knowledge of how the main areas of skeletal muscles function will help you develop a conducting technique free of unnecessary tension and unnecessarily restricted movement. The following exercises will help to acquaint you with muscle locations. Do them by tightening and releasing each muscle area in turn.

1 Stand with your feet at approximately a 45-degree angle. Slowly raise your heels and shift your weight toward the front of your feet. Feel the muscles contracting in your calves and thighs. Return to the starting position.

2 Slowly raise both arms, palms down, in front of your body to shoulder height and hold them parallel to the floor. Continue holding this position while again rising up on your toes. Slowly squeeze your hands into fists. Feel the tightening in your forearms, your biceps, your shoulders, and across your back. Return to the starting position and relax.

3 Again raise your arms to the position described in exercise 2. Squeeze your hands tightly into fists and then release the tension. Try to recall each area of tension and the way in which it was created and released.

4 Stretch your arms above your head and rise up on your toes, stretching upward as far as possible. Breathe in and out slowly and deeply. Begin contracting these muscle areas, trying a different sequence each time:

- Try moving the contraction and resulting tension upward from your feet through your calves, your thighs, and your back, and into your shoulders; continue the contraction through your arms and into your hands as you form a tight fist.
- Try to separate each main area of your body—arms, legs, head, upper torso, lower torso—and practice relaxation in one area while tightening the muscles in another.

These points of tension may occur later in actual conducting situations. Knowing how they originate and consciously relaxing the tension will help you to maintain a good physical and mental state.

Stretching is one of the best methods of alleviating tightness and stiffness, both while conducting and immediately following long conducting sessions. By learning the principles of tension and relaxation, a conductor may achieve a smoother, more flowing style and avoid excessive fatigue and soreness.

PERFORMANCE EXCERPTS FOR CHAPTER 1

Section Three, pages 163–171

1-1 Dello Joio, *Scenes from the Louvre,* second movement: "Children's Gallery"

1-2 Traditional, "Aura Lee"

1-3 Hanson, *Chorale and Alleluia*

1-4 Ravel, *Pavane pour une enfante défunte* ("Pavane for a Dead Princess")

1-5 Anonymous, *Dona nobis pacem* ("Give Us Peace")

1-6 Dvořák, Symphony No. 9, fourth movement

1-7 Weber, *Der Freischütz* ("The Freeshooter"), Overture

1-8 Sousa, *Semper Fidelis* March

CHAPTER 2

TWO-BEAT PATTERNS DYNAMICS

AMBIDEXTROUS CONDUCTING

COMMUNICATING THE ICTUS VISUALLY

ALTERNATIVE PATTERN STYLES

TWO-BEAT PATTERNS

Three variations of the two-beat pattern are shown in Figures 2-1, 2-2, and 2-3.

The pattern in Figure 2-1 is very simple and clear. It is excellent for fast tempos and is usually done with wrist motion only (there is little or no motion at the elbow or shoulder).

In the pattern shown in Figure 2-2, the rebound after the ictus of beat 1 prepares for a smaller motion on beat 2, visually emphasizing the different weight of the metric pulse on each beat. The angularity of the pattern is most appropriate for staccato or marcato styles. Remember to control the *size of the rebound.*

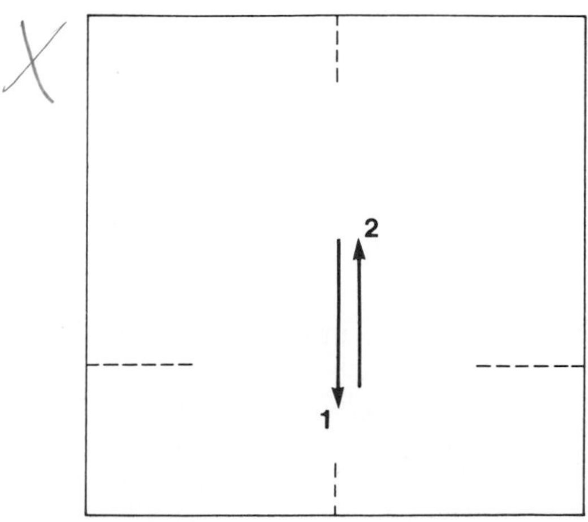

FIGURE 2-1
One version of the two-beat pattern.

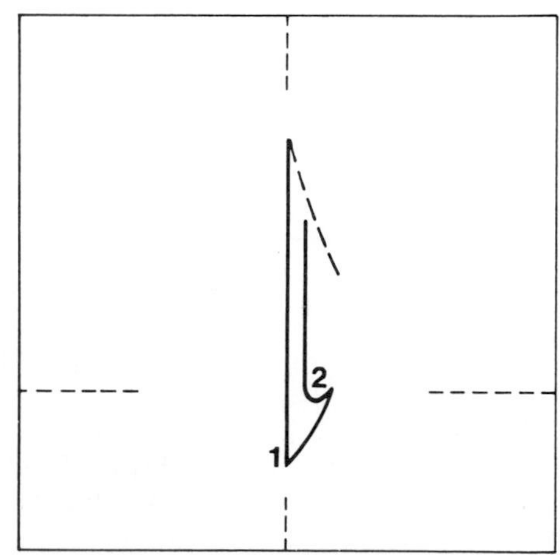

FIGURE 2-2
A second version of the two-beat pattern.

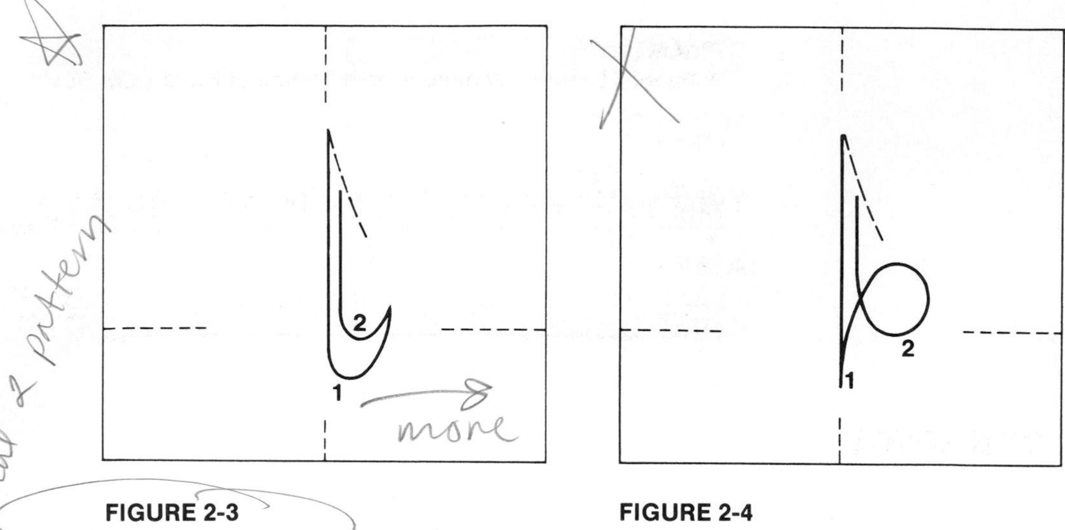

FIGURE 2-3
A third version of the two-beat pattern.

FIGURE 2-4
Two-beat pattern with loop.

The pattern shown in Figure 2-3 is usually used for slow, legato music. Notice that the motion for beat 2 is again smaller than the motion for beat 1.

A clockwise loop can be made for beat 2 to give increased weight or length to that beat, as shown in Figure 2-4. This pattern ordinarily would not be used for successive measures.

Often, two-beat patterns are not conducted clearly, usually as a result of an overly large rebound following beat 1. Notice, in Figure 2-5, that the two beats look nearly alike.

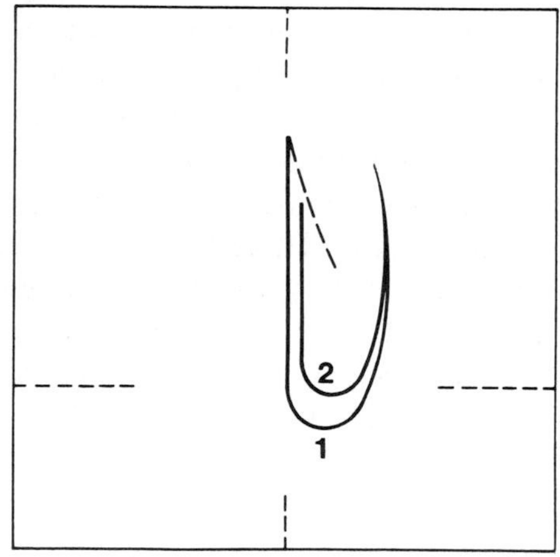

FIGURE 2-5
Two-beat pattern with rebound too large.

Sing and conduct the excerpts in Figures 2-6 and 2-7.

FIGURE 2-6
Béla Bartók, "Enchanting Song."

FIGURE 2-7
Johannes Brahms, Variations on a Theme of Haydn, Op. 56a.

DYNAMICS

Dynamic levels are indicated by the size of the beat pattern, by the overall intensity of gestures, and by special motions with the left hand. Here, we consider the first of these methods. (The others are discussed in later chapters.)

Varying the Size of Patterns

At a very soft dynamic level, the movement should take place mostly in the wrist and hand, with little perceptible motion at either the elbow or the shoulder. As the size of the pattern is increased, the larger radius of movement should be created by gradually transferring the main source of motion from the hand and wrist, first to the elbow and then to the shoulder. All the joints of the arm and shoulder, however, should feel flexible, regardless of where the main source of motion occurs.

As the motion is increased at the elbow, it should be proportionately decreased at the wrist. If the wrist motion is not decreased, the beat will have a whiplike appearance. Similarly, as the motion at the shoulder is increased, motion at the elbow should be decreased.

Another common problem is to use excessive shoulder motions—caused by unintentional rigidity in the elbow or wrist—as the main source of motion for all gestures, large or small. This should be avoided because (1) a pianissimo beat is much easier to "read" if the motion emanates from the wrist rather than from the shoulder, (2) constantly conducting from the shoulder creates a stiff and unnatural appearance, (3) flexibility and expressiveness are more limited, and (4) it leads to tired and sore muscles.

REMEDIAL EXERCISES

If there is any difficulty in making either the wrist or the elbow a primary center of motion, practice the following:

1. Hold your right upper arm with your left hand and practice beat patterns with your right hand and forearm by making the elbow the main source of motion.
2. Place your left arm in front of you and rest your right forearm on top of it. Practice conducting with only the wrist and hand.
3. Rest your right forearm on a table and conduct patterns with only the wrist and hand.

Crescendos and Decrescendos

An increase in dynamics can be shown by increasing the size of the beat pattern, and a decrease in dynamics by reducing the size of the pattern. Practice making crescendos and decrescendos in the patterns shown in Figure 2-8, noticing the shift in the source of motion as the size of the pattern changes.

FIGURE 2-8
Exercises for dynamic changes.

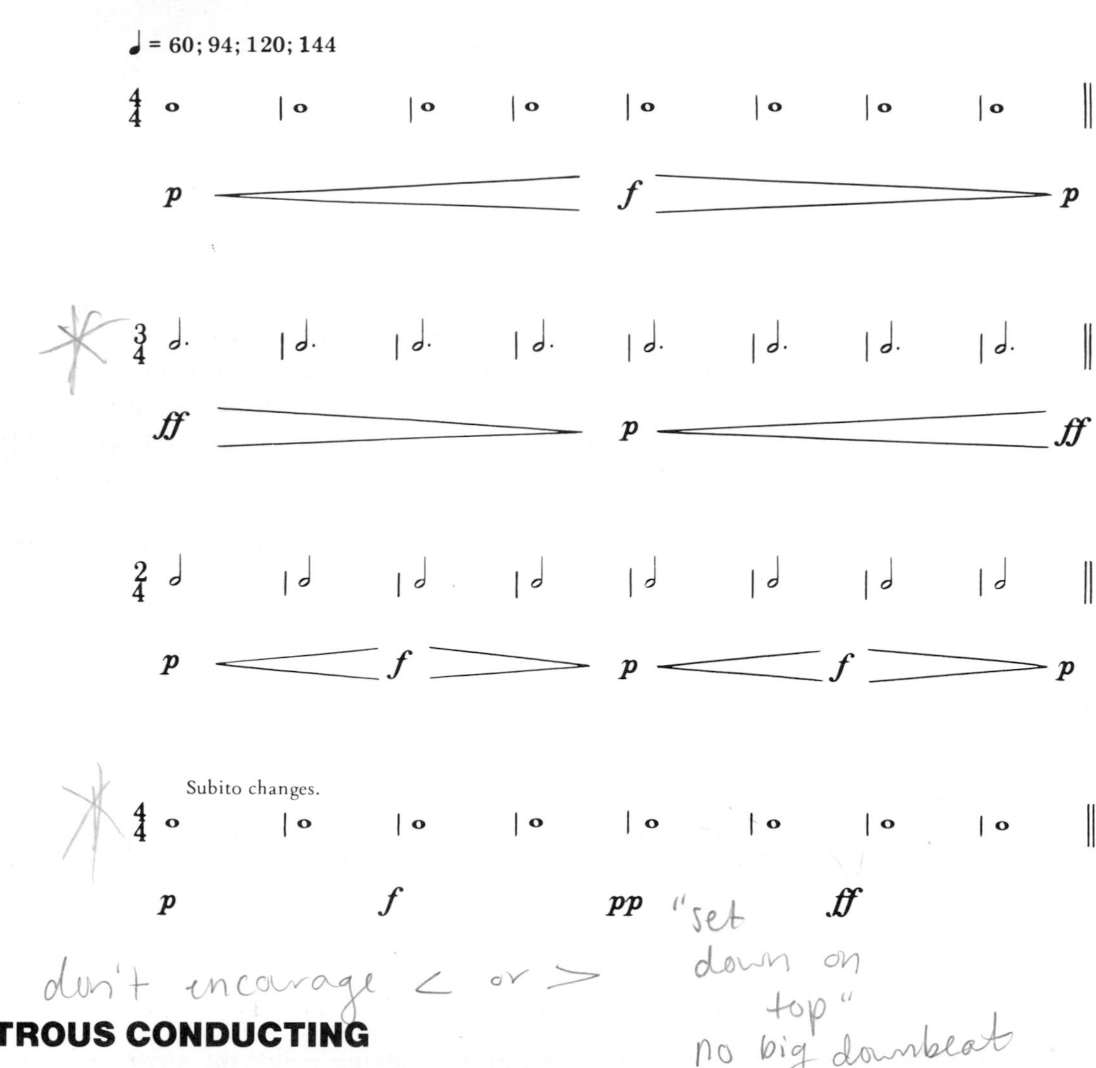

AMBIDEXTROUS CONDUCTING

The ability to conduct equally well with both hands should be acquired during the early stages. This will develop flexibility and coordination, which will reduce awkwardness later when both hands are needed for cues, dynamic indications, and separate patterns.

Practice the exercises in Figure 2-8 and the other exercises and excerpts in Chapters 1 and 2 with the left hand alone. Remember that the left hand will be performing patterns exactly opposite to those done by the right hand; that is, the left-hand patterns are a *mirror image* of the right-hand patterns, as shown in Figures 2-9 and 2-10. The hands should not cross on beat 2 of the four-beat pattern.

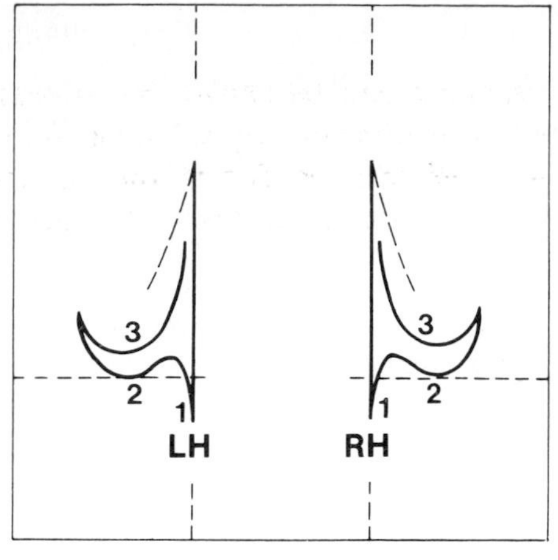

FIGURE 2-9
Three-beat pattern, both hands.

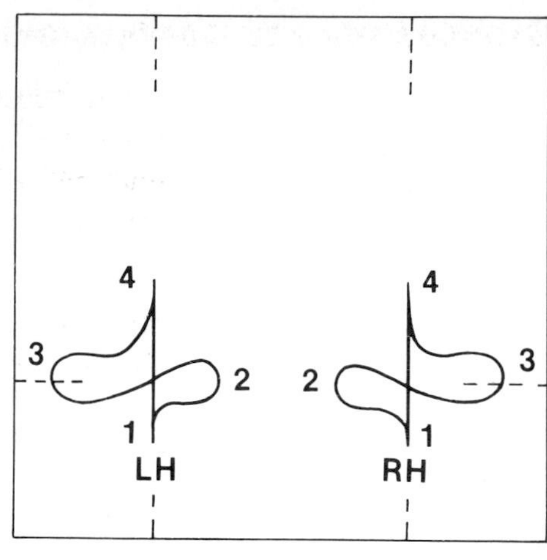

FIGURE 2-10
Four-beat pattern, both hands.

After practicing with the left hand alone, add the right hand and conduct with both hands simultaneously. *This style of conducting should not be overused:* far too many conductors use both hands in mirror image in much of their conducting, never realizing the potential of independent motions by each hand. However, the beginning conductor might spend some time practicing with both hands to develop a feeling for the correct size and placement of the left-hand patterns.

Practice the excerpt in Figure 2-11, alternating right-hand and left-hand patterns over one measure, two measures, and so on, to develop coordination and fluency in each hand. Both hands should be in the conducting position.

FIGURE 2-11
Peter Ilych Tchaikovsky, *The Nutcracker* Suite; exercise for alternating hands.

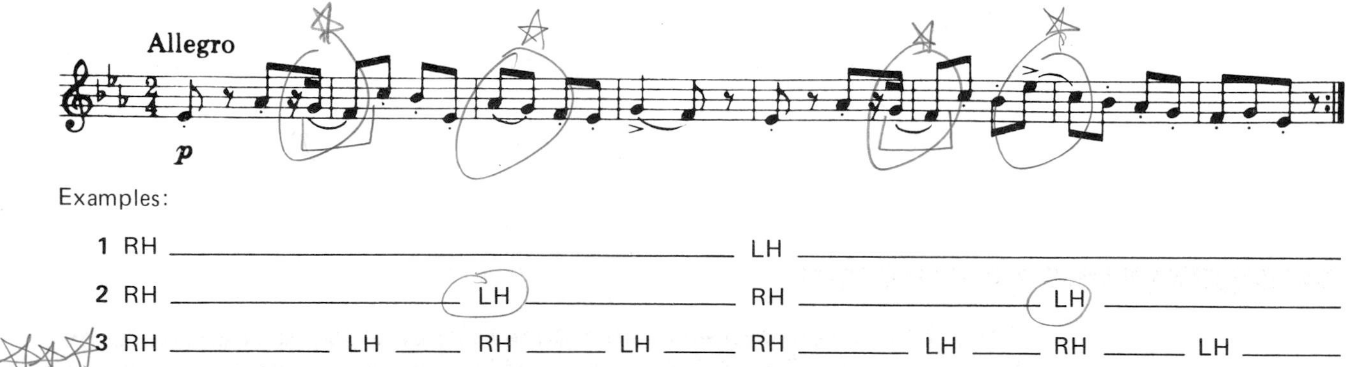

COMMUNICATING THE ICTUS VISUALLY

Visually conveying the ictus—the exact moment when the rhythmic pulse occurs—is usually not a problem in conducting staccato or marcato styles: the ictus will be created by an abrupt stopping of the motion or an abrupt change of direction. Conducting legato style, however, requires a more thorough understanding of how an ictus can be indicated.

An ictus can be shown by (1) a definite change in direction, such as a reversal in rebounding or an angular shape; (2) stopping or starting the travel; or (3) a change in the speed of travel combined with a change in direction. The ictus created by reversal of direction or angular shape has been illustrated by the staccato patterns. The following examples illustrate the other possibilities.

First, conduct a rounded four-beat pattern, this time stopping the motion slightly, as shown in Figure 2-12, to indicate each ictus. If the stop is very brief, there will be a feeling of only one ictus on each beat. If, however, the motion does not resume until the second half of the beat, the start of the travel will also create an ictus on the second half of the beat. The stop-start rhythm will create a subtle feeling of subdivision. The important point to notice is that both stopping and starting the travel create a feeling and appearance of ictus.

Conduct the rounded four-beat pattern again, as shown in Figure 2-13, increasing the speed of travel in the section indicated by the thin line and decreasing it in the sections indicated by the heavy line. You might try to feel as though your hand is falling into the beat and then moving more slowly until it falls into the next beat. Notice that this creates a subtle feeling of pulse. Also notice that the ictus can occur at the *lowest* point of each gesture—it does *not* have to be at the extreme left for two, the extreme right for three, or the very top for four.

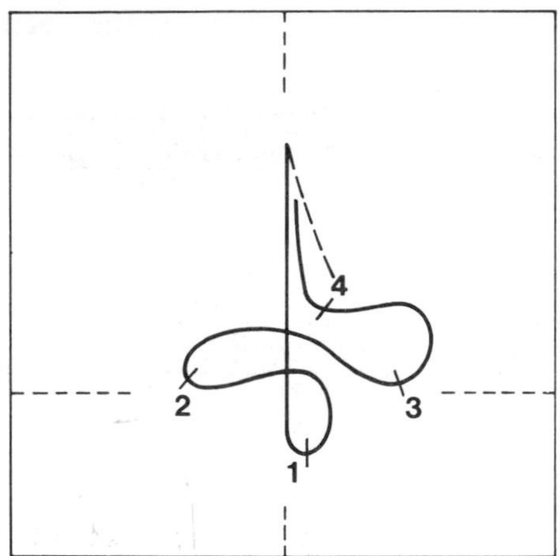

FIGURE 2-12
Stopping travel to indicate an ictus. / = slight pause.

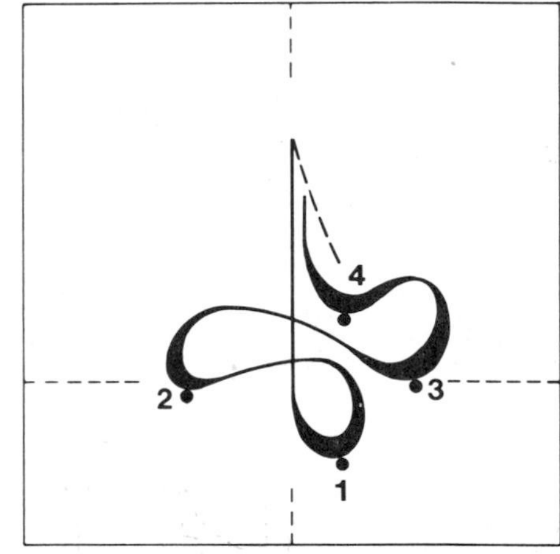

FIGURE 2-13
Changing travel and direction to indicate an ictus.

Next, try conducting a rounded pattern with absolutely no change in the speed of travel and see if it creates a feeling of pulse. What do you think creates a feeling of pulse with a rounded pattern like this: (1) placing the ictus at the bottom of each gesture, (2) changing the speed of travel, (3) combining both of these, or (4) using neither?

A light, smooth click beat may also indicate an ictus in legato patterns. As the hand arrives at the extremity of the pattern, add a small flicking motion of the wrist, as shown in Figure 2-14. This adds a slight point to an otherwise rounded pattern.

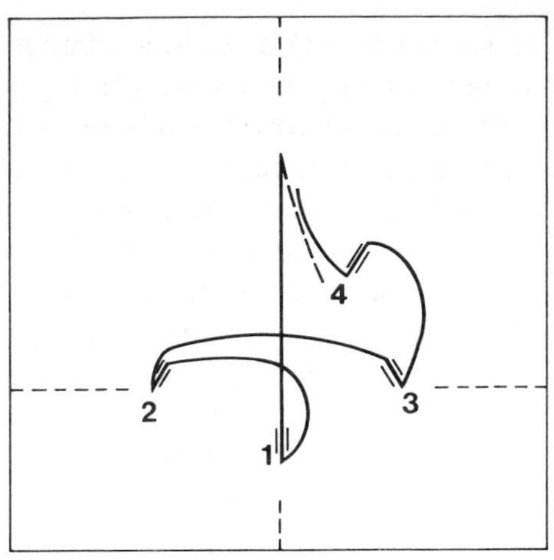

FIGURE 2-14
Legato pattern with click beat.

Practice slow, legato beat patterns, using each of the procedures described. Make small changes to vary the location, weight, and prominence of each ictus. Control the travel smoothly to indicate a sustaining and stretching out of the sound. Practice the excerpt in Figure 2-15.

FIGURE 2-15
Richard Wagner, *Lohengrin,* "Elsa's Procession to the Cathedral."

ALTERNATIVE PATTERN STYLES

Several distinctive approaches to beat patterns, with somewhat common terminologies, have evolved over the years. The differences in style depend primarily on the position of each ictus and the direction of travel following the ictus.

Below we describe the modified classical style, classical style, focal-plane style, and focal-point style.

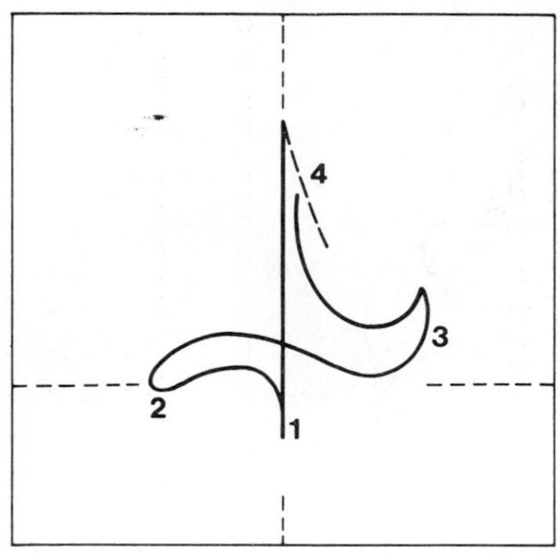

FIGURE 2-16
Modified classical style.

169

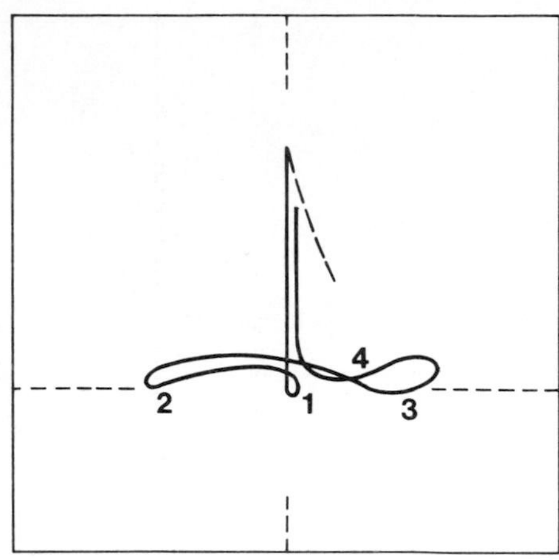

FIGURE 2-17
Classical style.

Modified Classical Style

The style illustrated in Figure 2-16 above, the modified classical style, places the ictus of each beat at the extremity of each direction in the pattern. The downbeat is on a lower horizontal plane than the sideward beats or the upbeat, and the ictus of beat 2, in a $\frac{4}{4}$ pattern for example, is at the leftmost position of the pattern.

Classical Style

The classical style, shown in Figure 2-17 above, places all the beats on the same horizontal plane. This style may tend to make the beats all look like downbeats unless the conductor takes special care to use sufficient horizontal motion for the sideward beats. Placing all the beats on the same horizontal plane also limits some instinctive, expressive motions.

Focal-Plane Style

In the focal-plane style, shown in Figure 2-18 (opposite page), each ictus is placed in the same vertical plane, the approximate center of the conducting area. The ictus is created by a change in the speed of travel, which is increased slightly as it approaches the ictus and then stopped briefly to create the ictus. Some conductors feel that this style enables them to use more travel for each beat, in order to stretch out beats where a flowing, sustained effect is required.

Focal-Point Style

The focal-point style, shown in Figure 2-19 (opposite), places each ictus on the juncture of the horizontal and vertical planes (or somewhat higher on the vertical plane). This approach focuses the performers' attention on one central area, indicated in Figure 2-19 by the circle. Distinguishing the beats from each other depends entirely on the direction of travel leading to each ictus. It is important to use a clear up-down motion after beat 4 to indicate the beginning of the new measure.

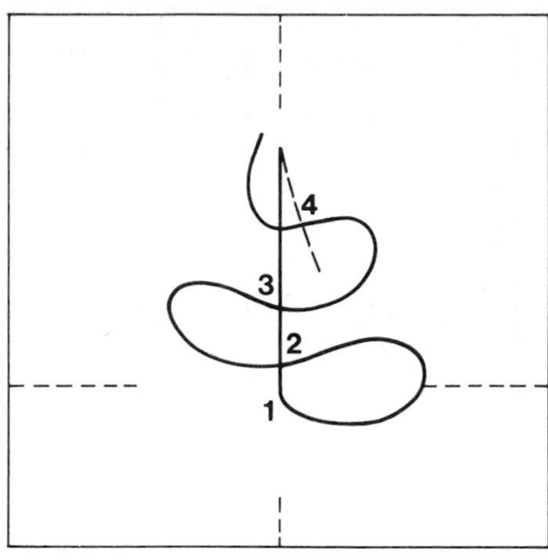

FIGURE 2-18
Focal-plane style.

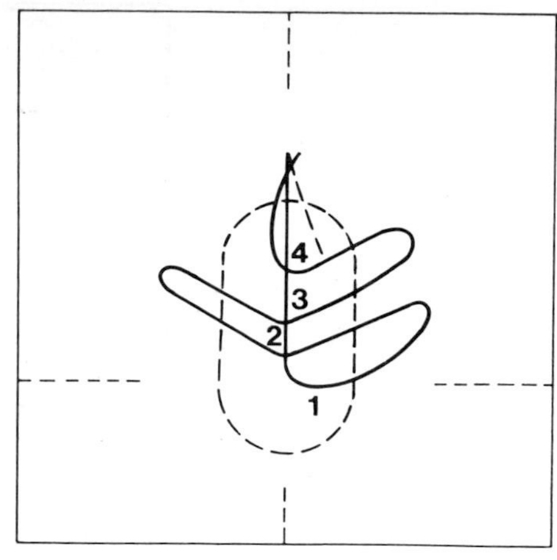

FIGURE 2-19
Focal-point style. *Note:* The vertical space shown in the illustration has been expanded for clarity. In this style the ictuses would occur at the same vertical and horizontal location.

ASSIGNMENT

Practice singing (using either neutral syllables or the text) and conducting the excerpts for Chapter 2 in the Anthology using the right hand only and the left hand only. Also practice alternating hands every few measures. When practicing alone, use a large mirror and check for the following:

1 Posture and stance
2 Arm and hand position
3 Plane of the beat pattern; ictus of each beat
4 Preparatory motion and downbeat
5 Size and style of the beat
6 Flexibility of the wrist, elbow, and shoulder
7 Location of the source of motion
8 Absence of tension

DAILY WARM-UP ROUTINE

Daily warm-up routines, similar in purpose to those used in singing or playing an instrument, should be used to refine and maintain your conducting technique. Do the following exercises in front of a mirror for 10 to 15 minutes every day.

1 Practice giving preparatory gestures and downbeats, varying tempo, dynamic level, and style. Practice releases in the same manner. Think of making a visual representation of the sound. Review Chapter 1.
2 Practice four-beat, three-beat, and two-beat patterns, gradually changing from a very staccato style to a legato style.
3 Practice very legato patterns, showing ictuses with varying degrees of emphasis or subtlety, (a) adding a click motion with wrist, (b) stopping the travel, and (c) changing both direction and speed of travel.

AURAL ANALYSIS FORM FOR CHAPTER 2

Name:______________________________ Date: __________

Tape-record at least four of the excerpts for Chapters 1 and 2 in the Anthology. As you listen to each one, imagine that it is a small segment for a professional recording and you can do one more "take." What needs to be done to make it more nearly perfect and more expressive? List the two or three top-priority items for each excerpt.

First excerpt: ______________________________

Second excerpt: ______________________________

Third excerpt: ______________________________

Fourth excerpt: ______________________________

Notes (list items that you should listen for more carefully):

AURAL ANALYSIS

Continue to practice the aural analysis exercises in Chapter 1. This can be done using the form provided above, or it can be done through class discussion. Listen more carefully in your ensemble rehearsals. Begin to think like a conductor, asking yourself, "What's good? What isn't good? What needs to be done?"

EVALUATION

The following optional form can be used for (1) self-evaluation of videotapes, as an assignment to be handed in; (2) evaluation during class by the instructor; or (3) evaluation of videotapes by the instructor.

EVALUATION FORM FOR CHAPTER 2

Name:______________________________________ Date: ____________

Choose an exercise or excerpt from Chapter 2 to show that you can do each of the following. Place a check mark or plus sign in the blank space to indicate that an item was done correctly and a minus sign to indicate that more work and review are needed.

Two-beat patterns with clearly defined downbeats and upbeats:

_____ Legato style

_____ Staccato style

Varying the size of four-, three-, and two-beat patterns to indicate dynamic levels:

_____ Wrist motion at piano levels

_____ Elbow motion at piano levels

_____ Shoulder motion at piano levels

_____ Wrist motion at forte levels

_____ Elbow motion at forte levels

_____ Shoulder motion at forte levels

_____ Smooth transition at wrist, elbow, and shoulder in changing dynamic levels

Ambidextrous conducting:

_____ Clear patterns indicated with the left hand

_____ Ability to change hands

Visually communicating the ictus:

_____ Legato style with a subtle but clear ictus

_____ Legato style with a click beat

PERFORMANCE EXCERPTS FOR CHAPTER 2

Section Three, pages 172–181

2-1 Billings, "Chester"

2-2 Wagner, *Lohengrin,* "Elsa's Procession to the Cathedral"

2-3 Schumann, Concerto for Piano, first movement

2-4 Jacob, *William Byrd Suite,* "The Earle of Oxford's March"

2-5 Thompson, *The Peaceable Kingdom,* "Say ye to the righteous"

2-6 Lasso, *Matona, mia cara* ("Matona, lovely maiden")

2-7 Parker (arr. Shaw), "What Shall We Do with the Drunken Sailor"

2-8 Bartók, "Enchanting Song"

CHAPTER 3

USING THE BATON
ONE-BEAT PATTERNS
THE LEFT HAND
ADDITIONAL RELEASES

USING THE BATON

A baton is usually used with large ensembles such as orchestras, wind bands, and large choruses because it can magnify and clarify physical communication to the performers, especially those who are at extreme angles to the podium or at a considerable distance from it. The baton is traditionally considered to be a natural extension of the arm.

Choral conductors often prefer conducting without a baton because they feel that they can be more clear and expressive without it. Also, the relatively compact arrangement and good sight lines of choral groups may make a baton unnecessary.

Wind band and orchestra conductors usually use a baton, but sometimes they too prefer to conduct without it in passages of extreme subtlety or flowing cantabile, preferring instead to "mold the sound" with the shape of their hands and flexible use of their fingers.

Baton Shapes and Materials

Batons are made in a wide variety of lengths, materials, and shapes, each with its own advantages and disadvantages. A baton with the following characteristics will help most students achieve good results in the initial stages: fiberglass shaft; 10- to 14-inch length; cork or wood handle.

The length of the baton and the shape of its handle can often influence conducting style. Large, long handles tend to be held firmly in the hand and may encourage more arm and shoulder motion. A tiny ball-shaped handle or no handle at all may encourage smaller patterns with more wrist motion.

With the type of baton recommended above, good results can be achieved by holding the baton by either the handle or the shaft. By holding the baton slightly back from the balance point, the weight of the shaft helps to create a more "live" feeling in the baton—a slight gravitational pull at the tip, which can be controlled to develop a clear and expressive technique.

Baton Grips

Either of the two basic grips described below (see Figures 3-1 and 3-2) will probably help you get good results; or your teacher may recommend a different alternative. In any case, it will be most helpful to begin with one grip and stay with it until it becomes comfortable. Then you can begin to experiment with other grips and analyze the differences among them. Figures 3-3 to 3-12 show some of the other grips and some common problems.

Basic Grip 1

For basic grip 1 (Figure 3-1), make a slight U shape with the forefinger. Grip the baton lightly between the thumb and the first joint of the forefinger so that the baton looks like an extension of the arm. The thumb and forefinger should contact the handle near the forward taper. The baton should be held with the pad of the thumb rather than the tip. Notice the natural curve of the thumb. The thumb should not be bent in either an extreme outward or inward position. The remaining fingers should curve naturally inward, almost touching the palm. The curve of the fingers can be opened slightly for a legato style or the grip can be closed firmly for a marcato style.

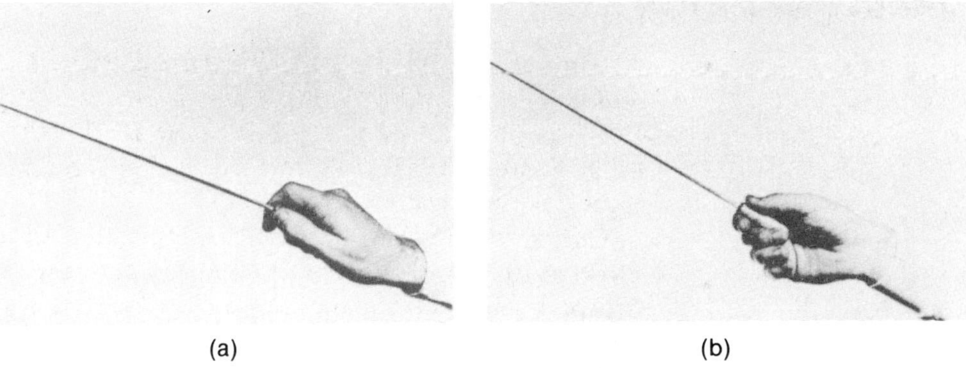

(a) (b)

FIGURE 3-1
Basic grip 1: (a) side view, (b) palm view.

Basic Grip 2

For basic grip 2 (Figure 3-2), point the baton in a more forward direction by holding the baton between the thumb and *second* finger. The first finger should rest lightly on the tapered part of the handle—*not on the shaft.* The other fingers should, again, curve in naturally.

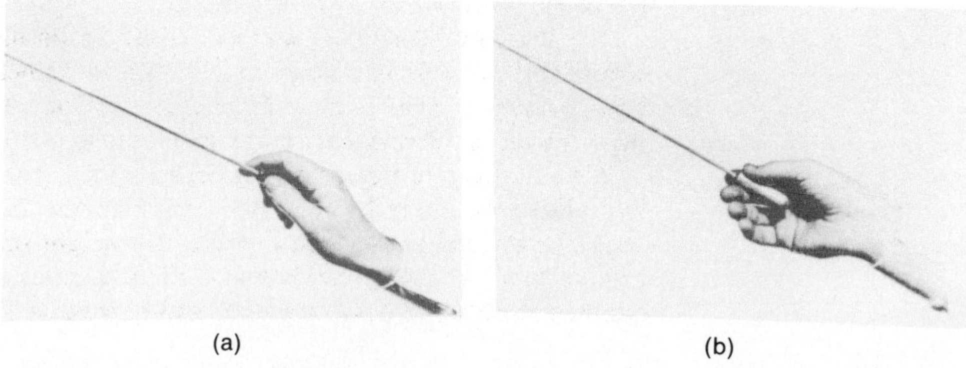

(a) (b)

FIGURE 3-2
Basic grip 2: (a) side view, (b) palm view.

Light Grip

When a very light and flexible grip is required, the baton can be held between the thumb and the first finger (between the tip and the first joint) with the first finger only slightly curved (see Figure 3-3). Again, allow the other fingers to curve inward. This grip is similar to the first basic grip (shown in Figure 3-1) because the thumb and the first finger contact the handle. The grip shown in Figure 3-3, however, is more open, with less curve to the first finger; and the baton contact is between the tip and first joint of the finger rather than precisely at the first joint. This grip works well for a light, legato style. Some conductors, however, tend to drop the baton occasionally when using this grip.

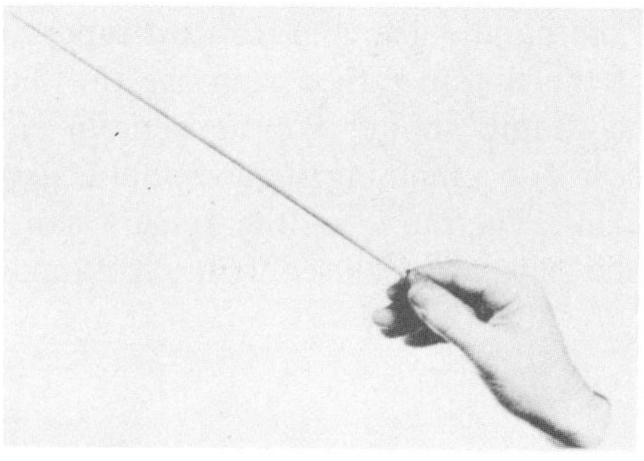

FIGURE 3-3
Light grip with thumb and first finger.

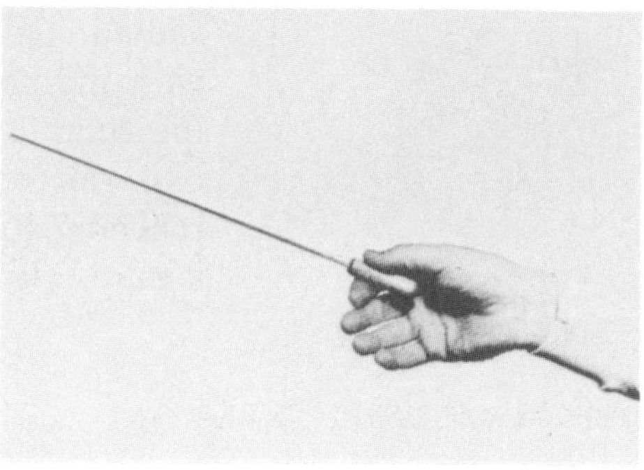

FIGURE 3-4
Grip with thumb and first finger, thumb up.

Grip with Thumb and First Finger, Thumb Up

Figure 3-4 shows the baton gripped as in Figure 3-1, but with the palm facing to the left and the thumb facing upward. The flexing of the wrist in this position can be used to emphasize the horizontal motion of patterns. Care must be taken, however, to ensure that the tip of the baton points downward far enough in giving downbeats. There is a tendency for the baton to point upward, with the ictus occurring in the hand rather than at the tip of the baton.

Grip with Handle against Palm

As shown in Figure 3-5, the baton can be held between the thumb and first finger, with the end of the handle firmly against the palm. This is a very secure and firm grip. Any grip that has three or more contact points with the baton, however, will not allow the baton to pivot. This grip may also produce tightness in the wrist and encourage more arm motion.

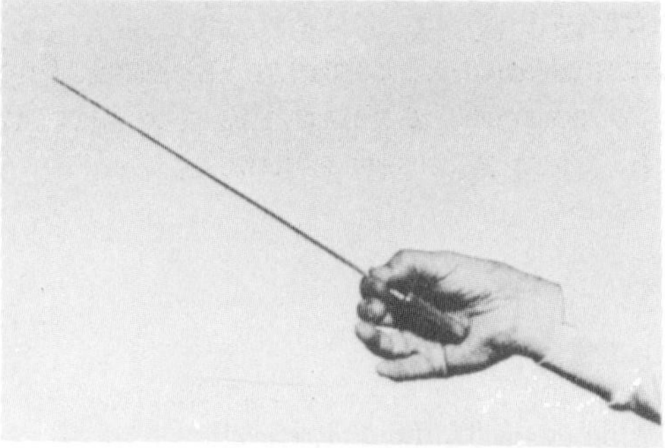

FIGURE 3-5
Grip with handle against palm.

Grip on the Shaft

The baton can be held between the thumb and first finger, contacting the shaft rather than the handle, as shown in Figure 3-6. This gives a more balanced feeling to the baton, which some conductors prefer.

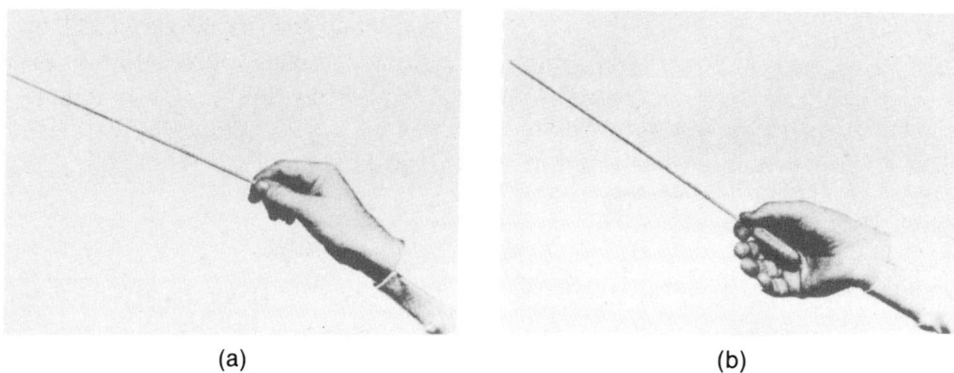

(a) (b)

FIGURE 3-6
Grip on the shaft: (a) side view, (b) palm view.

Problems with the Grip

Baton Pointing Excessively to the Left

Figure 3-7 illustrates a common problem, the baton pointing too far to the left. This is caused by positioning the thumb too far back in relation to the first finger. Correct this by moving the thumb forward or moving the first finger back. Notice how this makes the baton pivot.

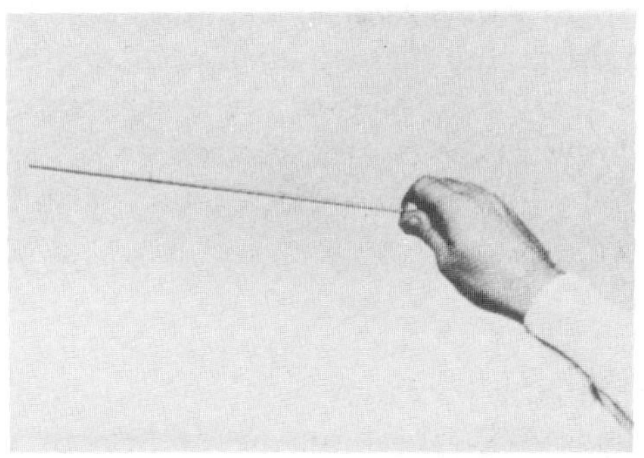

FIGURE 3-7
Baton pointing excessively to the left; incorrect thumb position.

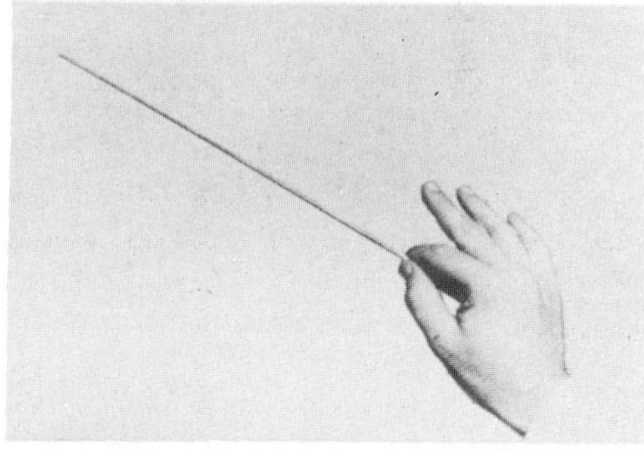

FIGURE 3-8
Fingers too straight.

Fingers Too Straight

Figure 3-8 illustrates another common problem: fingers that are straight and rigid-looking. To correct this, start the grip with the fingers closed against the palm; then let them open just a little.

Grip Too Close to End of Handle

In Figure 3-9, the contact point on the first finger is too high. This grip cannot be easily changed, and it usually does not provide good control of the baton. Remember that the contact point should be approximately at the *first* joint of the first finger.

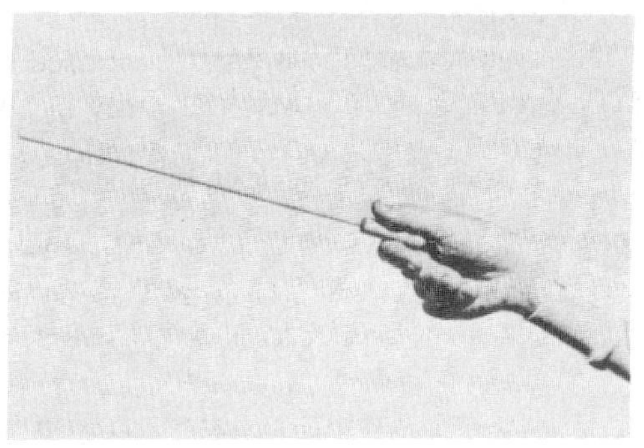

FIGURE 3-9
Grip too close to end of handle; contact point of first finger too high.

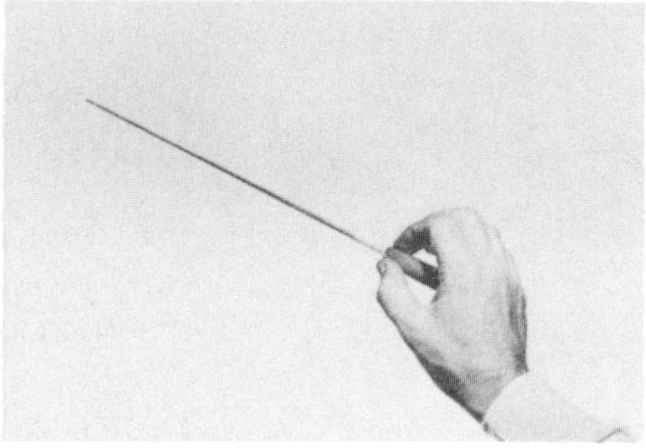

FIGURE 3-10
Overly light and open grip.

Overly Light and Open Grip

The grip shown in Figure 3-10 is very light and will make the baton pivot and float lightly, but this grip also makes it very easy to drop the baton.

Finger on Top of Baton

Placing the first finger on top of the baton, as shown in Figure 3-11, tends to produce a style with a very clear ictus, but it also eliminates flexibility in the grip, since there are three contact points.

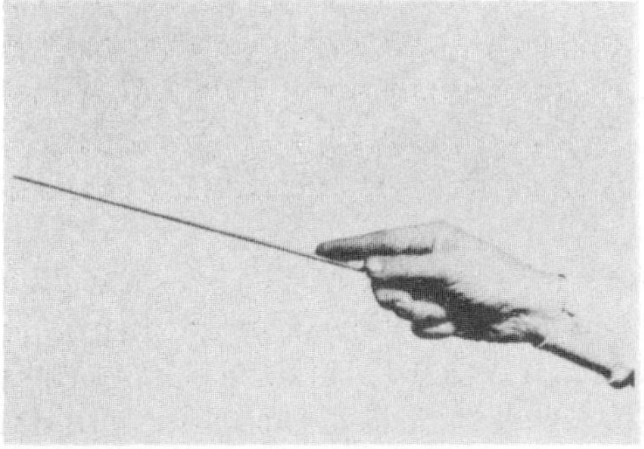

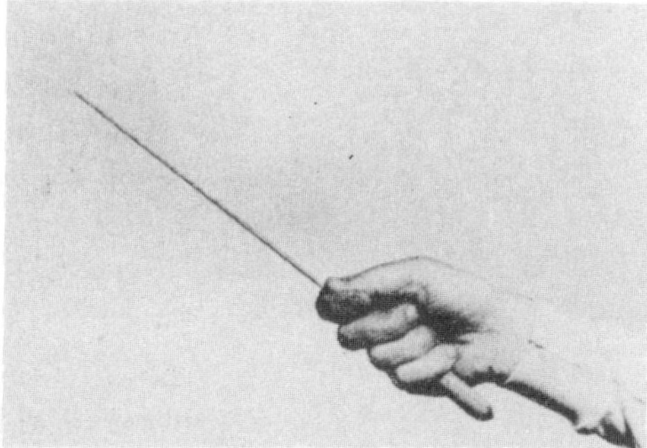

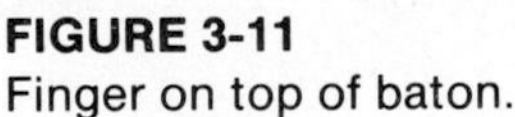

FIGURE 3-11
Finger on top of baton.

FIGURE 3-12
Handle extending beyond grip.

Handle Extending Beyond Grip

In Figure 3-12, the grip is too far forward on the shaft, with the handle extending beyond the back of the hand.

Analyzing Your Grip

Using a baton magnifies the beat pattern, but it can also magnify conducting problems. Problems that appear to be in the grip, moreover, sometimes actually begin in the wrist. A floppy wrist, for example, will look even more floppy with a baton, and a rigid wrist will look even more rigid. The foregoing discussion includes only the most common grips and problems—there are many other possibilities.

The first three grips described above can be used successfully by most people and are used by many professionals. Carefully analyzing how your grip looks and feels, however, is the only way to develop a grip that works well for you.

Review the musical excerpts in Chapters 1 and 2 and practice conducting basic and subdivided patterns in both legato and staccato style with the baton. Practice giving preparatory gestures and entrances. Check the following:

1. Feel where the contact points with the baton are located. For any style in which flexibility is required, there should be only two main contact points with the baton. Three or more contact points (such as two fingers and the thumb; or one finger, the thumb, and the palm) create a rigid grip, and the baton will not pivot. Test flexibility in the grip by holding the baton very lightly and making small down-up motions, allowing the baton to pivot slightly in the grip.
2. Notice the general shape of your hand and the curvature of all your fingers.
3. The ictus of the beat should always be focused in the tip of the baton. For example, when a beat is given to the right, the tip of the baton should make a larger motion in that direction than the hand or elbow. Some conductors prefer to lead with the wrist.

ONE-BEAT PATTERNS

One-beat patterns are used in compositions with a single pulse per measure, or whenever a duple- or triple-meter passage becomes too rapid for conducting the individual beats. Examples of the latter include waltzes ($\frac{3}{4}$), scherzos ($\frac{3}{4}$ or $\frac{2}{4}$), vivos ($\frac{2}{4}$), and galops ($\frac{2}{4}$). It is frequently necessary to make transitions between conducting the individual beats and conducting one beat to the measure.

The basic down-up motion of the one-beat pattern must be conducted in several different ways, depending on the metric and melodic accents of the music. The excerpt in Figure 3-13 on the following page requires a firm downward motion followed by a quick rebound that does not imply a subdivision of the measure, since this is not suggested by either the metric or the melodic structure.

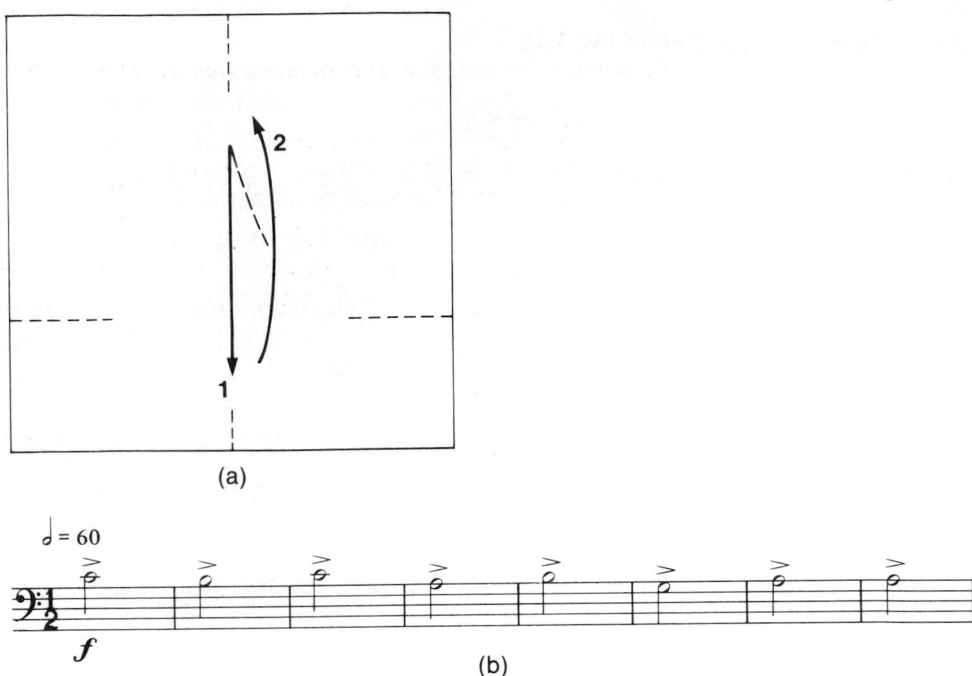

FIGURE 3-13
(a) One-beat pattern, quick rebound. (b) Traditional melody, *Dies irae.*

Legato Style in One-Beat Patterns

A simple down-up motion is usually appropriate in legato, flowing passages because the legato feeling is created by the flow of the phrase rather than by the beats within measures. However, conductors sometimes choose to add a curve to the down-up motion, as shown in Figure 3-14 to express a more legato style. An oval or circular pattern is also used, usually counterclockwise, as shown in Figure 3-15. The speed of travel usually accelerates toward the bottom of the pattern to give a light ictus. Practice the excerpt in Figure 3-16 using both of the patterns shown in Figures 3-14 and 3-15.

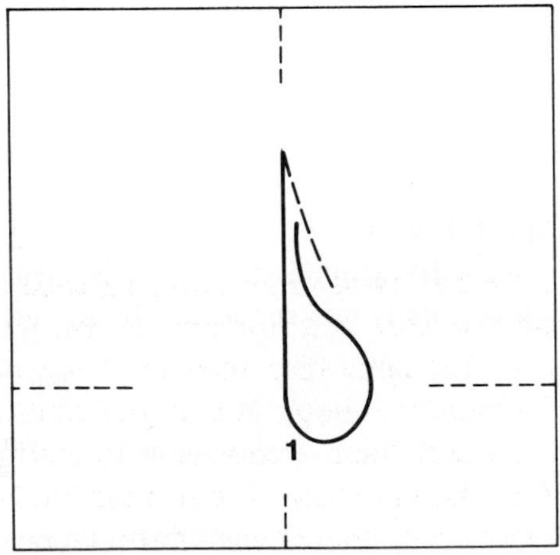

FIGURE 3-14
One-beat pattern, legato style.

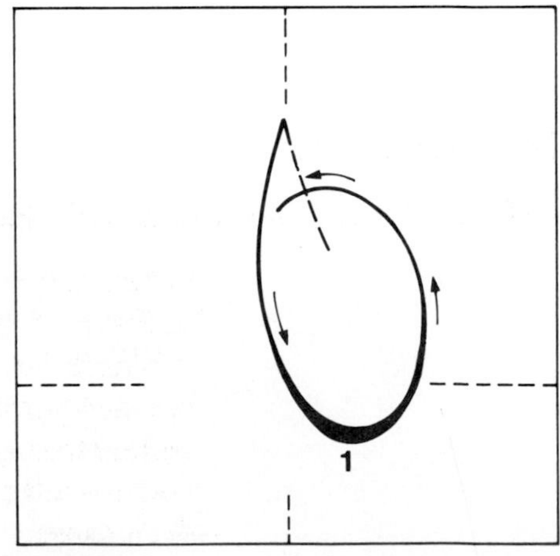

FIGURE 3-15
One-beat pattern, legato style, with oval or circular motion.

FIGURE 3-16
Peter Ilych Tchaikovsky, *The Sleeping Beauty, Thornrose* Waltz.

Shifting Between One-Beat and Three-Beat Patterns in Triple Meter

It is important to be able to shift smoothly between one- and three-beat patterns to indicate tempo changes or to emphasize different qualities of the music. If you are conducting in a fast three, for example, shifting to a legato one pattern will emphasize the flowing quality of the music and may allow you to shape the phrase more expressively. If you are conducting in one, you may want to shift to three to emphasize an accent on beat 2 or to bring out some other rhythmic quality of the music.

Practice the following:

1 Conduct a moderate one pattern. Without changing the tempo, add the rightward motion for beat 2 to make it a three pattern. Alternate between one and three patterns.
2 Conduct a one pattern at a fast tempo. Slow the tempo and add a very small second beat, gradually increasing the size of beat 2 as the tempo slows. Then increase the tempo, making the second beat gradually smaller until it feels natural to shift back into one.
3 Practice the excerpts in Figures 3-13 and 3-16 in different tempos, alternating between a one-beat pattern and multiple-beat patterns.

THE LEFT HAND

At-Rest Position of the Left Hand

When not in use, the left hand may hang naturally at the side or be held in front of the body, a little below chest height. From the latter position, it is easier to bring the left hand into and out of use. Both positions, however, are acceptable. Uncertainty about at-rest positions sometimes causes new conductors to use the left hand excessively to mirror the right hand, or—worse—to hold the left hand extended in front of the body without any reason or purpose. (Holding the left hand extended should be used only as an attention signal to precede an important indication, such as an entrance or a tempo change.)

Left-Hand Dynamic Indications

The left hand can be used to indicate dynamic changes while the beat pattern is maintained with the right hand. Using the left hand for this separate function usually increases the clarity and emphasis of the indications. (The size of the beat pattern must continue to indicate dynamic changes, even when the left hand is also used for that purpose.) Developing the ability to use both hands independently usually requires systematic practice over a long period of time. If you have practiced using the left hand as recommended in Chapters 1 and 2, it should not be difficult now to begin giving left-hand dynamic indications.

LEFT-HAND EXERCISES

1 Practice raising the left hand, palm up, with the fingers slightly spread, to indicate a crescendo; and lowering it, palm down, to indicate a diminuendo.

- Check the position of the upper arm, elbow, and forearm—which should be in essentially the same positions described in Chapter 1. Keep the upper arm away from the body, and not too far out in front of the body. Do not bend the wrist; rather, maintain a straight line from elbow to hand.
- The fingers should be slightly separated and have a natural curve. This basic shape may vary depending on the requirements of the music; however, a hand that is too open or too closed most of the time looks awkward.
- Many dynamic indications will be given in only the upper part of the conducting area—from about chest height to a little above head height. Right now, however, practice using all the vertical space for large dynamic indications.

With the left hand only, practice exercises 2 to 5 to a slow count.

2 Extend the left hand in front of your body, palm up.

- Hold in the extended position for four beats.
- Raise the hand for four beats.
- Hold in the upper extended position for four beats.
- Lower, palm down, for four beats.

3 Repeat exercise 2 with a count of six beats and then with a count of eight beats. Concentrate on making the motion smooth and flowing.

4 Repeat exercises 2 and 3 without the hold positions.

5 Conduct four-beat patterns with your right hand while practicing exercises 2 and 4 above. Practice until both hands can be used independently and smoothly.

Dynamic Indications with Alternating Hands

In a slow crescendo over several measures, it may feel unnatural to make one long and continuous left-hand motion. Moreover, when left-hand travel is slow and prolonged, the motion may not communicate a feeling of increasing intensity. In this case, it may sometimes be more effective to *repeat* the basic left-hand rising motion several times during the crescendo. To try this, make a crescendo for eight slow beats using the right hand in a $\frac{4}{4}$ pattern. Make the rising motion with the left hand for the first four beats, and then emphasize the crescendo with the right hand for beats 5 and 6. Repeat the left-hand rising gesture on beats 7 and 8.

Using the continuous left-hand motion for an extended diminuendo is less of a problem than the single left-hand motion for a crescendo, since the slow descending movement can communicate a gradual decrease in intensity. Even so, it will often be preferable to repeat the gesture.

When using the left hand, you may tend to mirror the motion of the right hand. Using the left hand in this manner may be valid at times, provided the mirroring does not continue too long. Check carefully if you tend to mirror for more than two or three counts, or if the mirroring begins to occur merely out of habit rather than for a definite purpose.

ADDITIONAL RELEASES

Releases can be given with either hand alone or both hands together. Nearly any decisive change in the speed or direction of travel will produce a release—the possibilities are infinite.

Practice indicating releases with the left hand. When a circular or loop pattern is used, it will usually be in a clockwise direction, mirroring the counterclockwise direction of the right hand. (See Figure 3-17.)

The location of the release pattern in the conducting area affects the dramatic qualities of the release. For example, the release shown in Figure 3-18, which occurs in the upper right section of the conducting area, will have a more dramatic effect than a release given near the center of the conducting area.

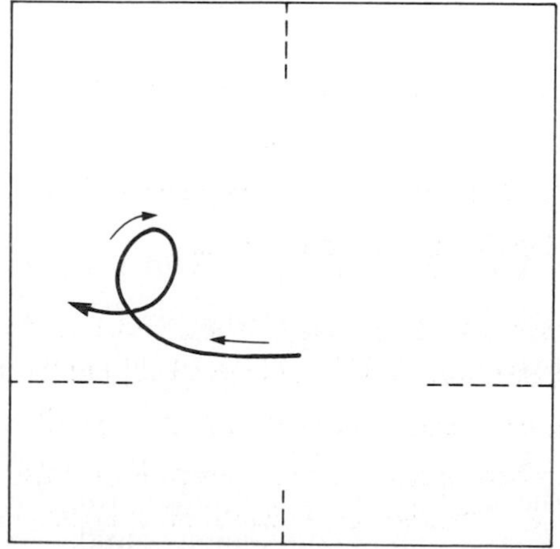

FIGURE 3-17
Left-hand release.

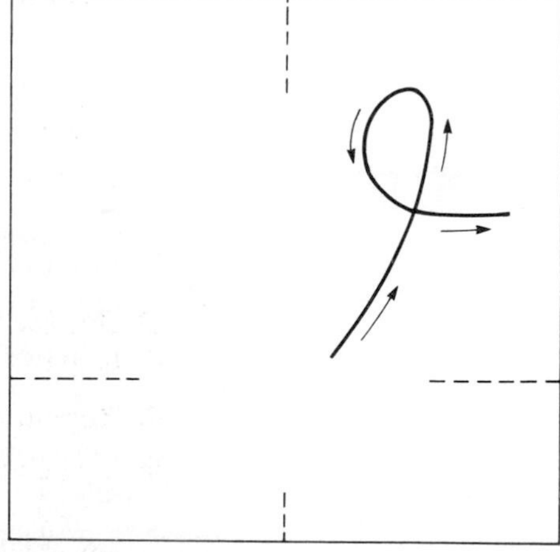

FIGURE 3-18
Right-hand release, high plane.

Concentrate on the sound of the ensemble as you conduct releases. The expressive quality of releases is a major factor in interpretation, one that you must be able to control with finesse. Also, give careful thought to how the release relates to the sound or silence following it. If the release is at the end of a main section or movement, the hands usually should be held in a "freeze" position for a few moments after the actual release. The moments of silence and concentration following a final release can be exquisite.

Practice releases at the end of each beat in a four-beat pattern. To give each beat full value, the release will frequently be on the ictus of the following beat; that is, the release of a note on beat 2 will usually be given on beat 3.

Practice the releases in the following ways:

1 Right hand alone
2 Left hand alone
3 Both hands
4 Soft, tapered releases
5 Loud, abrupt releases
6 Using different parts of the conducting area
7 Using different hand motions

AURAL ANALYSIS

As students conduct the excerpts for this chapter, one student should serve as a *designated listener*. This student should stand or be seated near the conductor. After the conductor evaluates and comments on the performance, the designated listener should make one or more additional observations. The designated listener will be the next person to conduct.

The designated-listener procedure doubles the amount of time for each student to focus on making an aural analysis in a realistic setting. Focusing on aural analysis as a designated listener helps students prepare to make more accurate observations as they conduct.

This procedure can also include a *designated observer,* who will make comments about the conductor's technique. In order to save time, students should rotate through the three positions, beginning as the designated observer, then becoming the designated listener, and then conducting.

Continue the aural analysis procedures from Chapters 1 and 2, focusing on dynamic contours and releases.

ASSIGNMENTS

1 Practice the excerpts for Chapter 3 in the Anthology. Practice in front of a mirror and carefully evaluate each aspect of your conducting.
2 Practice the exercises in this chapter for left-hand dynamic indications every day.
3 Find three excerpts in the Anthology for Chapter 3 that require different releases for the endings. Practice conducting the final phrase, striving for a musically expressive and convincing sound.

EVALUATION

Use the following evaluation form to review and check the fundamental techniques you have studied thus far.

EVALUATION FORM FOR CHAPTER 3

Name: ______________________ Date: __________

Section/Lab: ______________________ Grade: __________

CHECKLIST { + indicates exceptionally good
− indicates deficient or incorrect

Repertoire:

1 __________ 2 __________ 3 __________

ENVIRONMENT AND POSTURE

1	2	3	
☐	☐	☐	Stand position
☐	☐	☐	Eye contact
☐	☐	☐	Stance
☐	☐	☐	Facial expression
☐	☐	☐	Attention-ready position
☐	☐	☐	Elbows

BATON AND BATON ARM

Grip ☐ Fingers
☐ Wrist
☐ Baton tip

Pivots ☐ Wrist
☐ Elbow
☐ Shoulder

NONBATON ARM

1	2	3	
☐	☐	☐	At-rest position
☐	☐	☐	Mirroring
☐	☐	☐	Independent motion

BEAT PATTERNS

1	2	3	
☐	☐	☐	Horizontal motion - beat plane
☐	☐	☐	Beat patterns
☐	☐	☐	Preparatory gesture
☐	☐	☐	Clear ictus
☐	☐	☐	Size of beat and rebound

OTHER

☐ Verbal directions
☐ Shows confidence
☐

PERFORMANCE EXCERPTS FOR CHAPTER 3

Section Three, pages 182–189

3-1 Waldteufel, *España* Waltz
3-2 Delibes, Waltz from *Coppélia*
3-3 Morley, "Sing we and chant it"
3-4 Grainger, *Lincolnshire Posy,* "The Lost Lady Found"
3-5 Strauss, *Blue Danube* Waltz
3-6 Tchaikovsky, *The Sleeping Beauty, Thornrose* Waltz
3-7 Offenbach, *Orphée aux enfers* ("Orpheus in the Underworld"), Overture

CHAPTER 4

ENTRANCES ON BEATS 2, 3, AND 4

CUES　ENDINGS

ENTRANCES ON BEATS 2, 3, AND 4

In Chapters 1 to 3, all the excerpts and exercises began on the first beat, with the preparatory gesture being the previous complete beat—that is, the upbeat. When the entrance occurs on other beats, the usual preparatory gesture is also the previous complete beat in the pattern. An exception to this may occur when the entrance begins on beat 2: then you may give the preparatory gesture in the opposite direction of the entrance, because inhaling while giving a downbeat as the preparatory gesture may feel unnatural. Therefore, the general rule is: *The preparatory gesture is the beat pattern that precedes the entrance or a gesture in a direction contrary to that given for the entrance.* (See Figures 4-1 and 4-2.)

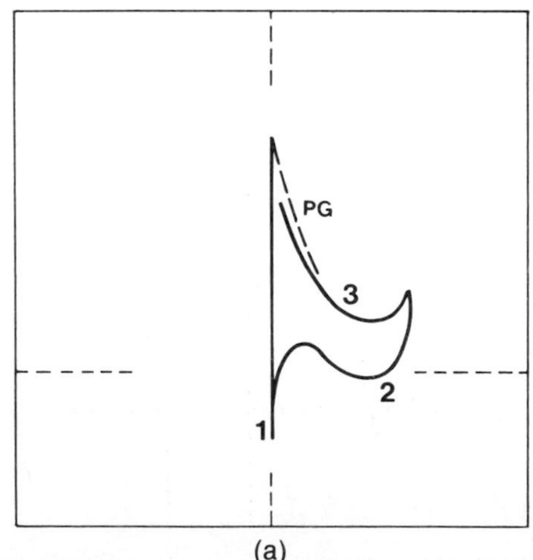

(a)

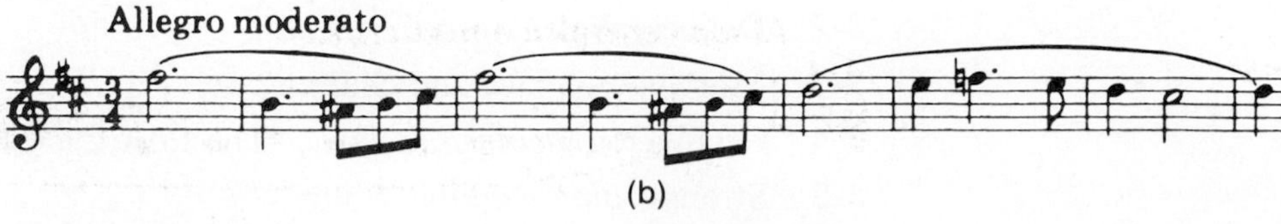

(b)

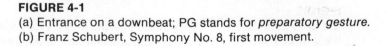

FIGURE 4-1
(a) Entrance on a downbeat; PG stands for *preparatory gesture.*
(b) Franz Schubert, Symphony No. 8, first movement.

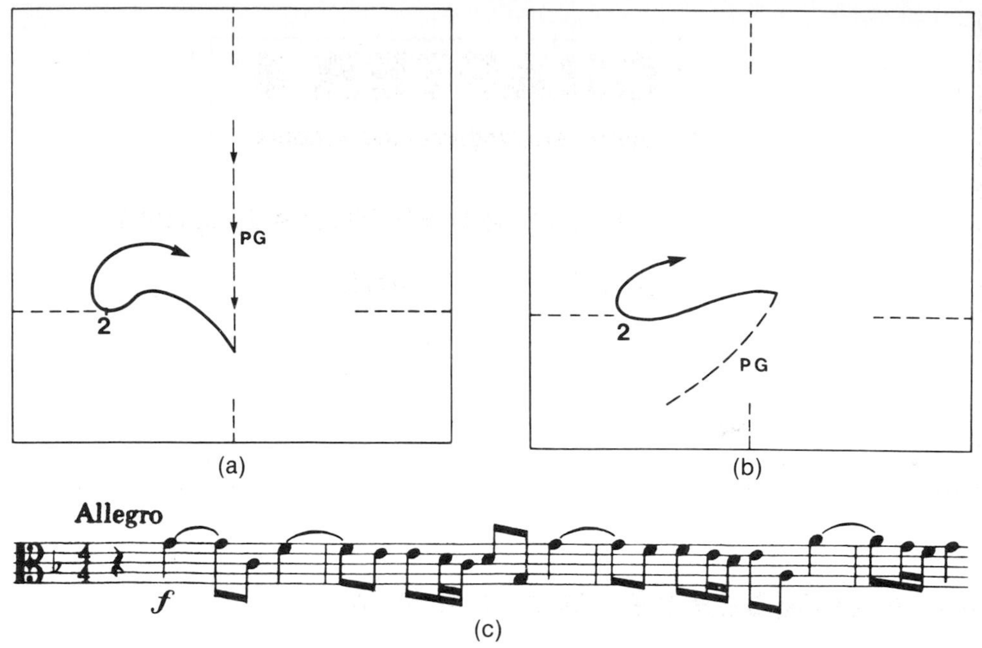

FIGURE 4-2
Entrance on a leftward beat in quadruple meter. (a) Preparatory gesture (PG) is the *previous beat*; notice that there is no upward motion before the downward preparatory gesture. (b) Preparatory gesture is from the *opposite direction.* (c) Arcangelo Corelli, Concerto Grosso for String Orchestra, Op. 6, No. 11, first movement.

Notice in the examples in Figures 4-3 through 4-5 that a slightly upward direction is used for each of the horizontal preparatory gestures to emphasize the breathing character. If a downward motion is used for the preparatory gesture, it should usually be short and light to ensure that it communicates preparation rather than entrance.

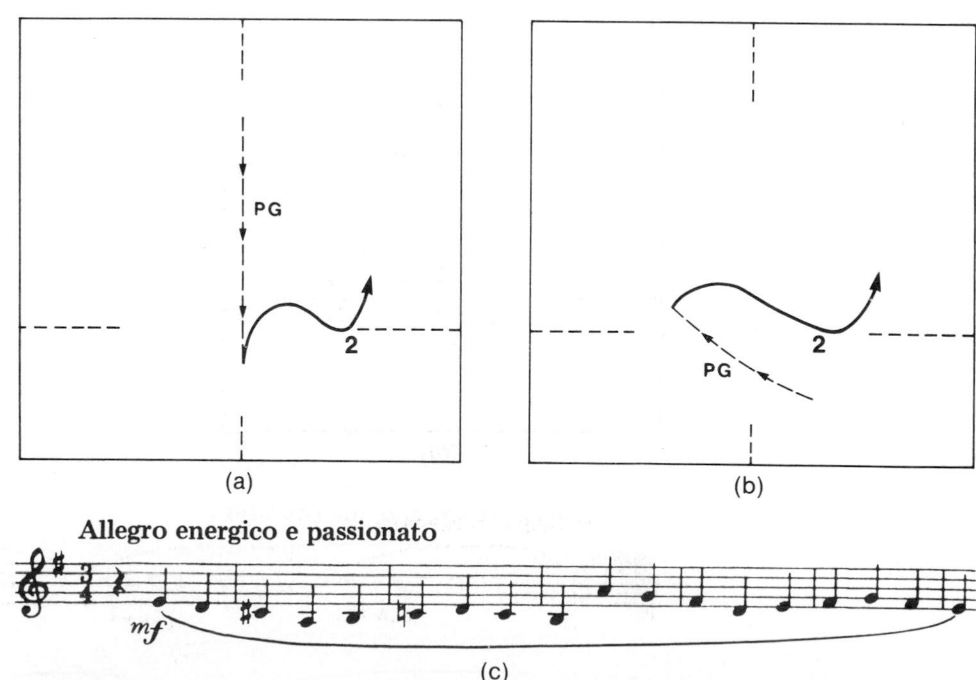

FIGURE 4-3
Entrance on a rightward beat pattern in triple meter. (a) Preparatory gesture (PG) is the *previous beat.* (b) Preparatory gesture is from the *opposite direction.* (c) Johannes Brahms, Symphony No. 4, fourth movement.

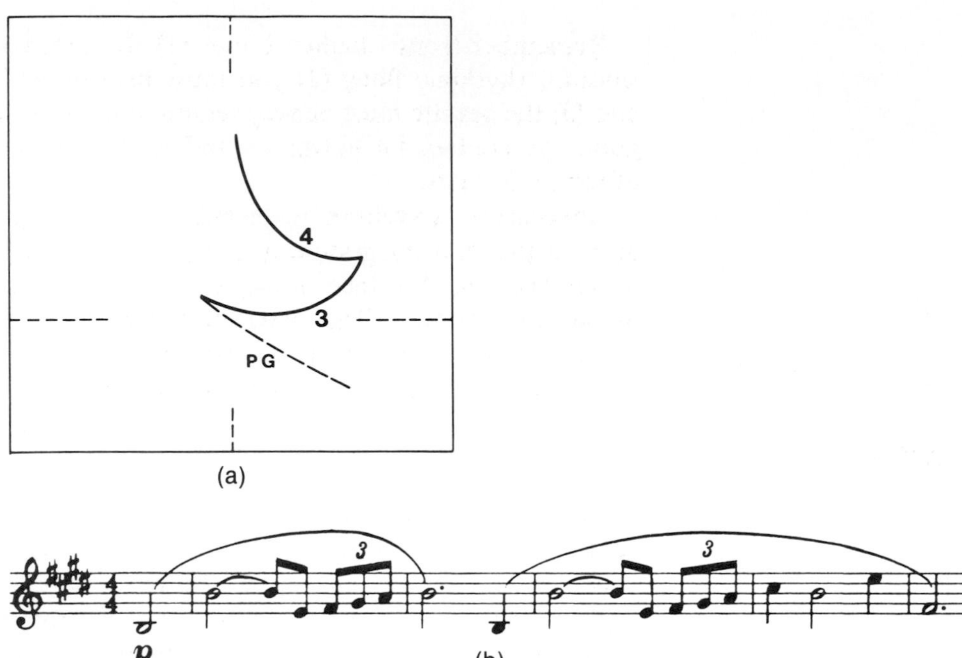

FIGURE 4-4
Above: Entrance on a rightward beat pattern in quadruple meter.
(a) Preparatory gesture (PG) is from the *opposite direction* and is also the *previous beat.*
(b) Richard Wagner, *Siegfried Idyll.*

FIGURE 4-5
Below: Entrance on an upbeat in quadruple meter.
(a) Preparatory gesture is from the *opposite direction* and is also the *previous beat.*
(b) Johannes Brahms, Symphony No. 1, fourth movement.

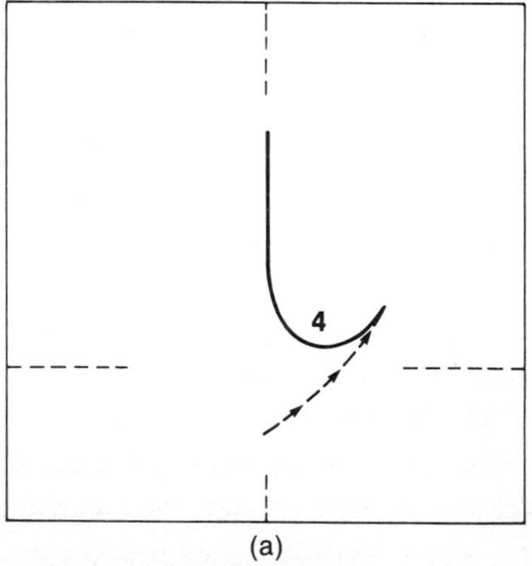

Remember from Chapter 1 that (1) the preparatory gesture must have a smooth, rhythmic flow; (2) you must breathe with the preparatory gesture; and (3) the gesture must convey tempo, dynamics, and style. Always establish good eye contact for entrances and wait until you sense the concentration of the performers.

Alternative procedures preferred by some conductors include giving an upward preparatory gesture and a downbeat for the entrance regardless of which beat the entrance is on, or giving one very small ictus before the preparatory gesture. The first alternative may be an advantage when the entrance is forte. The second alternative gives performers an extra beat in which to prepare, but it may also mislead them.

CUES

Cues assist performers in making precise, confident entrances. A cue should be given (1) for solo and sectional entrances, (2) for entrances that follow long rests, (3) for the beginning of any important musical event, and (4) in any other situation where it would help performers with a difficult entrance.

In some instances, it may not be possible to cue every entrance. For example, if several entrances occur in a few beats, the conductor could choose to cue only the first entrance. Performers making succeeding entrances would take their cue from the first entrance and mark in their parts where the first entrance occurs and who plays or sings it. The conductor could also choose to cue more than just the first entrance without cuing all entrances. It is sometimes helpful for the conductor to communicate the plan for cues verbally to the ensemble. In any case, consistency in cuing will usually lead to the most dependable results.

Procedure for Cues

The procedure for a cue is similar to that for any other preparatory gesture and entrance:

1 *Good eye contact must be established before the preparatory gesture.*
2 The preparatory gesture is given on the beat that precedes the entrance.
3 The preparatory gesture must communicate dynamic level, tempo, and articulation style.
4 The conductor's facial expression must be positive and supportive. (Many well-intentioned entrances have been undermined by inappropriate facial movements or grimaces by the conductor.)
5 The general effect must be decisive and reassuring to the performers, and the performers should acknowledge the cue whenever possible.
6 Reminders for cuing may be penciled neatly into the score to provide consistency in rehearsals and performance.

A cue may be given by:

- Right hand only, with special attention to making the required preparation and entrance beats distinguishable from the regular beat pattern
- Left hand only, independent of the right-hand beat pattern
- Head motion (this is more subtle than using either hand)
- Combinations of right hand, left hand, and head

Right-Hand Cues

When giving right-hand cues, the conductor should:

1 Turn and directly face the performers to be cued.

2 Maintain eye contact before, during, and after the cue.

3 Diminish the size of the beats preceding the preparatory gesture to make the cuing movements appear more prominent, or, if the regular size of the beat pattern should be maintained, enlarge the preparatory gesture and cue.

4 Raise the plane of the cuing movements (this is optional).

Study the sequence of events leading to the cue in Figure 4-6. The exact moment when eye contact is made will vary, depending on the tempo, the size of the ensemble, and other conditions.

FIGURE 4-6
Right-hand cue.

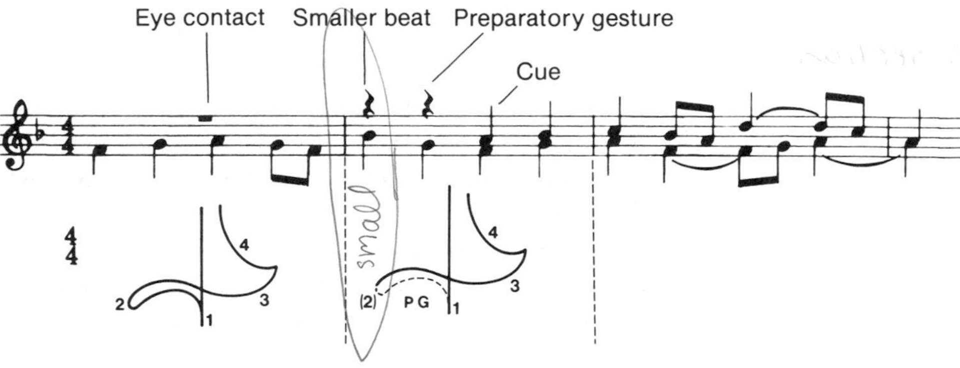

Left-Hand Cues

When giving left-hand cues, note the following:

1 The right hand can maintain the rhythmic pulse without assisting in the cuing process.

2 Raise the left hand to the attention position (arm extended and stationary, with hand at about head level) and establish eye contact before the entrance. The actual time before the entrance is determined by the tempo, the amount of rest that elapsed before the entrance, and the complexity of cues or the number of entrances requiring cues. Holding the left hand in the attention position longer increases the prominence of the cue.

3 Try not to mirror with the left hand; it detracts from the clarity of left-hand cues.

4 Avoid crossing hands in giving a left-hand cue such as that which might occur in cuing to the right on beat 2 of a four-beat pattern. Instead, give the cue with the right hand or turn far enough to the right to avoid the crossing. (Crossing looks awkward and is often difficult to follow.)

Study the sequence of preparation for a left-hand cue in Figure 4-7.

FIGURE 4-7
Left-hand cue. Preparatory gesture (PG) rises to avoid crossing of hands.

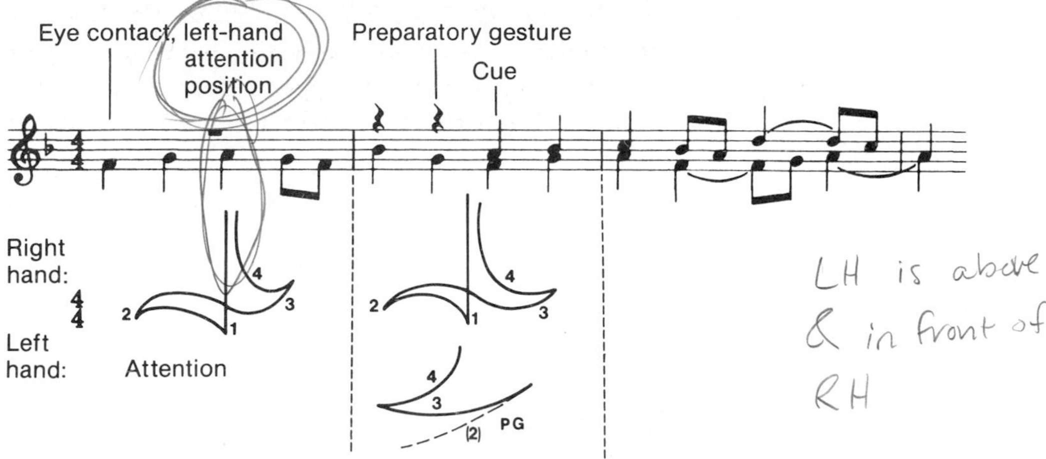

Head Cues

A cue can be given with a nod of the head by turning toward the entering performer, lifting the head slightly as a preparatory gesture, and lowering the head for the entrance beat. Good eye contact must be maintained throughout this process.

A downward-only motion of the head or a quick glance is *not* an adequate cuing gesture. A good cue *must* include a preparatory gesture, preceded and followed by eye contact. Eye contact alone may provide some reassurance—and some conductors do consider this in itself a cue—but it does not provide a complete cue because it lacks preparation and a definite ictus.

Excessive head motion may become distracting, so this type of cue should not be used too frequently.

Combinations of Cues

A head motion can be used with either or both hands, especially to communicate the breathing rhythm of the preparatory gesture. Both hands can also be used together, such as for a large tutti entrance. (See the example in Figure 4-8 on the following page.)

FIGURE 4-8
Entrance on beat 3, cue on a downbeat: Henry Purcell, *Dido and Aeneas*, "When I am laid in earth."

ENDINGS

The ending of a composition always deserves special attention. The conductor should decide how to approach the ending, what expressive effect should culminate the performance, and what to do after the ending.

Loud, rhythmic endings need to be conducted so that quality, blend, balance, and precision are not lost in the excitement. If rests are mixed with unison accents or chords, it is usually advisable to conduct only the notes, giving small marking beats on the rests or no beats at all. There should be a clear visual difference between the notes and the rests to reduce the possibility of a careless entry, which can seriously detract from a performance.

Listen carefully to the expressive effect of the ending. It may be necessary to hold the final tones longer than notated if the score does not have a fermata. Avoid the rather common tendency to hurry through the ending, losing much of its potential dramatic effect.

The visual presentation of the ending is also important. Think of the position and location of your hands for the final release. How long should they remain in a fixed position before you release the attention of the performers and the audience by moving? How should you move after the last tone is released?

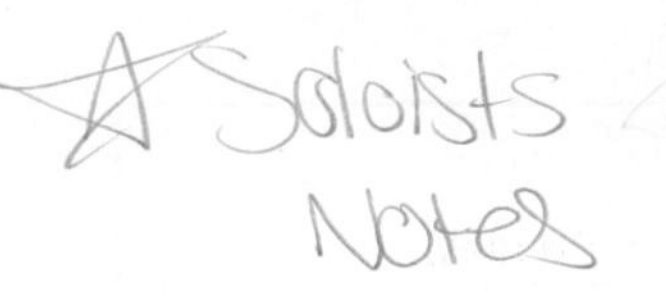

It is often helpful to make a notation at the end of the score to remind yourself which soloists should be acknowledged. After the applause begins, motion the ensemble to rise, bow to the audience pleasantly (do not allow yourself to have a grim expression), leave the stage quickly, and return quickly. At this time, acknowledge the concertmaster or concertmistress, the ensemble soloists, and the entire ensemble; then bow and leave again. Return for additional bows if the applause remains strong, but do not reappear if it is obviously about to stop.

AURAL ANALYSIS

Continue the procedures followed in Chapters 1, 2, and 3.

ASSIGNMENT

Practice the excerpts for Chapter 4 in the Anthology.

EVALUATION

Use the evaluation form on the following page to check basic techniques.

PERFORMANCE EXCERPTS FOR CHAPTER 4

Section Three, pages 190–214

4-1 Jacob, *Old Wine in New Bottles,* "Early One Morning"

4-2 Gabrieli, *Sacrae symphoniae, Canzon septimi toni à 8* ("Sacred Symphonies, Canzona on the Seventh Tone for Eight Voices")

4-3 Beethoven, Symphony No. 5, fourth movement

4-4 Billings, *Three Fuguing Tunes,* "When Jesus Wept"

4-5 Handel, *Messiah,* "And the glory of the Lord"

4-6 Pinkham, *Christmas Eve*

4-7 Bartók, "Don't Leave Me!"

4-8 Anonymous, *N'ia gaire que auvit* ("A Long, Long Time Ago")

4-9 Nelson, "Sleep Little One"

4-10 Moore, "The Minstrel Boy"

EVALUATION FORM FOR CHAPTER 4

Name:______________________ Date: __________ Grade: __________

Evaluate the following while conducting beat patterns or the excerpts for Chapter 4. A check mark or no mark indicates correct, + indicates exceptionally good, and – indicates deficient or incorrect.

POSTURE

_____ Foot position
_____ Knees
_____ Back
_____ Shoulders
_____ Neck
_____ Head
_____ Upper arm (angle from body)
_____ Upper arm (forward angle)
_____ Elbow (angle of bend)
_____ Forearm (4–5 and 7–8 o'clock)
_____ Wrist
_____ Fingers

Review the lessons if you are in doubt about correct positions.

ENTRANCES AND CUES

_____ Eye contact
_____ Rhythmic breathing motion
_____ Smooth preparatory gesture
_____ Appropriate tempo
_____ Appropriate dynamics
_____ Appropriate style
_____ Clear ictus
_____ Confident and assuring

RELEASES

_____ Circular
_____ Up-down
_____ Appropriate size
_____ Musical effect

BEAT PATTERNS

_____ Horizontal plane
_____ Rebound control
_____ Clear ictus on each beat
_____ Vertical plane
_____ Adequate horizontal motion

Each of the following beat patterns should be conducted with the right hand, left hand, and both hands together.

_____ Four _____ Three _____ Two (three variations)
_____ One (three variations)

Change the size and style of the beat patterns:

_____ Small _____ Medium _____ Large _____ Staccato _____ Legato

BATON GRIP

_____ Good contact points
_____ Curve of fingers
_____ Curve of thumb
_____ Direction of baton
_____ Ictus always at baton tip

LEFT-HAND DYNAMIC INDICATIONS

_____ At-rest position, side
_____ At-rest position, front
_____ Smooth, independent motions
_____ Hand shape, crescendo
_____ Hand shape, diminuendo

CHAPTER 5

SCORE STUDY **CLEFS AND TRANSPOSITIONS**
SAMPLE SCORES **USEFUL TERMINOLOGY**
REHEARSALS

SCORE STUDY

The learning process involved in score study brings into focus all the areas of education and experience encountered thus far. Every *note, symbol,* and *marking* on the page must be learned and placed in its appropriate relationship to the composition as a whole.

Appropriate conducting gestures grow out of the musical requirements indicated in the score; all you must do is find and identify these requirements and then apply the right set of gestures. In other words, your gestures should be a physical reflection of the sound being created by the ensemble. There is no problem involving general patterns of conducting, or specific gestures, that cannot be analyzed and worked out if you consider the needs of the performers and the musical clues in the score.

The primary route to comfort and security on a podium is knowledge and command of the score, and possession of the physical skills necessary to portray the composition visually. Each conductor must develop his or her own individual skills, based on personal capabilities, for score study and conducting. We recommend a three-phase series of study sessions, each accomplishing specific goals until the score is finally learned in every detail.

Phase 1: Title Page and Overview

A first look at the score, or a cursory overview of it, begins with page 1, which usually contains a large amount of information. Be sure that you have a thorough grasp of every word and marking on this page. Use reference books such as *Baker's Guide to Music and Musicians, Grove's Dictionary of Music and Musicians,* and the *Harvard Dictionary of Music* to find whatever additional information you may need to answer the following questions.

1 Composer. Where and when was this piece written? What do you know about other works by this composer? Who (if anyone) was the *editor,* the *arranger,* the *transcriber,* or the *orchestrator?*

2 *Title.* What can be inferred from the title? What do you know about the *genre*? Does the *opus number* indicate whether this is an early, middle, or late work by the composer? Is the *date of composition* given?

3 *Dedication.* If there is a dedication, what does it imply? For example, was the piece written for an ensemble or artist, and does that suggest anything about its *level of difficulty*?

4 *Historical context.* How does the work fit into the composer's overall output? What do you know about the style of the period and its performance practices? What do you know about the composer's style? Are you familiar with recorded performances of the work by different ensembles?

5 *Instrumentation.* Identify the instrumentation, and review *transpositions* and *ranges.* Is the piece for a standard grouping of instruments or voices? What is special or different in the listing? (Information on clefs, transpositions, and foreign terms for instruments will be presented later in this chapter.)

6 *Clefs.* What clefs are used? It is important to become fluent in reading clefs and transpositions, in order to know how the score should sound at concert pitch (untransposed). A conductor loses credibility quickly if he or she cannot read clefs or transpositions correctly in rehearsal and is unable to determine correct notes for the performers. Practice reading the clefs and transpositions on pages 54–61.

7 Is the score in concert pitch (C) or *transposed?* (Note: The abbreviation C is frequently used for *concert pitch,* and a concert-pitch score is called a *C score.*)

8 What are the *tempo indications* and *metronome markings*?

9 Do you understand all the *expressive markings* and all the *dynamic markings*?

10 *Text.* If there is a text, is it in the original language or is it a *translation*? Who (if anyone) is the translator?

11 *Publisher.* Does the name of the *publisher* imply anything about quality?

12 Is there an explanation or description of *unusual notation* or *effects*?

Phase 2: Structural Features

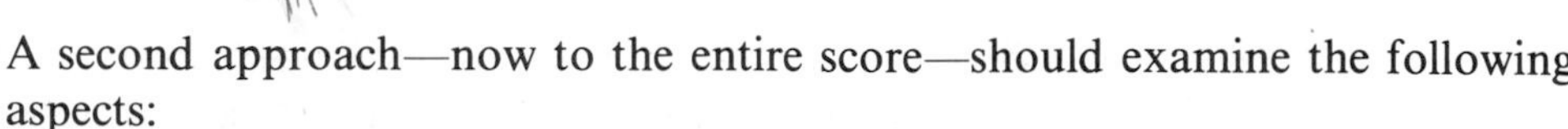

A second approach—now to the entire score—should examine the following aspects:

1 *Formal design.* How many sections are there? What are the characteristics of each section? Consider making a chart or table of the sections, listing their distinctive features.

2 *Melodic development.* Identify the main melodic materials. Think about their characteristics. Look for *motives* and *imitation.* What technical problems are there in the melodic material? Are there any awkward intervals or extreme tessituras? Do you find inherent intonation problems in unison and doubled parts? What are the problems of balance in doublings and unison?

3 *Harmonic organization.* Look at key signatures and the bass line to make preliminary decisions about large tonal areas. Look for pedal points, inverted pedal points, and main cadences. Then examine specific areas in detail to notice the type of chord structures used and the harmonic movement. Does the harmonic background merely support the melodic material, or is it rhythmically aligned? Make a diagram of the tonal outline of the piece.

4 *Rhythmic development.* What are the distinctive rhythmic qualities of the piece? How do they change throughout each main section? Are there sections or passages that will probably require special rehearsal?

5 *Texture.* Is the texture polyphonic, homophonic, or monophonic? Does the scoring or instrumentation change within small or large formal areas? If so, what is the effect of each change? How does the *density* (sparse, thick, heavily doubled, widely spaced, etc.) within small or large formal areas affect the flow of the music?

6 *Text.* If the music has a text, examine it. Look at the relationship between expressive features of the music and the meaning of the text. Make sure that you know the correct pronunciation of every word and the diction and vocal techniques involved in singing the text.

7 *Conducting problems.* Analyze each change of meter, of cadence, of tempo, etc. Mark areas of concern in the score for future reference, study, and practice. Practice singing and conducting each major section and finally the entire score. Can you hear the lines and timbres in your mind as you conduct? You should be able to compare details of this work with similar details of other works in your aural memory.

Phase 3: Interpretation

The third approach is to interpret the composition. Examine the following:

1 What distinctive characteristics of the composition should be emphasized? Consider melodic, rhythmic, and harmonic qualities; tension and release; timbres; and structural design.

2 Can you feel and set a correct tempo for each section? Check your concept of tempos with a metronome repeatedly until you can accurately remember the right tempos.

3 How does the structure of the piece evolve? Think in terms of bringing out the new structural features of each section so that the audience will hear them.

4 How do you want your audience to respond to this work? How can you project your concept to the audience? You and the performers must hear and feel your own interpretation with such intensity and involvement that the audience will also hear and respond to it. This is similar to an actor's feeling and projecting fear or happiness with such intensity that the audience experiences the same emotion.

5 Listen to recordings of other compositions by the same composer, or in the same style, or of the same genre. How does your interpretation compare with the musical thoughts and expression of other conductors and performers?

CLEFS AND TRANSPOSITIONS

Alto and Tenor Clefs

As music notation and calligraphy developed over the past four centuries, a system of movable clefs evolved that placed C^1 (middle C) on various lines of the five-line staff. Each of the human voices had its own movable C clef (soprano clef, mezzo-soprano clef, and so on), which tended to place most of the written notes in the general range of the staff, thus eliminating excessive use of leger lines. This system has remained in use today, with two primary C clefs employed in addition to the treble and bass clefs—the *tenor* and *alto* clefs. Conductors must be able to read alto and tenor clefs with ease. Reading C clefs should not be considered transposition; all notes are at concert pitch. The alto and tenor clefs are shown in Figures 5-1 and 5-2.

FIGURE 5-1
Alto clef.

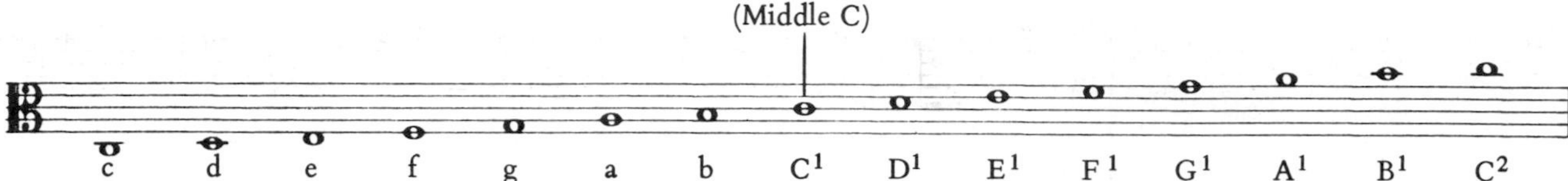

FIGURE 5-2
Tenor clef.

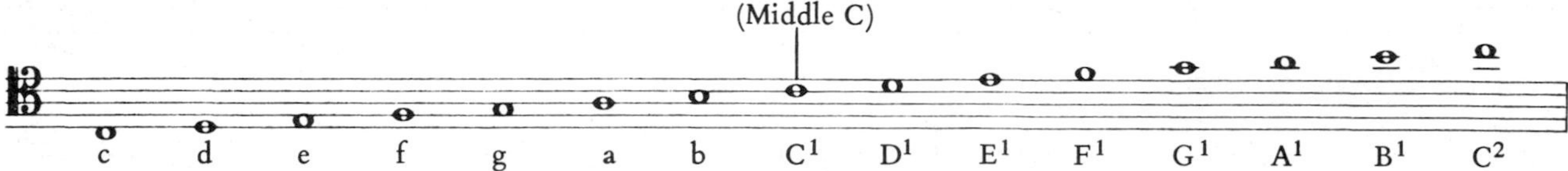

Practice the excerpts in Figure 5-3, singing the names of the notes or playing the notes on the piano.

Additional examples in alto clef can be found in viola parts in orchestral and chamber music; additional examples in tenor clef can be found in cello, trombone, and bassoon parts.

FIGURE 5-3
Reading exercises in the alto and tenor clefs: (a) Peter Ilych Tchaikovsky, *March Slav;* (b) Edward Elgar, *Enigma* Variations; (c) Michael Haydn, Quintet in F Minor; (d) Johannes Brahms, Concerto No. 2 for Piano and Orchestra, third movement.

(a) *March Slav.*

FIGURE 5-3
(Continued)

(b) *Enigma* variations.

(c) Quintet in F Minor.

(d) Piano Concerto No. 2.

Vocal Transpositions

Vocal music normally uses only one transposed voice, the tenor part, which sounds one octave lower than written.

Instrumental Transpositions

Transposing instrumental or vocal parts to concert pitch is one of the conductor's constant tasks. The individual performer sees only one or two written lines in a part and frequently needs instant confirmation or correction of that part from the conductor.

Understanding the process of transposition requires understanding the system of intervallic relationships that includes the *concert pitch* (the pitch that is heard) and the *transposed pitch* (the pitch that is written at some interval from the concert pitch). An inexperienced performer will frequently think only in terms of the written pitch in the transposed part, not of the concert pitch relationships with the rest of the ensemble. But each performer can become more aware of these ensemble relationships through constant reference by the conductor to concert pitch during rehearsals.

Theoretical and Historical Background

One basis for the transposition process that we use is the *harmonic series,* a succession of pitches produced when a pipe is blown and overblown or a string is set into vibration by being plucked or struck. The lowest pitch of the harmonic series is called the *fundamental,* and the subsequent tones are called *overtones.* Another term for the fundamental is the *first partial,* with each successive partial numbered consecutively.

The harmonic series of a pipe with a fundamental of C below the bass staff would produce the tones shown in Figure 5-4. The two commonly used systems of enumeration are indicated: the one above the staff is the fundamental with subsequent overtones, and the one below the staff lists each tone by partial number. The noteheads in black—partials 7 and 11—are badly out of tune and must be adjusted by performers.

FIGURE 5-4
Harmonic series in C.

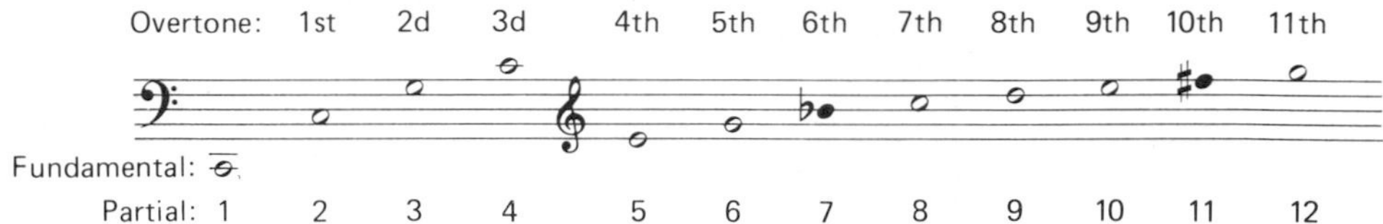

Before the invention of valves for brass instruments, during the second decade of the 1800s, the horns and trumpets of the orchestra and wind band were mainly restricted to the tones of the harmonic series. Pitches between series tones were possible, however, through hand positioning in the horn bell and through lip manipulation with the mouthpiece. When a composition required harmonic or melodic resources other than the tones in the C harmonic series, the performer changed the length of tubing on the instrument through the use of crooks or slides, producing a new fundamental and overtone series. (The trombone is an excellent example of this process; its seven positions produce seven harmonic series—B-flat, A, and so on, through E.) Horn players of the late 1700s used a basic instrument of circular tubing with crooks that put the horn into harmonic series based on B, B-flat, A, A-flat, G, F, E, E-flat, D, C basso, and B-flat basso. Thus it became the performer's task to find a way to perform the part as the harmonic language of the classical period assumed more of a chromatic nature.

The excerpt in Figure 5-5 illustrates the principle of transposition with the famous "horn fifths," a set of harmonic-series tones that produced a sixth, a fifth, and a major third between the two voices. This is probably the most common open-horn passage of the prevalve era, other than unisons and octaves. The concert-pitch result is shown in Figure 5-6.

FIGURE 5-5
Franz Joseph Haydn, Symphony No. 103, fourth movement.

Allegro con spirito

1 2 3 4 5 6 7 8

Flauti

Oboi

Clarinetti in B♭

Fagotti

Corni in E♭

p

Trombe in E♭

Timpani in E♭, B♭

Violino I

p

Violino II

Viola

Violoncello e Basso

FIGURE 5-6
Haydn, Symphony No. 103, C reduction.

Common Transpositions: C, B-Flat, F, and E-Flat

The conductor will occasionally find other transpositions in various keys in baroque, classical, and impressionist music, but the primary transposition requirements for most nineteenth- and twentieth-century music are:

- *C.* One or more octaves upward or downward
- *B-flat.* Major second, major ninth, major ninth plus one octave lower, minor seventh higher
- *F.* Perfect fifth lower (if in bass clef, perfect fourth up or perfect fifth down as specified)
- *E-flat.* Major sixth lower, major sixth plus one octave lower, minor third higher

Occasional use of A (minor third lower) and G (perfect fourth lower) will also be encountered.

C transpositions are described in Figure 5-7.

FIGURE 5-7
C transpositions, one or more octaves: (a) octave higher; (b) two octaves higher; (c) octave lower in vocal music; (d) octave lower in instrumental music.

(a) Octave higher (8va). Instruments using 8va: piccolo; celesta.

Written: Sounds:

(b) Two octaves higher (15va). Instruments using 15va: orchestra bells (glockenspiel).

Written: Sounds:

(c) Octave lower (8ba), vocal music. Used for tenor voices.

Written: Sounds:

(d) Octave lower (8ba), instrumental music.
Instruments using 8ba: guitar, string bass (also uses 𝄞 for upper tessitura); contrabassoon.

Written: Sounds:

B-flat transpositions sound a major second (M2), major ninth (M9), or major sixteenth (M16) lower than written and may also transpose upward a minor seventh (m7). The written part uses the key signature a major second above concert pitch; thus, the concert pitch of the example is F and the key signature of the written, transposed part is G. B-flat transpositions are shown in Figure 5-8.

FIGURE 5-8
B-flat transpositions: (a) major second lower; (b) major ninth lower; (c) major fifteenth lower.

(a) Major 2d lower. Instruments using M2 lower: B-flat clarinet, soprano saxophone, B-flat trumpet, B-flat cornet, flügelhorn.

Written: Sounds:

(b) Major 9th (octave plus M2) lower. Instruments using M9 lower: bass clarinet, tenor saxophone, treble clef baritone.

Written: Sounds:

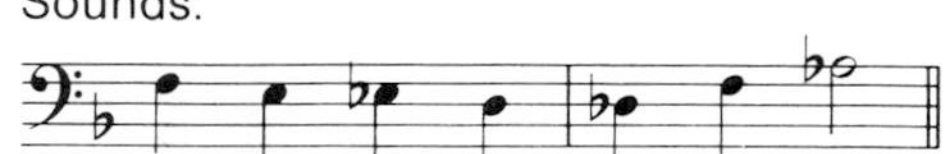

(c) Major 16th (two octaves plus M2) lower. Instruments using 16ba lower: BB-flat contrabass clarinet; bass saxophone.

Written: Sounds:

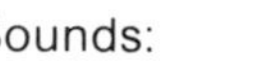

F transpositions (see Figure 5-9) sound a perfect fifth (P5) lower than written. The written part uses the key signature a perfect fifth above concert pitch; thus in Figure 5-9 the concert-pitch key signature is F and the key signature of the written, transposed part is C.

FIGURE 5-9
F transposition: perfect fifth lower.

Written: Sounds:

Transpositions in E-flat (see Figure 5-10) sound a major sixth (M6) or an octave plus a major sixth lower than written. The written part uses the key signature a major sixth above concert pitch; thus, in Figure 5-10 the concert pitch is F and the key signature of the written, transposed part is D. E-flat transpositions also occur upward (E-flat clarinet and E-flat trumpet; concert pitch is a minor third higher than the written pitch).

FIGURE 5-10
E-flat transposition: major sixth lower.

Written: Sounds:

Quick-Check Transpositions for Orchestras and Wind Bands

Today, typical orchestra and band scores include the following instruments and transpositions. All other instruments listed on a score should be assumed to be written and sounding at concert pitch unless a key designation is given.

Instrument	Sounds	Written Sounds
C piccolo	Octave higher	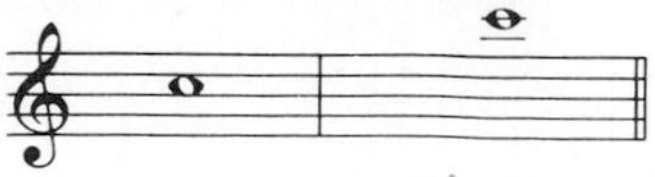
English horn	P5 lower	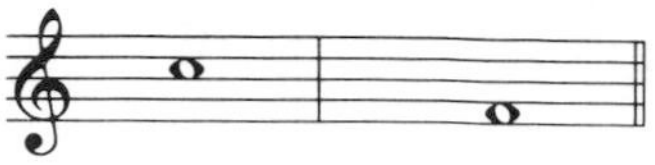
E-flat clarinet (transposes upward)	m3 higher	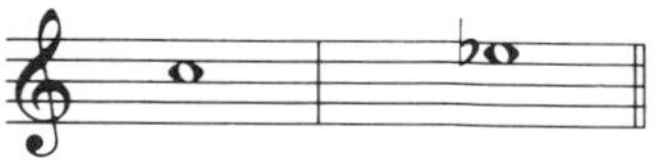
B-flat clarinet	M2 lower	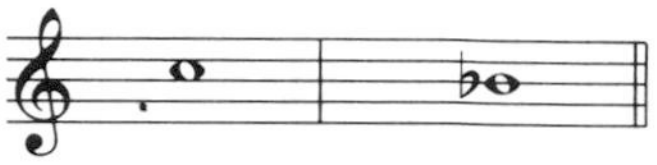
A clarinet	m3 lower	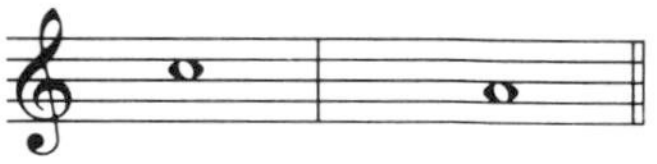
Alto clarinet	M6 lower	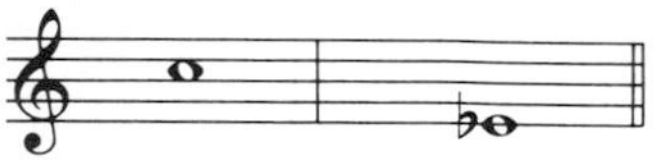
Bass clarinet	M9 lower	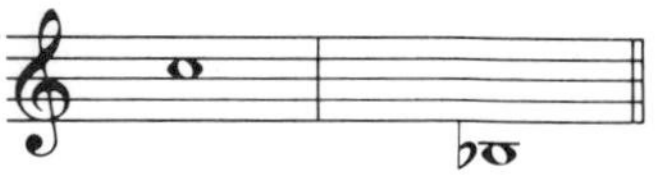
EE-flat contra-alto clarinet	M6 plus octave lower	
BB-flat contrabass clarinet	M16 lower (two octaves plus M2 lower)	
Contrabassoon	Octave lower	

Instrument	Sounds	Written	Sounds
Soprano saxophone	M2 lower		
Alto saxophone	M6 lower		
Tenor saxophone	M9 lower		
Baritone saxophone	M6 plus octave lower		
F horn	P5 lower		
C trumpet	Concert pitch		
B-flat trumpet	M2 lower		
D trumpet (transposes upward)	M2 higher		
B-flat piccolo trumpet (transposes upward)	m7 higher		
String bass	Octave lower		
Celesta	Octave higher		
Orchestra bells	Two octaves higher (15va)		

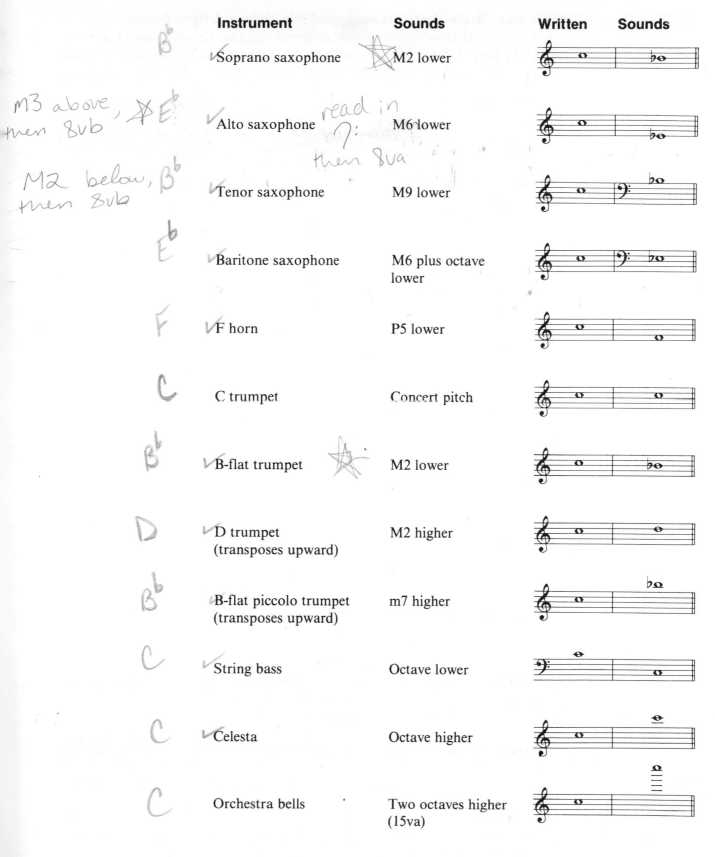

SAMPLE SCORES

Multistaff Vocal Scores

Choral music is normally written as a four-part score with one staff each for the soprano (S), alto (A), tenor (T), and bass (B) parts—referred to as an SATB score. Each part can be divided into separate voices by writing *divisi* on one staff or by using additional staffs. Each type of vocal ensemble is identified by the number of treble or bass parts: SSA, SSAA, TBB, and so on.

All voices except the tenor part are nontransposing. The tenor part sounds one octave lower than its treble-clef notation.

Piano reductions are often included with vocal scores for rehearsal purposes. Figure 5-11 (opposite page) shows a typical SATB score, with piano accompaniment for rehearsal only.

The Condensed Instrumental Score

The condensed (short or reduced) score has been in common use in nonclassical compositions for more than a century. Although generally an inferior guide to the intricacies of orchestration, it has served musical theater, ensembles of the salon orchestra type, military and concert bands, and, more recently, jazz ensembles. The primary disadvantage of the condensed score is that it has only two or three staffs, so that creative orchestration indications are precluded and octave distributions of tones are not always indicated. Correcting mistakes in rehearsal is often a problem because the conductor cannot be certain about the accuracy of each individual part; many hours must be spent before rehearsal comparing parts with the score and adding additional markings to the score where necessary. On the positive side, condensed scores are easy to read—even though the information is incomplete—and placing more bars of score on each page greatly reduces page turning during performances. All parts in condensed scores are written in concert pitch, except for some European wind band scores that are printed in B-flat transposition.

Several publishers have attempted to upgrade the usual two- or three-line wind band score by increasing the number of staffs and assigning a treble staff and a bass staff to both the woodwind and the brass families. This four-staff version also has a separate line or group of lines for the percussion. Regardless of what efforts are made, however, condensed scores are usually an impediment to efficient rehearsing. Nevertheless, there are still in existence many works for which only a condensed score is available; therefore, every conductor should learn how to cope with these scores.

An example of a Broadway musical score, with a voice line and text plus a piano reduction of the orchestration, is the song "The Company Way" from *How to Succeed in Business without Really Trying* (Figure 5-12, page 64). In this example, as in those that follow, the conductor must assume that "tutti" does indeed include all the voices available and that doublings will continue until canceled.

The three scores in Figures 5-13 to 5-15 (pages 65–67) illustrate varying amounts of information. Each is a setting for concert band using complete instrumentation.

FIGURE 5-11
Four-part vocal score: Orlando di Lasso, *Matona, mia cara* ("Matona, lovely maiden"). (English version by William Alexander Barrett; edited by H. Clogh-Leighter.)

FIGURE 5-12
Frank Loesser, *How to Succeed in Business without Really Trying,* "The Company Way."

FIGURE 5-13
Georges Bizet, *L'Arlésienne* ("The Woman of Arles"), Suite No. 1, Prelude. (Arranged by L. P. Laurendeau.)

FIGURE 5-14
Roger Nixon, *Fiesta del Pacifico.*

FIGURE 5-15
Vincent Persichetti, *O Cool Is the Valley.*

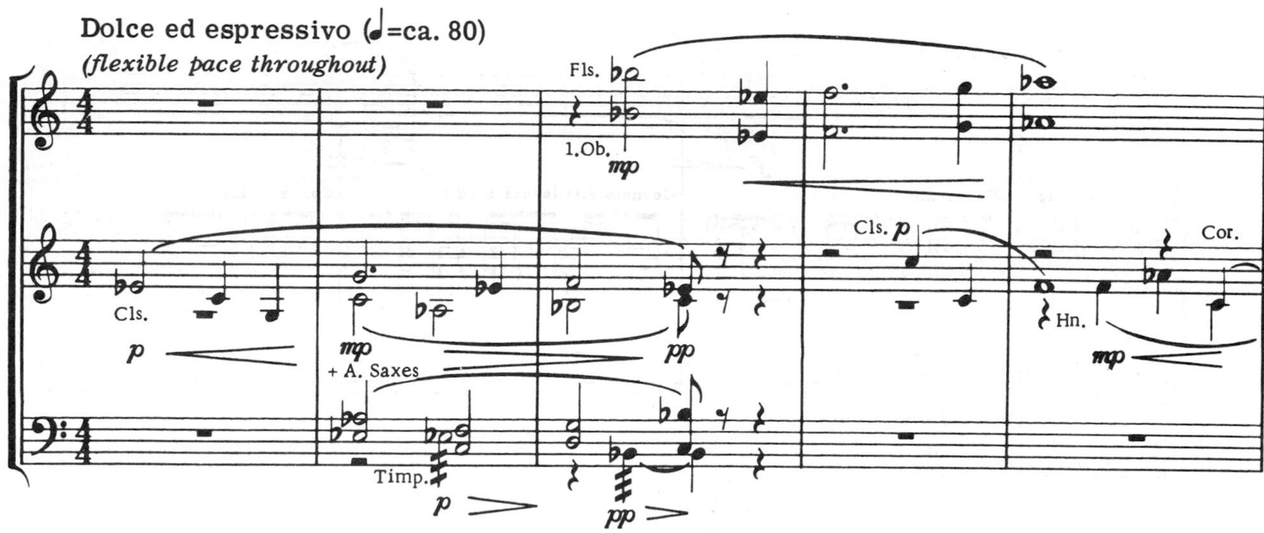

The jazz ensemble score (or *chart,* as it is frequently called) is found in several forms. Figure 5-16 (page 68) is a typical jazz score. It shows the notation for every instrument, with each section of the ensemble grouped on one or two staffs. Harmonic relationships between sections can be quickly seen, because all parts are in concert pitch. A piano–string bass part with harmonic chord symbols is shown in Figure 5-17 (page 69).

FIGURE 5-16
Don Sebesky, *Meet a Cheetah.*

Note: Hand clappers may be added on beats 2 and 4 from [A] on. They should rest in solo breaks. (ex. 9-14 after [A] at [E] etc.) Any Alto, Trumpet, or Trombone part may be doubled at will. Tenor Saxes and Baritone Sax may be omitted if necessary.

FIGURE 5-17
Manny Albam, *Pennies for Evan,* rhythm section score.

USEFUL TERMINOLOGY

Foreign Names of Instruments

English	Italian	German	French
Woodwinds			
piccolo	flauto piccolo ottavino	kleine Flöte	petite flûte
flute	flauto	Flöte, grosse Flöte	flûte
oboe	oboe	Oboe or Hoboe	hautbois
English horn	Corno Inglese	Englisch Horn	cor anglais
clarinet	clarinetto	Klarinette	clarinette
bass clarinet	clarinetto basso	Bassklarinette	clarinette basse
bassoon	fagotto	Fagott	basson
contrabassoon	contrafagotto	Kontrafagott	contre-basson
saxophone	sassofone	Saxophon	saxophone
Brass			
horn	corno	Horn	cor
trumpet	tromba	Trompete	trompette
cornet	cornetto	Kornett	cornet à piston
Fluegelhorn	flicorno	Bugle	bugle
trombone	trombone	Posaune	trombone
euphonium	baritone saxhorn	Baryton	basse à pistons
tuba	tuba di basso	Basstuba	tuba basse
Percussion			
timpani or kettledrums	timpani	Pauken	timbales
xylophone	silofone	Sylophon	sylophone
marimba	marimba	Marimba	marimba
glockenspiel	campanelli	Glockenspiel	jeu de timbres or carillon
vibraphone	vibrafono	Vibraphon	vibraphone
bells or chimes	campane	Glocken	cloches
snare drum	tamburo	kleine Trommel	tambour or caisse claire
field drum	tamburo	Rührtrommel	tambour
bass drum	(gran) cassa	grosse Trommel	grosse caisse
cymbals	piatti	Becken	cymbales
suspended cymbal	piatto sospeso	hängendes Becken	cymbale suspendé
gong or tam-tam	tam-tam	Tam-tam	tam-tam
triangle	triangolo	Triangel	triangle
tambourine	tamburino	Schellentrommel or Tambourin	tambour (de Basque)
castanets	castagnette	Kastagnetten	castagnettes
rattle (or ratchet)	raganella	Ratsche	crécelle
wood block	cassa di legno	Holzkaste	bloc de bois
cowbells	campanelli di bacca	Heerdenglocken	grelots de vaches
sleighbells	sonaglia	Schellen	grelots
slapstick or whip	frusta	Peitsche	fouret
celesta	celesta	Celesta	célesta

English	Italian	German	French
Strings			
harp	arpa	Harfe	harpe
violin	violino	Violine	violon
viola	viola	Bratsche	alto
violoncello or cello	violoncello	Violoncell	violoncelle
double bass	contrabasso	Kontrabass	contrebasse

String Bowings and Articulations

Term	Definition
am Steg (German)	At the bridge of a stringed instrument.
an dem Griffbrett (German)	Play stringed instruments on the fingerboard.
a punto d'arco (Italian)	With the point of the bow.
archet (French)	With the bow.
arco (Italian)	With the bow.
Bogen (Bog.) (German)	With the bow.
corda (Italian)	String.
détaché (French)	Each note bowed separately, played broadly.
Fr., Frog	To be played near the frog.
jeté (French)	"Thrown" bow (flying staccato).
legno (Italian)	Wood.
col legno (Italian)	With the stick of the bow.
L.h.	Lower half of the bow.
M	Middle of the bow.
pizzicato (pizz.) (Italian)	Pluck string(s) with finger(s).
ponticello (Italian)	A light tone, sounding upper partials by bowing near the bridge of a stringed instrument.
Pt., Point	To be played near the point of the bow.
saltando (salt.) (Italian)	Bounce the bow off the string, using short, quick bow strokes.
scordatura (Italian)	Special tuning of a stringed instrument.
spiccato (spicc.) (Italian)	A light, bouncing bow movement.
spitze (German)	Point of the bow.
sul (Italian)	On (as in *sul D,* on the D string).
sulla tastiera (Italian)	On the fingerboard.
sul tasto (Italian)	On the fingerboard.
sur la touche (French)	On the fingerboard.
sur le chevalet (French)	Bow close to the bridge.
sur une corde (French)	Play on one string.
⊓	Down bow.
V	Up bow.

Term	**Definition**
U.H.	Upper half of the bow.
W.B.	Whole bow.
bowed tremolo	Very fast separate strokes on the same pitch, near the point for soft dynamics and near the middle for louder dynamics.
détaché	Played with separate bows; in a very rapid détaché, the bow bounces (spiccato) from the string (sautillé).
fingered tremolo 	Played like a trill, for intervals larger than a whole step. Played with left-hand fingers and a single bow.
harmonic, artificial	Lower note is stopped by the first finger and upper note by the third or fourth finger.
harmonic, natural	String is touched lightly at the point indicated by the diamond-shaped note, thus dividing the string and producing a natural overtone.
glissando (gliss.) 	Slide.
louré 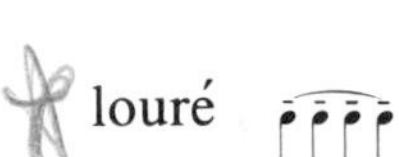	Notes under the slur are played with one bow direction. Bow pressure is released slightly to make a subtle articulation of each tone.
martelé 	Heavy accent with clear separation between notes.
portamento  	A smooth, short slide leading to a note.
left-hand pizzicato	String is plucked with the finger(s) of the left hand.
ricochet 	Bow moves in one direction for each slur and bounces for each note. (Actually two or more spiccatos with one bow direction.)
slur 	Bow moves smoothly in one direction while the left-hand fingers change the notes.
slurred staccato 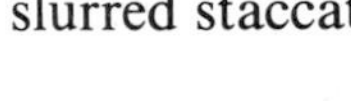	Played in one bow, stopping between notes to articulate.
spring bow arpeggio 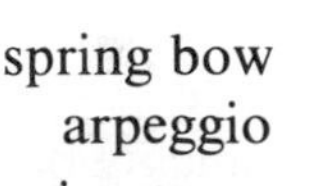	Bow bounces across the strings, playing each string in sequence.
spiccato 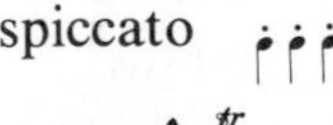	Bouncing bow. Bow leaves the string between notes.
trill 	A rapid alternation to the half step or whole step above.

REHEARSALS

Rehearsal Planning

The planning recommendations that follow focus only on understanding the composition and leading the ensemble. Specific aspects of vocal or instrumental technique, such as articulation, tone production, and diction, are not within the scope of this book. Other sources which cover those areas are listed in Appendix 8. You should make these books a part of your personal and professional library.

Your study of the score must lead to a clear, detailed mental image of the piece, and ultimately to your own interpretation of it. You should also determine the strengths and weaknesses of the ensemble, anticipate what will need to be done in problem areas, and establish specific objectives. Prioritize the objectives and plan a rehearsal procedure for each. In some cases, the performers will be able to accomplish an objective simply by being told or shown through musical examples; in other cases, you will need to have a plan for isolating individual problems and using specific rehearsal procedures.

Rehearsal Procedures: A Basic Repertoire

Successful conductors develop a repertoire of rehearsal procedures for teaching specific concepts and correcting common problems. This personal repertoire of analytical and rehearsal techniques may be expanded by observing other conductors, by creating new ideas yourself and trying them out in rehearsal, and by reading additional books, such as those listed in Appendix 8. As a conductor, you will decide what needs to be done and how to do it. Be prepared with two or three alternative approaches for each potential problem. If the first approach doesn't work, try to achieve the desired result with a different approach. This calls upon all your musical experience and knowledge and is one of the most challenging and gratifying aspects of conducting.

In selecting procedures, it is always necessary to consider the experience and maturity of the performers. The list below includes some ideas that would work only with professional-level musicians, and others—intended for younger students—which would seem condescending if they were used with good high school or college students.

The list is a *basic repertoire* of procedures. Evaluate these as you see them used in the conducting class and in rehearsal or performances of all types of ensembles. Discard those that don't work for you and try developing other ideas. Expanding this repertoire and refining your skill in using it will be a gratifying lifelong pursuit.

Style

1 Use concert pitch, not transposed pitch, when demonstrating or discussing melodic and harmonic material.

2 Sing to demonstrate. Describe the style in musical terms. Avoid using street language to describe an artistic event.

3 Work on one small section of the piece that embodies the essence of its style. Establish a concept of style in this segment by rehearsing it thoroughly and then ask the performers to extend this concept to similar sections of the piece.

4 Play recordings to illustrate other approaches to the work, or to works in a similar style.

5 Ask individual players to demonstrate their concept of the style. When you find someone who does it well, use that as an example to establish the concept for everyone, pointing out why it is a good example.

Rhythm

1 Identify each problem and give clear, positive instructions for correcting it.

2 Demonstrate the correct rhythm by singing it or tapping it.

3 Teach the rhythm to everyone. Have everyone sing it in unison or play it at a designated unison concert pitch.

4 Write it on a chalkboard and have everyone sing or play it in unison.

5 Have everyone say it in rhythm syllables.

6 Have everyone conduct while singing or saying the rhythm in order to feel the pulse.

7 Have one or more students play the part melodically while others say the rhythm in syllables.

Intonation

1 Always tune to a reliable reference pitch. Use an electronic tuner.

2 Tune to more than one note.

3 Encourage students to work with a visual and audio tuner outside of rehearsal to learn the intonation characteristics of their instruments. In addition to checking the visual tuner, have them listen to beats between their own pitch and that of the tuner. (Beats are pulsations in sound created by two pitches that are very close together.)

4 Make the players and singers feel individually responsible for intonation. Don't give them the impression that it is the conductor's responsibility to make decisions for every performer.

5 When you hear an intonation problem, ask the performers to listen to it and to decide how they can solve it, rather than just telling them how to correct it. This will take longer at first, but it will help them develop independence, which will eventually save time.

6 Tell performers who are out of tune to listen and tune to someone who is in tune. Instead of "Clarinets, you're out of tune," consider saying "Clarinets, the trumpets are in tune. Listen to them and tune to them."

7 Developing a good sense of intonation is an absolute necessity for a successful conductor. Even though errors of precise pitch determination may occur, do not allow these to deter you from working to develop finely tuned aural skills.

Balance and Blend

1 Describe problems of balance and blend, saying what needs to be louder or softer.

2 Ask the performers to listen and identify balance problems.

3 Discuss timbre of the instruments to create a blended sound.

4 Balance a single chord to establish the sound of the correct balance, and then ask them to play or sing the section with that balance.

5 Create the chord from the bottom to top: "Basses. Now tenors. (Etc.)" Reverse the procedure.

6 Ask for parts of the chord: "Let's hear everyone who has the root. Now add the third. (Etc.)" Make ear training part of every rehearsal.

Technique

1 Isolate the problem and work on it. Give appropriate instructions.

2 Take a very slow tempo and work for precision and control. Immediately repeat the section several times, gradually increasing the tempo.

3 If more than one section of the ensemble is involved, it may be helpful to rehearse the sections separately.

4 Find one or more performers who can perform the problem area correctly and have them demonstrate. Having them model a correct performance enables the others to hear the concept.

Warm-Ups

1 The warm-up should produce physical and mental readiness for the rehearsal.

2 Warm-up materials should be related to the music to be rehearsed.

3 Especially for younger performers, the warm-up period is an ideal time to work on perfecting fundamentals of tone production, technique, and articulation.

4 Emphasize listening. Emphasize concentration.

5 Introduce enough variation into the warm-up exercises each day to keep them from becoming a mindless ritual.

6 Keep track of the time and avoid spending more time than you planned for.

Organizing Rehearsal Time

1 In general, rehearsals should begin and end with a piece or section which the ensemble is able to perform with a satisfying musical effect and which establishes a refined ensemble sound with good balance and blend. Avoid starting or ending the rehearsal with a piece or section that leaves many of the performers uninvolved or is unmusical because of technical deficiencies.

2 Maintain a balance between working on individual parts or detail and working with the whole ensemble. Remaining inactive for long periods is frustrating, even for mature players, and is a major cause of discipline problems for young players.

3 In general, think in terms of working from the large scale to smaller, individual parts and back again to the whole. This could mean reading a piece through to get a general concept, working on details, and then playing the piece or large sections through to relate details to the whole. This concept can apply to entire compositions or to large or small sections, but there may be reasons for making exceptions to it. If a read-through is too poor to give a good impression of the style or flow of the music, it may be better to establish a concept by first taking a small section and working on it until it gives a sense of the essence of the piece, and only then reading through the whole work.

4 Try posting a weekly rehearsal schedule with specific sections of works identified for each rehearsal. This will allow performers to set priorities and prepare for each rehearsal. Make a long-term rehearsal plan for several weeks of work to set long-range goals. Each schedule should contain clear, attainable goals for the ensemble and for yourself. Review your long-term rehearsal plans and continually revise and modify them on the basis of the progress of the ensemble.

Developing Musicianship and Musical Literacy

Too often, students graduating from high school after being in music classes and ensembles for several years know very little about music—even the music that they have performed. Conductors who work with student groups can easily improve this situation by teaching the students at least two or three things about each piece that they perform. A particular composition, for example, might have motives and a change from polyphonic to homophonic texture. Point out these features and ask students to identify them in other pieces. Ask students to point out specific structural features as they learn more. This is a very modest goal, but the results over time will be substantial, and the possibilities for extending this process are endless.

Leadership

You probably have definite ideas about the kind of rapport that should exist between conductor and performers, based on performing for conductors you have liked and disliked. As a conductor, developing that rapport in a positive way will be one of your major responsibilities. Clarify goals for yourself and discuss them in class. This is an individual, personal matter, but consider the following:

1 Treat your performers with dignity and respect.

2 Do not embarrass or humiliate anyone, especially less-developed performers.

3 Do not use intimidation to accomplish your goals.

4 Use first names often, to validate the performers as individuals.

5 Many music teachers and conductors give mostly negative feedback. Make a point of listening for improvement and giving enthusiastic praise. If the number of problems seems so overwhelming that it is hard to find anything to praise, the music you have selected is probably too difficult, or you haven't used a well-organized approach to teaching and rehearsing it.

6 You should always challenge the group to do better. They should have to work hard to satisfy your standards, but they should see this as a sign of your respect for their ability and potential.

7 Make a point of giving each section of the ensemble positive feedback on a regular basis. Some conductors make a habit of focusing on some sections while ignoring others.

8 Teach the performers to follow your conducting gestures. Sometimes it is better to say "You're not following my indications; please watch more carefully," than to say "Make more crescendo in measure 4."

9 Conductors often ask verbally for results that they have failed to indicate through gestures. (An example is the conductor who gives an instruction for an accent or a dynamic change but didn't indicate one.) When you give a verbal instruction, ask yourself if you did your best to communicate it through your physical conducting.

Postrehearsal Evaluation

After the rehearsal, make an evaluation, reflecting on the results of what you did. What worked? What didn't work? What needs to be done at the next rehearsal? How did the players respond? Did you use time effectively? Were you a confident leader? Did you provide useful assistance to the performers? Did you communicate clearly? Did you give feedback to every section of the ensemble? Were there any conducting problems that made you feel uncomfortable? Did you check all aspects of the performance?

You can make and review an audiotape or videotape as a part of this procedure. If you tape a rehearsal, check the percentage of time you spent talking to the ensemble and compare it with the percentage of time you spent actually performing.

We want to emphasize again that this list is only a beginning, a way for you to establish a concept of how to organize your knowledge of rehearsal procedures. You must continue to add to your knowledge and skill in a systematic way throughout your musical lifetime.

ASSIGNMENTS

1 Rewrite the short sections of the score in Figure 5-18 (pages 78–80) to make a concert C score from the transposed score.

2 Write out parts for French horn and clarinet for the first two measures of the excerpts in Figure 5-19 (page 81).

3 At the piano, play the concert pitches that will sound for each excerpt in Figure 5-19 as though it were written for each of the following:

- English horn
- French horn
- Clarinet
- Orchestra bells

4 At the piano, play the concert pitches that will sound for each of the excerpts in Figure 5-20 (page 81) as though it were a part written for each of the following:

- Alto saxophone
- Celesta
- EE-flat contralto clarinet
- Trumpet
- Alto clarinet
- Tenor saxophone
- Baritone saxophone
- B-flat clarinet

Optional written assignment: Write out two measures of a transposed part for each of the above instruments, for the excerpts in Figure 5-19. (Assume that it is in C.)

5 Practice the excerpt for Chapter 5 in the Anthology.

PERFORMANCE EXCERPT FOR CHAPTER 5

Section Three, pages 215-225 **5-1** Holst, *Five Folksongs,* "Swansea Town"

FIGURE 5-18
Léo Delibes, *Coppélia.*

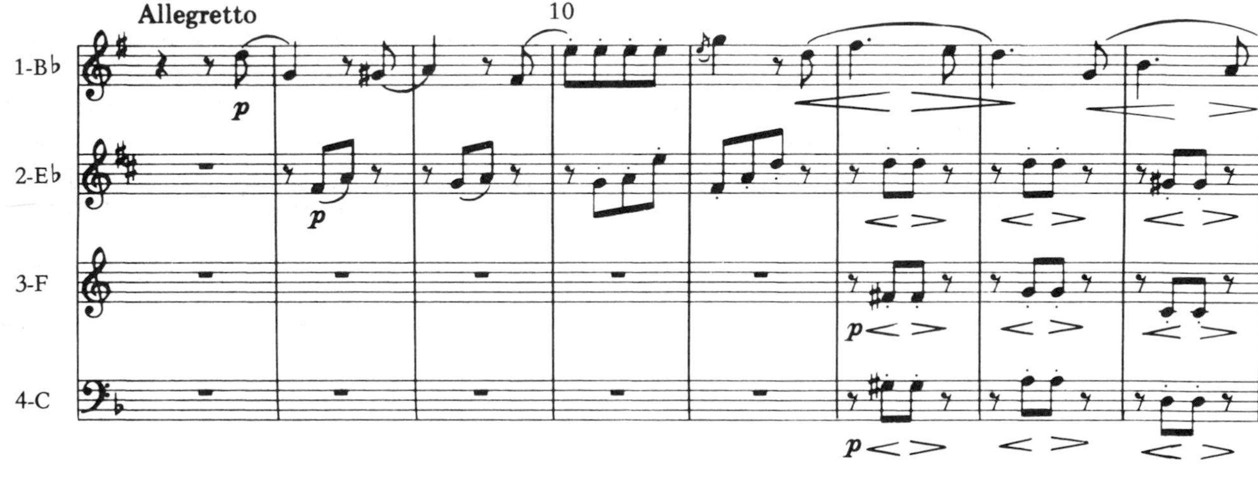

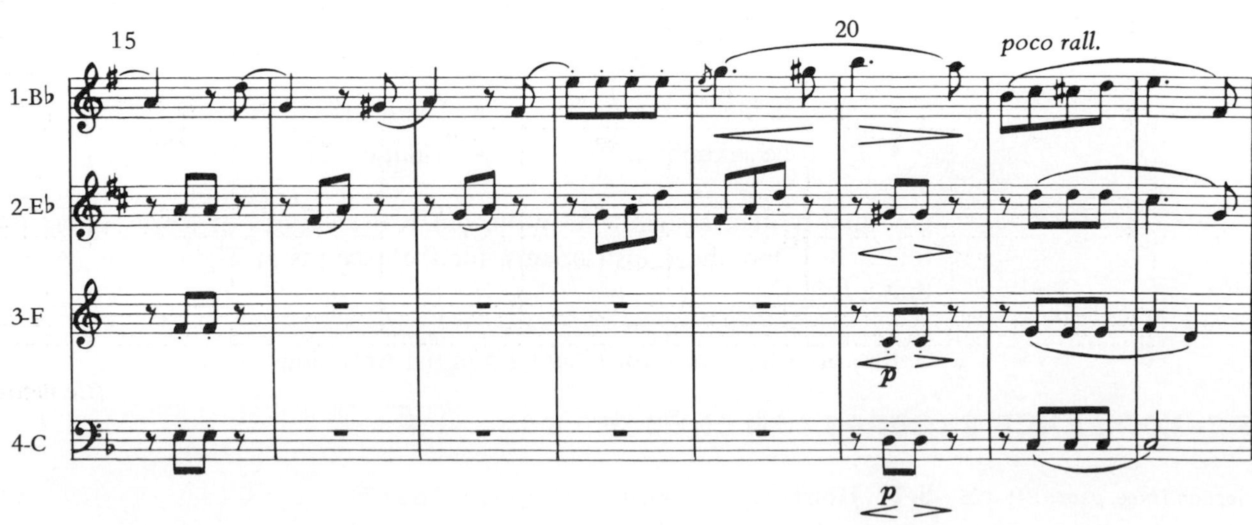

a tempo
25
1-B♭
2-E♭
3-F
4-C
p
p
p
p

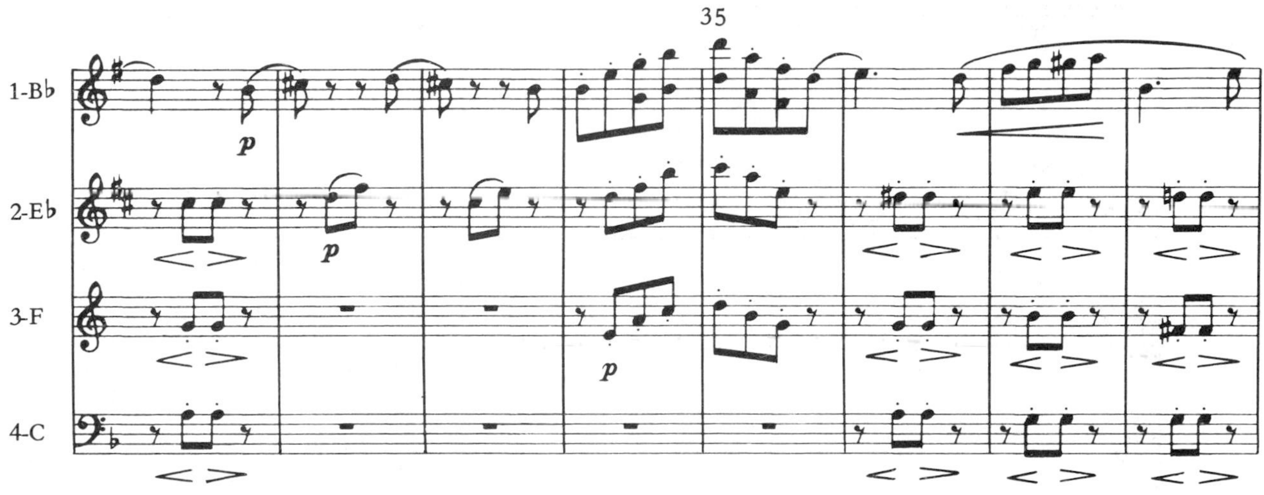
35
1-B♭
2-E♭
3-F
4-C
p
p
p

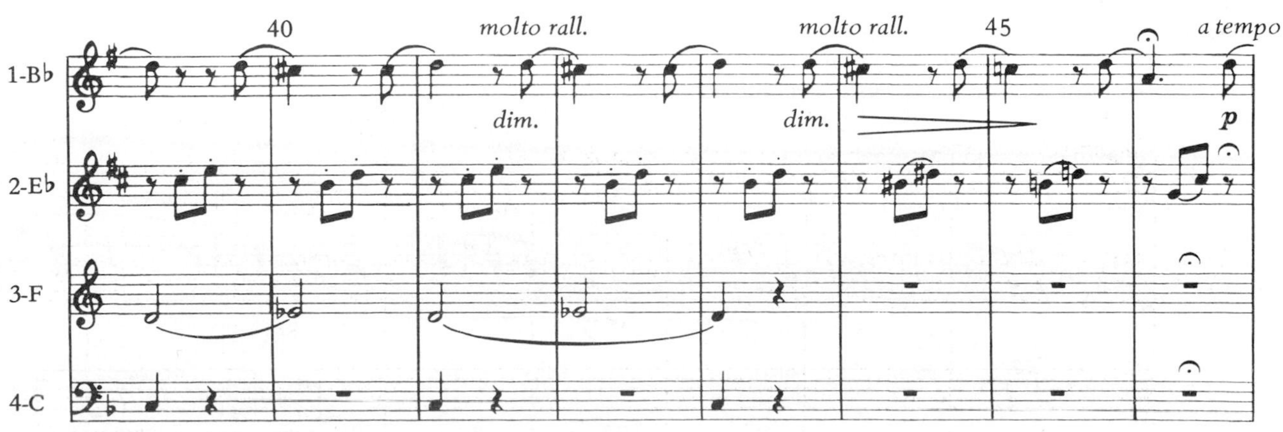
40
molto rall.
molto rall.
45
a tempo
1-B♭
2-E♭
3-F
4-C
dim.
dim.
p

(Continued)

FIGURE 5-18
(Continued)

FIGURE 5-19
Excerpts for transposition practice: (a) Carl Maria von Weber, *Der Freischütz* ("The Freeshooter"); (b) Giovanni Gabrieli, *Canzon septimi toni à 8* ("Canzona on the Seventh Tone for Eight Voices"); (c) Antonin Dvořák, Symphony No. 9, second movement.

(a) *Der Freischütz.*

FIGURE 5-19
(Continued)

(b) *Canzon septimi toni à 8.*

(c) Symphony No. 9.

FIGURE 5-20
Excerpts for practice, E-flat transpositions: (a) Alexander Borodin, *Prince Igor,* "Polevetsian Dances"; (b) Richard Wagner, *Tannhaüser,* "Fest March"; (c) Wolfgang Amadeus Mozart, *Eine kleine Nachtmusik* ("A Little Night Music"), third movement: menuetto, trio.

(a) "Polevetsian Dances."

(b) "Fest March."

(c) *Eine kleine Nachtmusik.*

CHAPTER 6

SUBDIVISION OF BEATS

ENTRANCES ON INCOMPLETE BEATS

SUBDIVISION OF BEATS

At a very slow tempo, the beats may be so far apart that it is difficult to perceive the rhythmic pulse. In such cases it is often helpful to subdivide the beats. Subdivision is also used to increase rhythmic precision during ritards or in other instances where it may help to clarify the rhythmic structure.

Subdivision in Simple Meters

In simple meters, subdivisions can be shown in three ways: the rebound style, the continuation style, and a combination rebound-continuation style.

Rebound Style

To provide a clear division with a strong pulse on the subdivision, let the hand rebound slightly from the ictus of the beat and place an additional, smaller beat in approximately the same location. This style is very clear and easy to follow. Some modifications can be made for a more elegant appearance, such as reversing the direction of the subdivision on the upbeat (instead of giving left-left, give left-right). In the pattern shown in Figure 6-1, the subdivisions appear to be in slightly different locations from the primary beats, but this is only to make it possible to show them in the drawing.

Practice rebound subdivisions of four-beat, three-beat, and two-beat patterns in both legato and staccato style, varying the speed of travel and the angularity or roundness of the motions. (See Figures 6-2 and 6-3.)

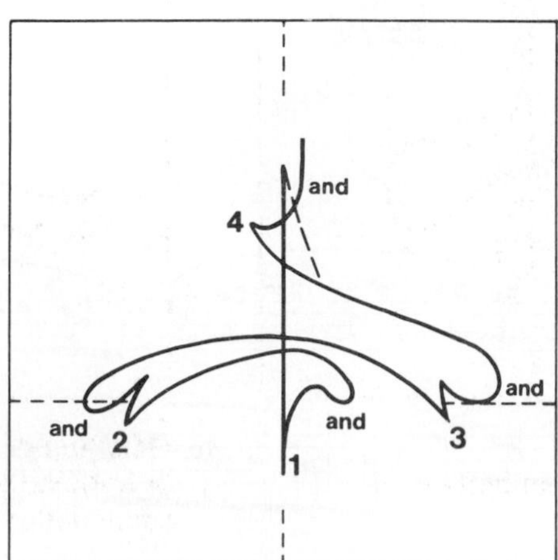

FIGURE 6-1
Subdivided four-beat pattern, rebound style.

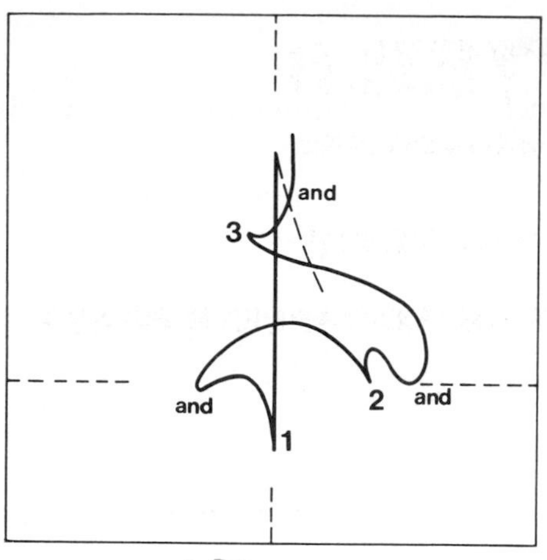

FIGURE 6-2
Subdivided three-beat pattern, rebound style.

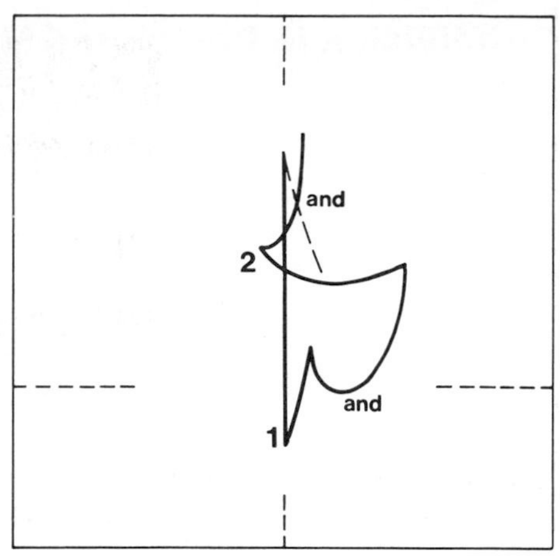

FIGURE 6-3
Subdivided two-beat pattern, rebound style.

Continuation Style

Subdivisions can also be indicated by using a continuous motion without rebound. Rather than rebounding as described above, make a slight pause on the beat, as indicated by the X in Figure 6-4, and continue in the same direction, as in a legato-style pattern. Notice that the subdivision of beat 1 goes in the opposite direction from beat 2. This is also true of the three-beat pattern. Stopping the motion marks the location of the primary beat, and restarting it marks the subdivision.

Continuation style is particularly useful for indicating a light pulse and emphasizing the flowing quality of phrases, but it can also be done very abruptly to indicate marcato.

Continuation-Rebound Style

The continuation-rebound style is similar to the continuation style, but it changes to a slightly more angular pattern, as shown in Figure 6-5, by making an upward lift after each primary beat, stopping to indicate the subdivision, and then continuing to the next primary beat.

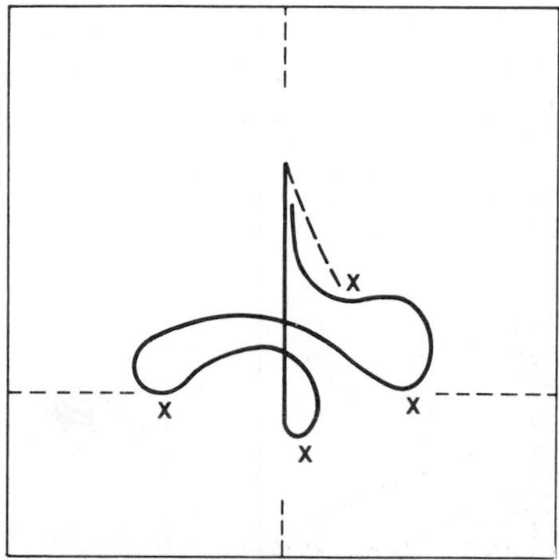

FIGURE 6-4
Subdivided four-beat pattern, continuation style.

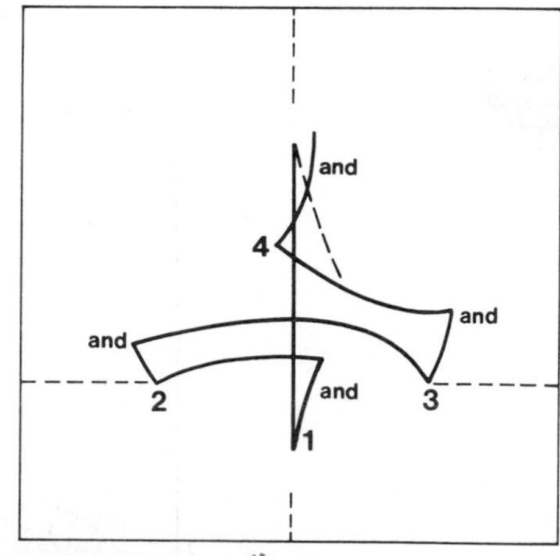

FIGURE 6-5
Subdivided four-beat pattern, continuation-rebound style.

Subdivision in Compound Meters

In compound meters, the rebound style of subdivision is usually used when beats are divided into three or more subdivisions. The continuation style is also possible, but stopping the motion three times on each primary beat may look and feel awkward unless the distance of travel for each subdivision is very short—which may make it difficult to see the subdivisions. The continuation-rebound style is not usually possible in compound meters.

Practice the patterns shown in Figures 6-6, 6-7, and 6-8 with the rebound style. On the final beat of the measure, the direction of the subdivisions may alternate (left-right-left rather than left-left-left). This approach is arbitrary, however; giving all the motions leftward and upward is also completely acceptable. Although for the purpose of illustration the subdivisions appear to be in slightly different locations from the primary beats, they will actually be given in approximately the same locations. Practice the six, nine, and twelve patterns; and practice conducting the excerpts in Figures 6-9, 6-10, and 6-11.

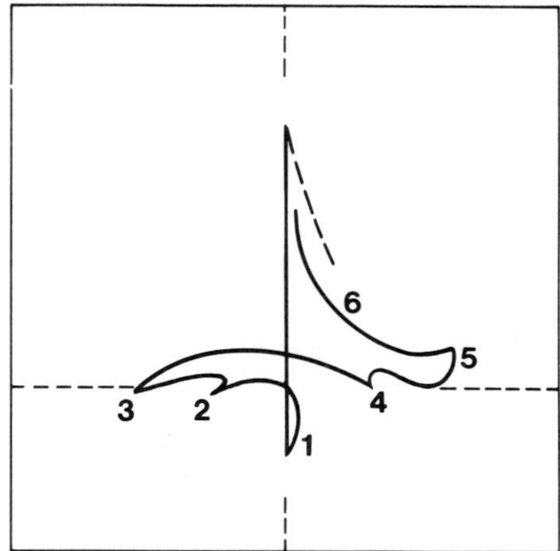

FIGURE 6-6
Six-beat pattern, traditional.
Crossing the body on the fourth pulse indicates a large subdivision in 2.

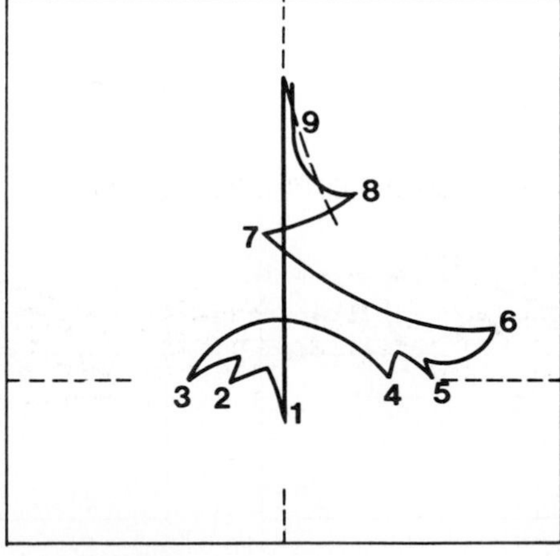

FIGURE 6-7
Nine-beat pattern.

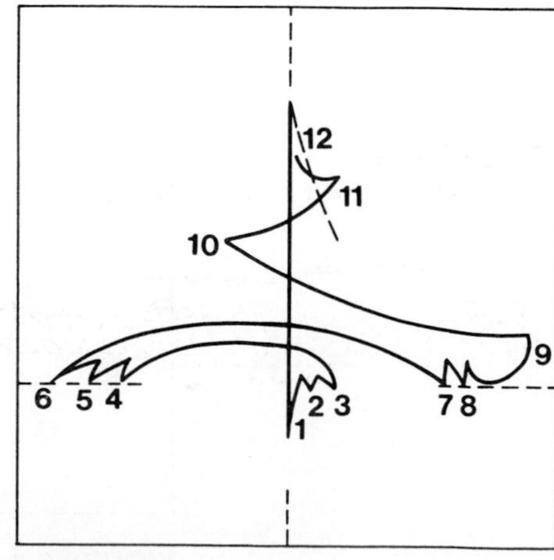

FIGURE 6-8
Twelve-beat pattern.

FIGURE 6-9
Six-beat pattern: Wolfgang Amadeus Mozart, Symphony No. 40 in G Minor, K. 550, second movement.

FIGURE 6-10
Nine-beat pattern: Claude Debussy, *L'Après-midi d'un faune* ("Afternoon of a Faun").

FIGURE 6-11
Gian Carlo Menotti, *Amahl and the Night Visitors,* "Shepherds' Chorus."

ENTRANCES ON INCOMPLETE BEATS

Entrances on incomplete beats are usually conducted as though they were *on* the beat, because the performers must see two ictuses (a preparatory ictus and the entrance ictus) before they enter. Both excerpts in Figure 6-12 are therefore conducted in the same way.

FIGURE 6-12
Entrance on an incomplete beat: (a) on ictus; (b) after ictus.

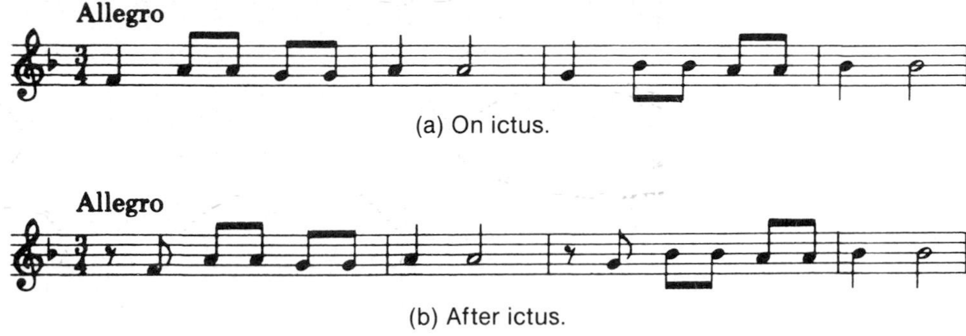

(a) On ictus.

(b) After ictus.

Sometimes, after an ensemble has rehearsed a work sufficiently to retain a close approximation of each change of tempo, the conductor may give only one ictus before an entrance on an incomplete beat, with good results. However, this gives the performers very little time for preparation and depends largely on the performers' having prior knowledge of the conductor's tempo, which enables them to enter with some precision. Therefore this procedure will not be as consistently precise as using two ictuses.

A good rule to remember is this: Always prepare your gestures as though the ensemble were reading the work for the first time and needed the utmost clarity in your beats. This may be modified, of course, as comprehension of the music increases through rehearsal.

Rests before Entrances

In general, the conductor should account for every beat of the entrance that is notated, including rests. If there is only one beat of notated rest, this will be given as the preparatory gesture. If there are several beats of rest, the pattern for the rests before the preparatory gesture can be given with a very small, light motion called a *marking beat.* Players will not enter by mistake on marking beats, because they have not been given a preparatory gesture and because the character of the marking beats should indicate that their function is only to show beats of rest. Figure 6-13 (page 88) illustrates the pattern for marking rests.

Analyze and practice the excerpts in Figures 6-14 and 6-15 (page 88). Evaluate the results.

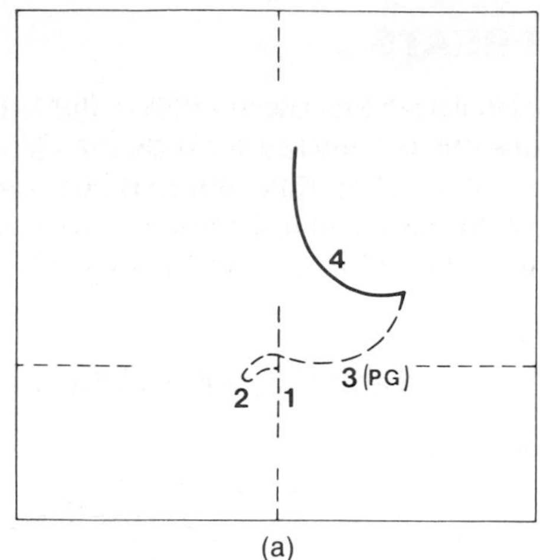

(a)

(b)

FIGURE 6-13
Above: (a) Marking rests. (b) Johannes Brahms, Symphony No. 1, fourth movement.

FIGURE 6-14
Below: Franz Joseph Haydn, Symphony No. 86, fourth movement.

FIGURE 6-15
Felix Mendelssohn, Symphony No. 4 *(Italian),* third movement.

Entrances at Slow Tempos

When an entrance occurs on an incomplete beat in a slow (or subdivided) meter, as shown in Figure 6-16, the *subdivision* preceding the entrance can be given as the preparatory gesture. Notice that this actually amounts to the most common procedure for preparatory gestures—giving the previous beat in the pattern for preparation.

FIGURE 6-16
Peter Ilych Tchaikovsky, Romance in F Minor.

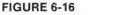

Ornamented Entrances

When an entrance begins with a note or notes of less than a half-beat's duration, the preparatory gesture is sometimes given for the main beat that *follows* the short note or notes, rather than for the beat on which the short notes occur. This is often the case when the short notes function like a grace note, ornamenting the note that follows, as in Figure 6-17.

FIGURE 6-17
J. Offenbach, *Orphée aux enfers* ("Orpheus in the Underworld").

Cuing Entrances

The choice of procedure for cuing an entrance on an incomplete beat depends mainly on two factors: (1) the part of the beat on which the entrance occurs, and (2) the tempo. The most common procedure is to give the cue on the beat—just as if the entrance were on the beat. This is particularly true if the entrance is within the first half of the beat, as in Figure 6-18.

FIGURE 6-18
Cuing an entrance on an incomplete beat: cue on the beat.

If an entrance occurs on the last half of the beat, such as a sixteenth note in common time, it may be more satisfactory to give the cue for the beat that follows, letting the performers treat the first note in the manner of a grace note (but with specific duration). (See Figure 6-19.)

FIGURE 6-19
Cuing an entrance on an incomplete beat: cue for the following beat.

FIGURE 6-20
Gioacchino Rossini, *L'Italiana in Algeri* ("The Italian Girl in Algiers").

Additional Preparatory Beats

It is sometimes helpful to give several marking beats before an entrance to establish the tempo. At an extremely fast tempo, for example, a single preparatory gesture may be almost imperceptible. Marking beats are small, nonexpressive motions given with the wrist which convey tempo only. Preparation should *not* be given for the first marking beat; this will decrease the possibility that players will accidentally enter on it. You will need to give a very decisive preparatory gesture after the marking beats.

Marking beats should not be overused. They can be a visual distraction and they may sidestep, rather than solve, the problem of learning to communicate clear preparatory and entrance gestures.

Conduct members of the class in the excerpt from *L'Italiana in Algeri* ("The Italian Girl in Algiers") in Figure 6-20 (opposite page). Analyze the entrance after the fermata at the allegro. First, give only beat 3 for the entrance. To analyze the function of a preconceived concept of tempo, conduct the excerpt once again at an unexpected tempo. Next, use a preparatory gesture and ictus before beat 3 (conduct as though the entrance were on beat 3). Again, try an unexpected tempo and analyze the results. A single melodic line with a piano part is included in the Anthology (Excerpt 7-2).

DAILY WARM-UP ROUTINES

1 Practice patterns with three different types of subdivision.

2 Practice conducting entrances on incomplete beats for each beat in a four-beat pattern.

3 Practice slow, legato patterns, creating a feeling of resistance. Vary the prominence of ictuses by using a click, stopping the travel, or changing both the direction and the speed of travel. Practice singing and conducting slow melodies such as Wagner's "Elsa's Procession to the Cathedral" from *Lohengrin* (Excerpt 2-2 in the Anthology).

AURAL ANALYSIS

Make an audio recording of three excerpts for Chapter 6 in the Anthology. Play each excerpt two or three times, to identify at least three things that need to be done to improve each performance. List them in a logical order for rehearsing. Briefly describe possible rehearsal procedures. Discuss the results in class.

ASSIGNMENTS

1 Practice the excerpts for Chapter 6 in the Anthology until the preparatory gestures are fluent and consistent—that is, until they become a natural reflex motion.

2 Conduct the class in singing or playing the Anthology excerpts. Evaluate the following aspects of each entrance:

a Eye contact
b Wait for concentration
c Breathing with the preparatory gesture
d Smooth, rhythmic flow

e Shape and direction of the preparatory gesture
f Tempo, dynamics, and articulation style of the preparatory gesture
g Number of ictuses before entrance
h Unnecessary motions
i Marking beats if necessary
j Overall confidence and assurance

EVALUATION

Use the following evaluation form to review and check the fundamental techniques covered thus far.

EVALUATION FORM FOR CHAPTER 6

Name:________________________________ Date: __________

Section/Lab ___________________________ Grade: __________

CHECKLIST { + indicates exceptionally good
− indicates deficient or incorrect }

Repertoire:

ENVIRONMENT AND POSTURE

1 2
☐ ☐ Stand position
☐ ☐ Eye contact
☐ ☐ Stance
☐ ☐ Facial expression; confidence
☐ ☐ Attention-ready position
☐ ☐ Verbal directions

BATON AND BATON ARM

Grip ☐ Fingers
☐ Wrist
☐ Baton tip

Pivots ☐ Wrist
☐ Elbow
☐ Shoulder

NONBATON ARM

1 2
☐ ☐ At-rest position
☐ ☐ Mirroring
☐ ☐ Independent motion
☐ ☐ Meaningful and worthwhile use

BEAT PATTERNS

1 2
☐ ☐ Horizontal motion; beat plane
☐ ☐ Beat patterns
☐ ☐ Preparatory gesture
☐ ☐ Clear ictus
☐ ☐ Size of beat, rebound

OTHER

1 2
☐ ☐ Fermata
☐ ☐ Cutoffs
☐ ☐ Dynamics, phrasing, musicality, tempo changes
☐ ☐ Cues ☐ Left hand ☐ Right hand

PERFORMANCE EXCERPTS FOR CHAPTER 6

Section Three, pages 226-252

6-1 Strauss, Serenade, Op. 7
6-2 Berlioz, *Roman Carnival* Overture
6-3 Jacob, *William Byrd Suite,* Pavana
6-4 Rimsky-Korsakov, *Scheherazade,* third movement
6-5 Purcell, "In these delightful, pleasant groves"
6-6 Traditional, "The Riddle"
6-7 Handel, *Royal Fireworks Music, La Paix* ("Peace")
6-8 Mozart, Symphony No. 36, second movement
6-9 Tchaikovsky, Symphony No. 4, second movement
6-10 Irish tune, "My Gentle Harp"

CHAPTER 7

DYNAMIC ACCENTS SUBITO DYNAMIC CHANGES

SYNCOPATIONS TEMPO ALTERATIONS

TENUTO FERMATAS

DYNAMIC ACCENTS

A dynamically accented note must contrast in intensity with the notes that surround it, particularly those that precede it. The physical gesture for indicating an accent is similar to that for an entrance or a cue in that it also requires a preparatory gesture leading to the accented beat. The preparatory gesture should communicate the amount of dynamic change and the style of articulation. The motion leading to the accented ictus should be larger than the rest of the pattern; this can be emphasized by decreasing the size of one or two beats before the preparatory gesture.

Practice the exercise in Figure 7-1 with the right hand alone. On each repeat, change the location of the accent in the second measure to one beat later. Preparation for the accent begins two beats before the accented ictus with a deemphasized pattern; one beat before the accent, the size of the preparatory gesture indicates the degree of accent.

FIGURE 7-1
Exercise: accents. Practice (a) and (b) in varying tempos.

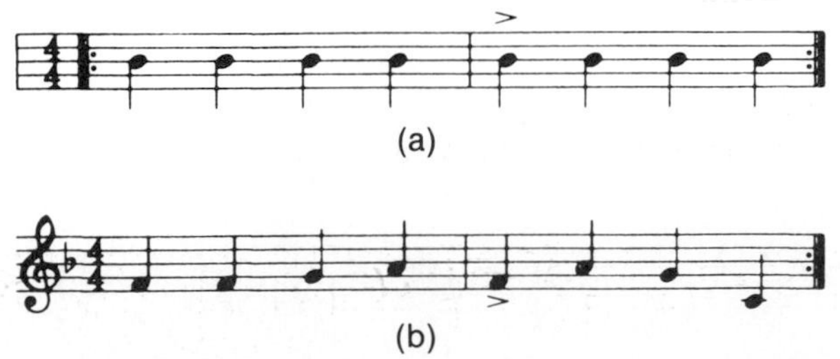

Try conducting this exercise without a preparatory gesture before the accent. This will demonstrate fully the function and necessity of the proper preparation sequence.

Adding the left hand for the preparatory gesture and accent will greatly increase the prominence of the accent gesture. Take care, however, to avoid mirroring the beat pattern for additional beats, because this will negate the emphasis of using the left hand.

SUBITO DYNAMIC CHANGES

The procedure for making an abrupt change to a louder dynamic level is the same as for indicating an accent, except that the larger beat pattern is now continued. As with the accent, the left hand can mirror the preparatory gesture and following beat for increased emphasis. The left hand may also be held in a stationary attention position for several beats before the impending dynamic change.

A subito change from a loud to a soft dynamic level also requires a preparatory gesture. Raise the left hand, palm down, on the preparatory beat and bring it downward on the motion leading to the softer beat in a manner that shows a decrease of volume.

Practice subito dynamic changes by rotating the location of the change in the second measure of Figure 7-2.

FIGURE 7-2
Exercise:
subito dynamic changes.

Achieving abrupt dynamic changes with an ensemble may sometimes be difficult even if the conducting gestures are correct and clear. Rehearsal may be required to correct the common tendency of performers either to anticipate the new dynamic level by changing too early or to drift into the change late.

You should practice the exercise in Figure 7-2 daily in front of a mirror until you can perform it with ease. Also practice conducting the excerpts in the Anthology for Chapter 7 (and for the preceding chapters) until the dynamic indications look convincing and feel natural.

SYNCOPATIONS

Syncopations are conducted in several different ways, depending on their musical context. Syncopations in long note values that occur on the beat, such as those in Figure 7-3, are prepared in the same manner as other accents on the beat.

FIGURE 7-3
Syncopations in long note values.

♩ = 112

If syncopated notes are not accented, as in Figure 7-4, a regular beat pattern should be maintained, with an emphasis on clarity. Performers who need to place syncopation on an upbeat must be able to see and feel a clear beat pattern.

FIGURE 7-4
Unaccented syncopation.

When an accent must be shown on a subdivision of a beat, the preparation emphasizing the accent is the beat *preceding* the accent. The procedure is similar to bouncing a ball—the harder the throw, the higher the rebound. (The ictus is comparable to the point where the ball hits the floor, and the accent is like the rebound.) The speed of travel and the size of the motion leading to the ictus will indicate the articulation style and the dynamic level of the syncopation accent that follows. Another approach uses a stop beat (no motion) on the beat before the motion for the syncopated accent, but this procedure may sometimes give more emphasis than is desired.

The two passages in Figure 7-5 can be conducted in exactly the same way. Notice that the preparatory ictus (discussed in Chapter 1) for the accent will be on beat 2.

FIGURE 7-5
Accented syncopation.

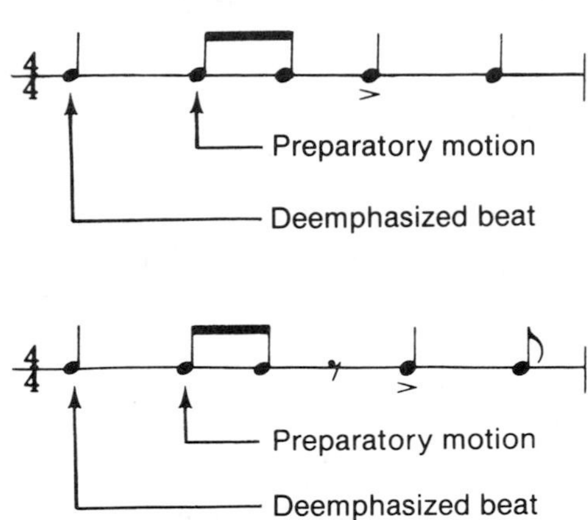

In another style of conducting syncopations—one that gives a visual representation of the rhythm—a motion is given for the beginning of each tone. Since there is no preparation for the accent, however, this is not really conducting the ensemble, and it may also be confusing if there are several accents in close succession.

In general, do not attempt to conduct syncopated accents by subdividing the beat or displacing the ictus from the beat. Performers are able to place the accent without these techniques, and "spoon feeding" of this type is unnecessary and may be somewhat confusing or, on the other hand, degrading.

Practice conducting the single-pitch exercise in Figure 7-6.

FIGURE 7-6
Single-pitch exercise for syncopations.

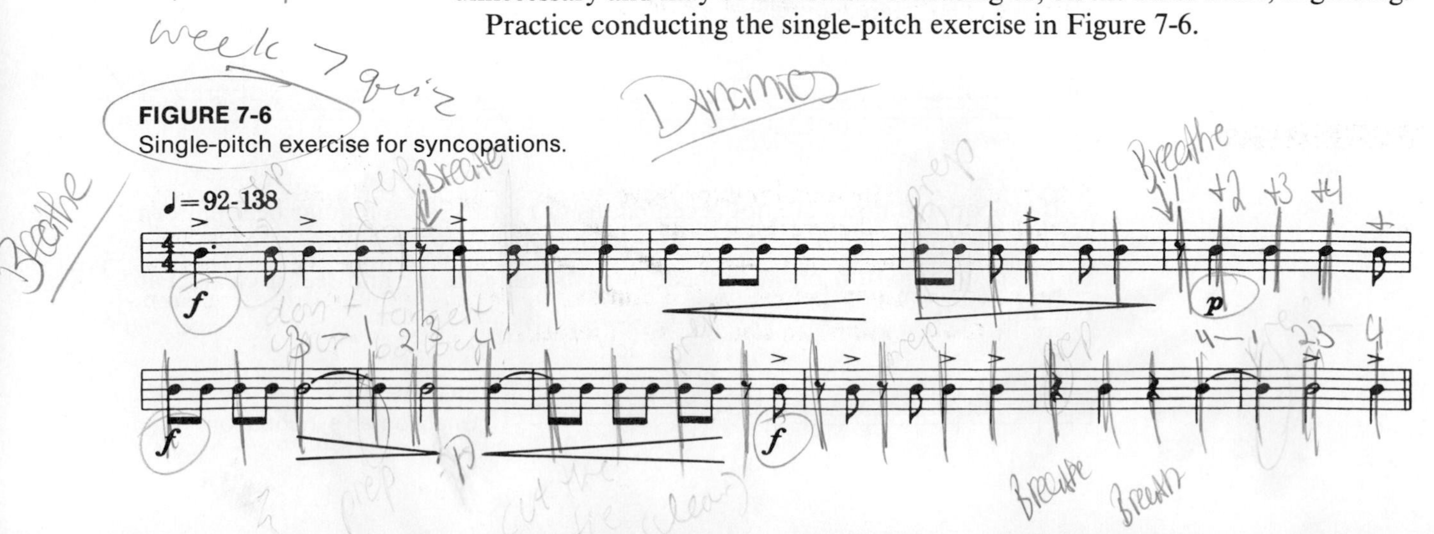

TEMPO ALTERATIONS

Special attention must be paid to any deviation from rhythmic pulse, such as a ritard, accelerando, subito tempo change, tenuto, or fermata. Always prepare a designated change of tempo or pulse by thinking of the existing tempo, the new tempo, and the change to be undertaken. To clarify the relationship among these three things, it may be helpful to identify the point at which the new tempo is fully established and then work back to the point where the old tempo begins to change.

Good eye contact with the performers is essential throughout the musical sections surrounding a tempo change. The conductor must be sensitive to the responsiveness of the ensemble and make very clear indications, becoming more deliberate and compelling as necessary. The final result should feel and sound perfectly natural and should be consistent with the overall style of the composition.

Sing and conduct the excerpt in Figure 7-7.

FIGURE 7-7
Henry Carey, "America."

TENUTO

A tenuto marking, requiring a broadening of the sound, can usually be accomplished by stretching out the travel or enlarging the pattern. Notes with tenuto marks are sometimes given additional emphasis by slightly increasing or decreasing the dynamic level.

Practice the exercise in Figure 7-8.

FIGURE 7-8
Exercise: tenuto.

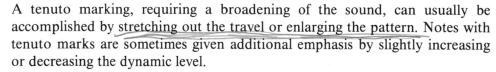

FERMATAS

A fermata is usually a major expressive event. Preparation, duration, dynamic level, and release all contribute to its musical effectiveness. Thus, it is important to analyze the function of each fermata and type of release (three types of release are described below) in the context of the entire composition. Listen carefully to the expressive effect of each fermata.

Location of the Fermata

The fermata occurs on the beat on which the rhythmic motion in all the parts stops. In Figure 7-9, the fermata is given on beat 1, because conducting the first two beats and holding beat 3 would be visually inconsistent with the musical flow. In this example, the conductor must make clear that the release motion that follows is both the release of the sound in the style of the music and the preparation for the downbeat of the next measure.

FIGURE 7-9
Location of fermata on beat 1.

In Figure 7-10, the fermata occurs where the rhythmic motion of the inner voices stops—in this case on beat 2.

FIGURE 7-10
Location of fermata on beat 2: Johann Sebastian Bach, *Wir glauben all' an einen Gott.*

FIGURE 7-10
(Continued)

Travel during Fermatas

As a general rule, either the right or the left hand should remain in motion—however slow—during a fermata, to indicate that the sound is being sustained. If this is indicated with the left hand, the right hand may remain in the approximate position of the ictus. When the right hand is used to indicate a short fermata, the motion of the baton may be continued, following the ictus, in the same direction as the beat.

For a long fermata with the right hand, it may be necessary to curve back gradually from the direction of the ictus so that the beat can be repeated as a preparatory gesture.

Carefully analyze and practice the examples in Figures 7-11 through 7-14. The wide line illustrates the travel during the fermata, and the X indicates the location of the ictus. Preparatory gestures are indicated by broken lines.

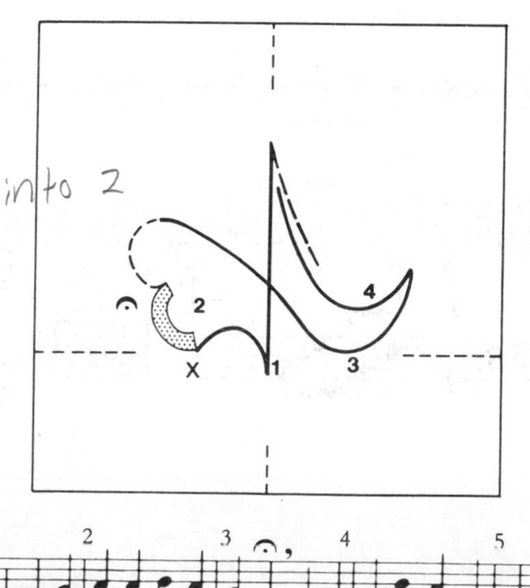

FIGURE 7-11
Short fermata on beat 2.
Note: In Figures 7-11 to 7-14, *wide line* indicates travel during the fermata; *dashed line* indicates release and preparation during the fermata.

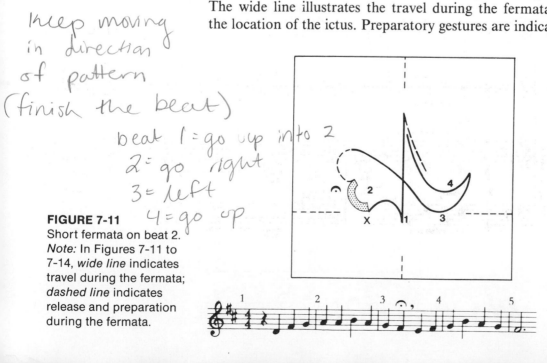

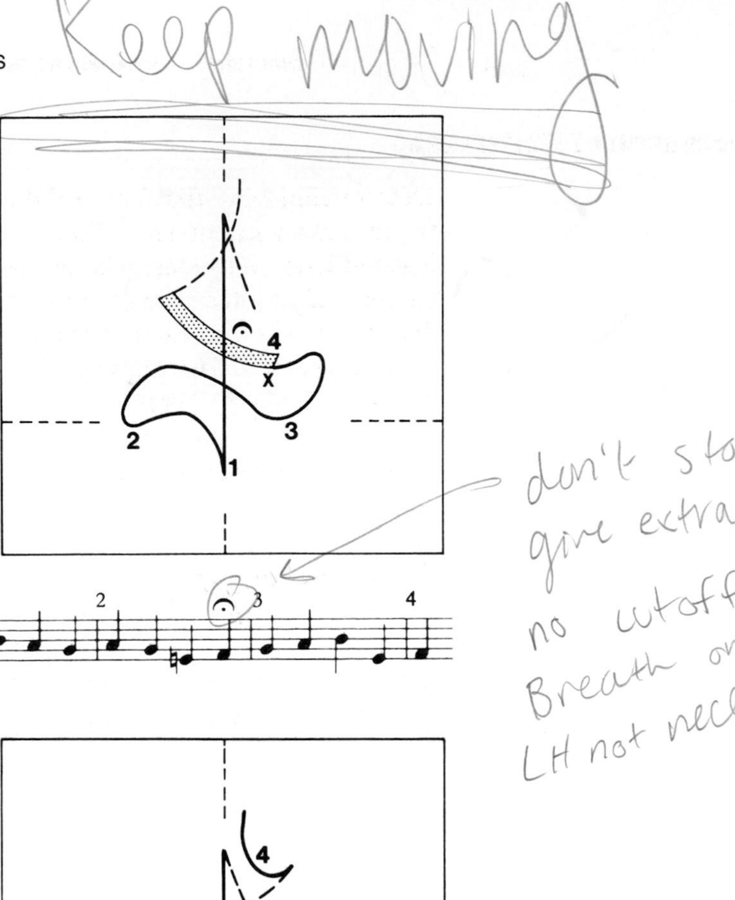

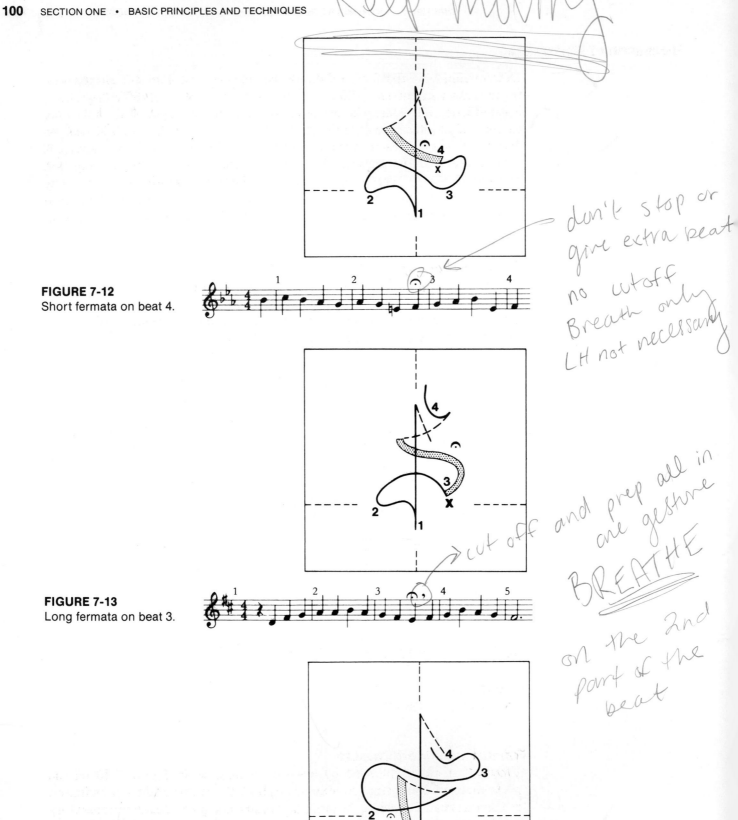

FIGURE 7-12
Short fermata on beat 4.

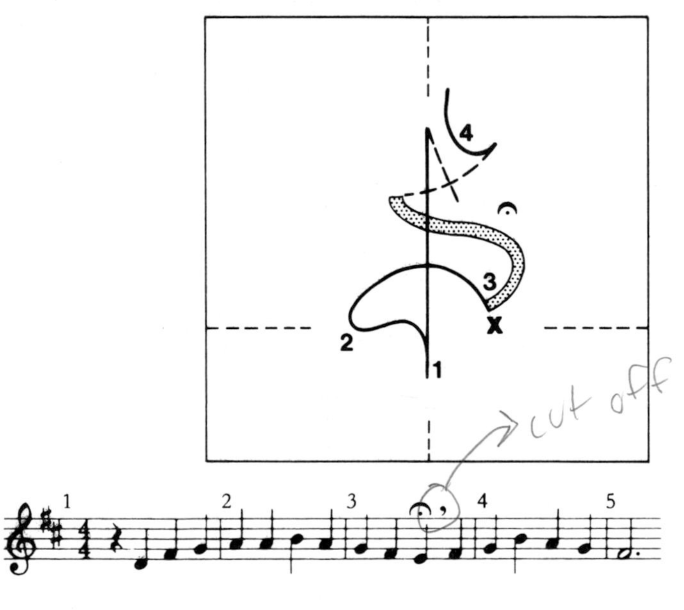

FIGURE 7-13
Long fermata on beat 3.

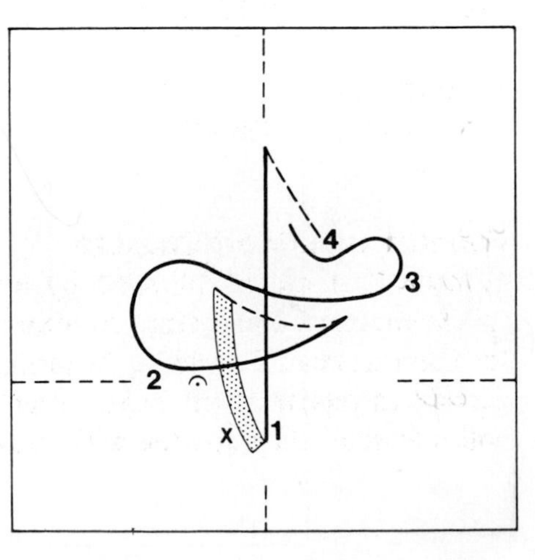

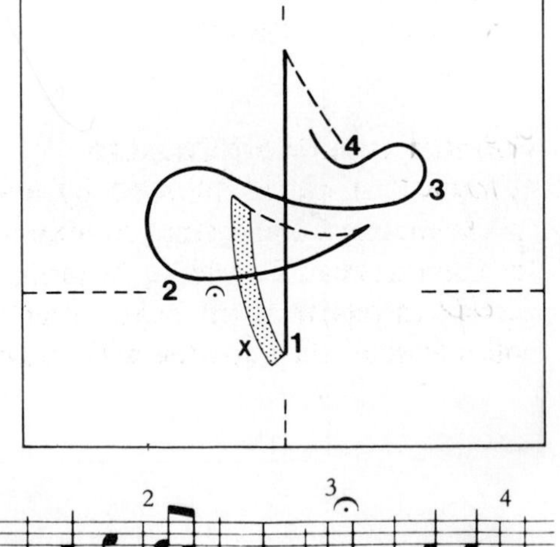

FIGURE 7-14
Long fermata on beat 1.

Releases of Fermatas

Determining how the fermata should be released and how the preparation for the following entrance should be given is usually the most difficult problem in conducting fermatas. The decision depends on the length of the following caesura, if any (*caesura* literally means "cut" or "break"). You will need to determine whether each fermata should be followed by a long caesura, a short caesura, or no caesura. Practice the releases shown below until you understand all the types and can conduct them confidently. If there is any question about what type of release should be used, try each of the logical possibilities and make a decision by listening carefully to the expressive musical effect.

Fermata with Long Caesura

When a fermata is followed by a long rest or caesura, one motion is required to make the release, the hands remain motionless for a moment, and a separate motion is required for the preparation of the next sound (a regular preparatory gesture). Practice the exercise in Figure 7-15.

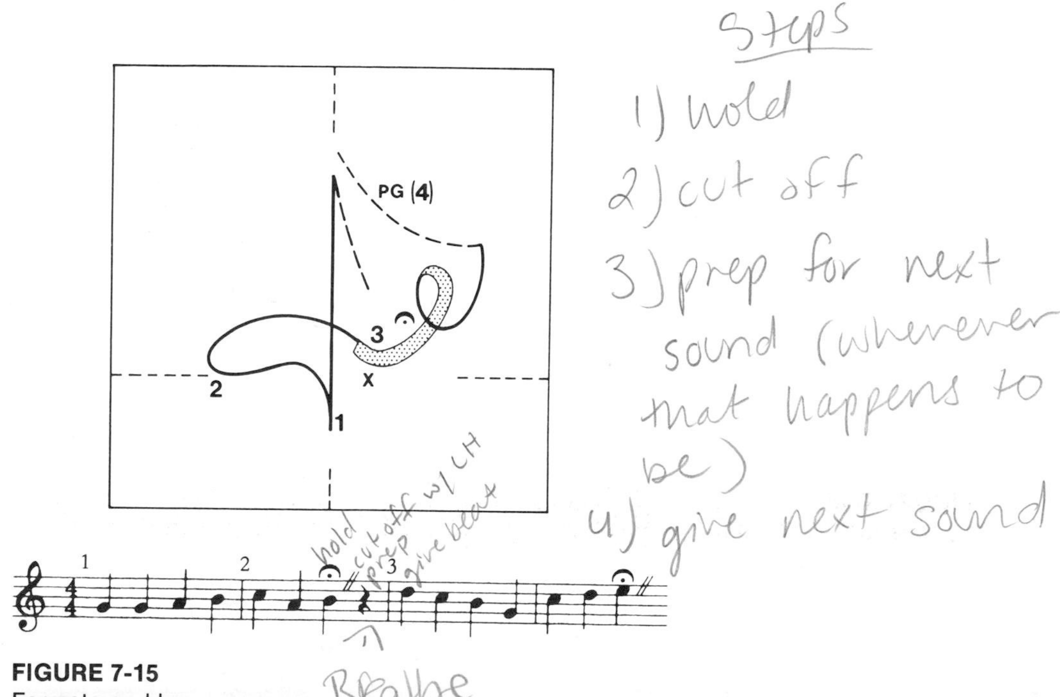

FIGURE 7-15
Fermata and long caesura.

Fermata with Short Caesura

When a fermata is followed by a short caesura, as in Figure 7-16 on the following page, one gesture communicates both the release and the preparation for the next beat. To release the fermata, breathe and give a decisive preparatory gesture (a repeat of the beat on which the fermata occurred); the performers will release as they breathe with the preparatory gesture.

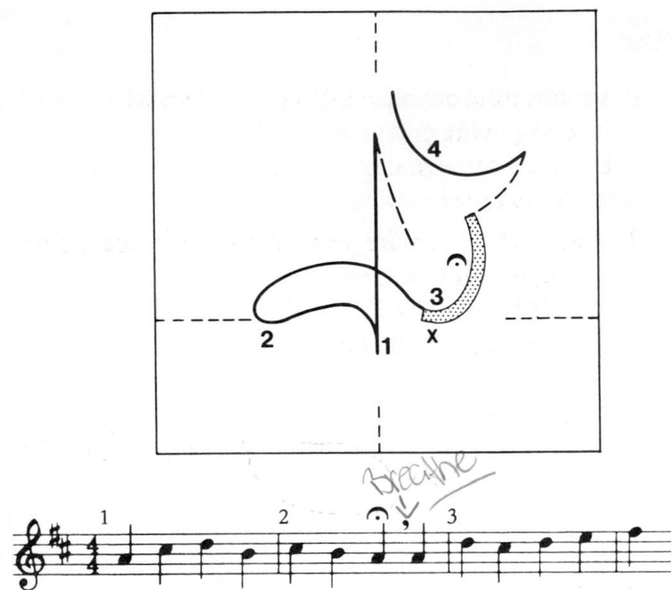

FIGURE 7-16
Fermata and short caesura.

Fermata with No Caesura

In Figure 7-17, the fermata is not released. You will find, however, that if you hold beat 3 and move directly to beat 4, the performers will have difficulty following you. Therefore, give a light, smooth preparatory gesture on the beat following the fermata, to aid in ensemble precision. In this gesture, smoothness and subtlety are essential, since a large or abrupt gesture would suggest a release. The left hand can be used to indicate that there is no break.

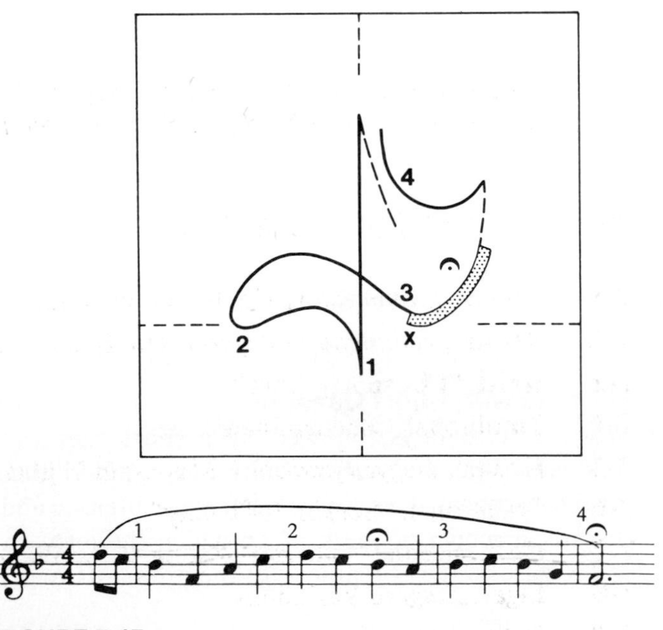

FIGURE 7-17
Fermata with no caesura.

FERMATA EXERCISE

1 Practice the exercise in Figure 7-18 with
- **a** Long caesura
- **b** Short caesura
- **c** No caesura

2 Practice the fermata gesture and the release gesture with
- **a** Right hand alone
- **b** Left hand alone
- **c** Both hands together

This exercise should be used as part of your daily warm-up routine for a period of several weeks. When you conduct fermatas, the mechanics of approach, hold, and release should be almost automatic so that you can concentrate completely on the musical phrase. When practicing the exercise in Figure 7-18, vary the tempo and change the location of the fermata to beat 1, 2, 3, or 4, or into measure 1.

FIGURE 7-18
Exercise:
fermatas and caesuras.

AURAL ANALYSIS

Take turns as designated listeners and observers (this procedure is described in Chapter 3) as each student conducts the excerpts for Chapter 7 in the Anthology. Comment on the expressive effect of the concepts covered in this chapter.

ASSIGNMENT

Practice conducting the excerpts for Chapter 7 in the Anthology. Try all three types of release for each fermata. Listen to the expressive effect of your conducting.

PERFORMANCE EXCERPTS FOR CHAPTER 7

Section Three, pages 253–289

- **7-1** Schubert, Symphony No. 8, first movement
- **7-2** Rossini, *L'Italiana in Algeri* ("The Italian Girl in Algiers"), Overture
- **7-3** Holst, "I Love My Love"
- **7-4** Traditional, "Shenandoah"
- **7-5** Kodály, *Hegyi Éjszakák* ("Mountain Nights")
- **7-6** Traditional, "Seekin' for a City"
- **7-7** Holst, Second Suite in F, "Song of the Blacksmith"
- **7-8** Elgar, *Enigma* Variations
- **7-9** Delibes, *Coppélia*
- **7-10** Haydn, Symphony No. 104 *(London),* first movement
- **7-11** Schubert, Mass in F *(Deutsche Messe)* ("German Mass")

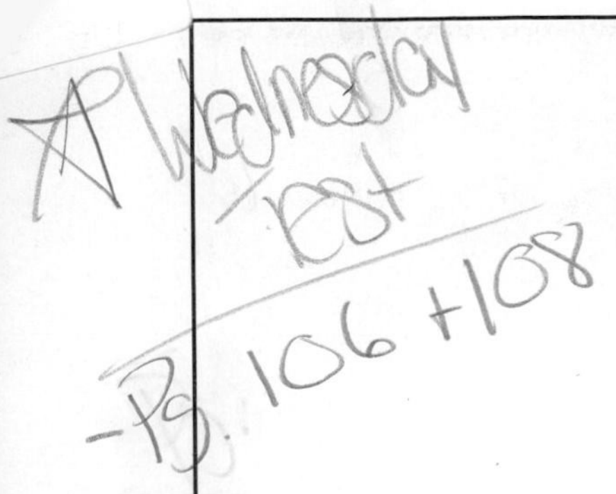

CHAPTER 8

ASYMMETRICAL METERS

CONDUCTING PATTERNS FOR ASYMMETRICAL METERS

ASYMMETRICAL METERS

In asymmetrical meters, such as $\frac{5}{4}$, $\frac{7}{4}$, and $\frac{11}{4}$, measures are divided into unequal groupings which create an uneven metrical pulse. A $\frac{5}{4}$ measure, for example, is ordinarily perceived as either a long pulse followed by a short pulse (3 + 2) or the reverse—short followed by long (2 + 3).

CONDUCTING PATTERNS FOR ASYMMETRICAL METERS

Conducting patterns for asymmetrical meters can be devised in three different ways:

1. One of the regular symmetrical patterns can be altered; for example, a beat can be eliminated from a six-beat pattern to create a five-beat pattern.
2. The *length* of one beat in a regular pattern can be decreased or increased; for example, one of the beats in a three-beat pattern can be lengthened to create a $\frac{7}{8}$ pattern.
3. Two or more different symmetrical patterns can be conducted consecutively; for example, a five-beat pattern can be made by combining a two-beat and a three-beat pattern.

Choosing the best alternative for a composition or passage requires careful analysis of its metric organization and tempo, and knowledge of how to alter or combine patterns. Personal preference is also a factor. Most conductors, for example, avoid combining patterns because they feel that two downbeats should not be given in one measure, even if the first is more prominent than the second. But some conductors prefer to combine patterns because they feel that the results are clear and easily understood.

Altering Symmetrical Patterns

Conduct the following patterns by adding one beat to, or omitting one beat from, a regular symmetrical pattern. Alternate back and forth between the symmetrical pattern and the asymmetrical pattern created by the modification.

Five-Beat Pattern, 3 + 2
Omit one of the rightward movements from the regular six pattern. (See Figure 8-1.)

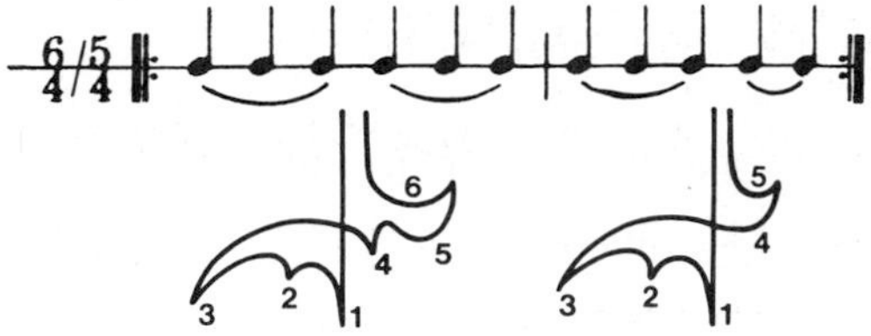

FIGURE 8-1
Shortened six-beat pattern:
one rightward movement omitted.

Five-Beat Pattern, 2 + 3
Omit one of the leftward movements of the regular six pattern. (See Figure 8-2.)

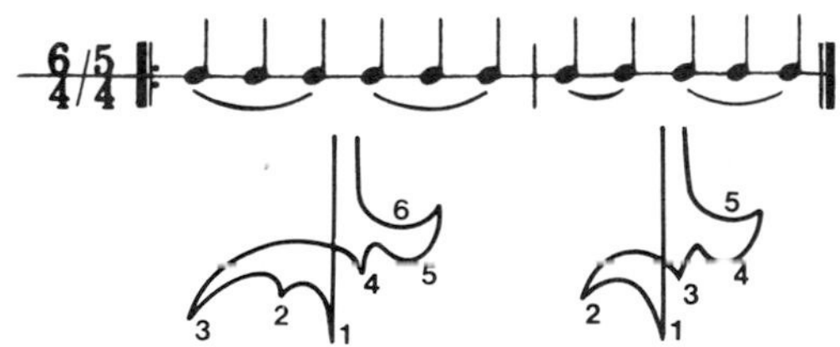

FIGURE 8-2
Shortened six-beat pattern:
one leftward movement omitted.

Seven-Beat Patterns
Conduct a subdivided three pattern. Lengthen each beat in turn by adding a subdivision. The subdivision pattern is shown below the beat numbers:

1-2 3-4 5-6-7	1-2 3-4-5 6-7	1-2-3 4-5 6-7
1 & 2 & 3 & &	1 & 2 & & 3 &	1 & & 2 & 3 &

Eleven-Beat Patterns
Conduct a twelve-beat pattern and omit a beat. For example:

1-2-3	4-5-6	7-8	9-10-11
1 & &	2 & &	3 &	4 & &

Practice leaving a beat out of each of the other three-beat groups to create the three other eleven-beat patterns.

Creating Other Patterns
The foregoing are the most common possibilities for altering patterns. You may find rare instances, however, that require the creation of other patterns. An eight-beat pattern, for example, could be asymmetrical (3 + 3 + 2 or 2 + 3 + 3 or 3 + 2 + 3) and could be conducted by modifying a nine-beat pattern.

Changing Length of Beats

Frequent changes in meter including asymmetrical meters at fast tempos (Figure 8-3) are characteristic of twentieth-century music and require special study by both conductors and performers. In such music (e.g., Figure 8-4 on the opposite page), note values remain constant from one meter to the next, unless otherwise indicated. The travel following the ictus in the longer measure will be slower, owing to the addition of the extra duration, and may require special attention.

FIGURE 8-3
Example of alternation of basic pattern and asymmetrical derivation.

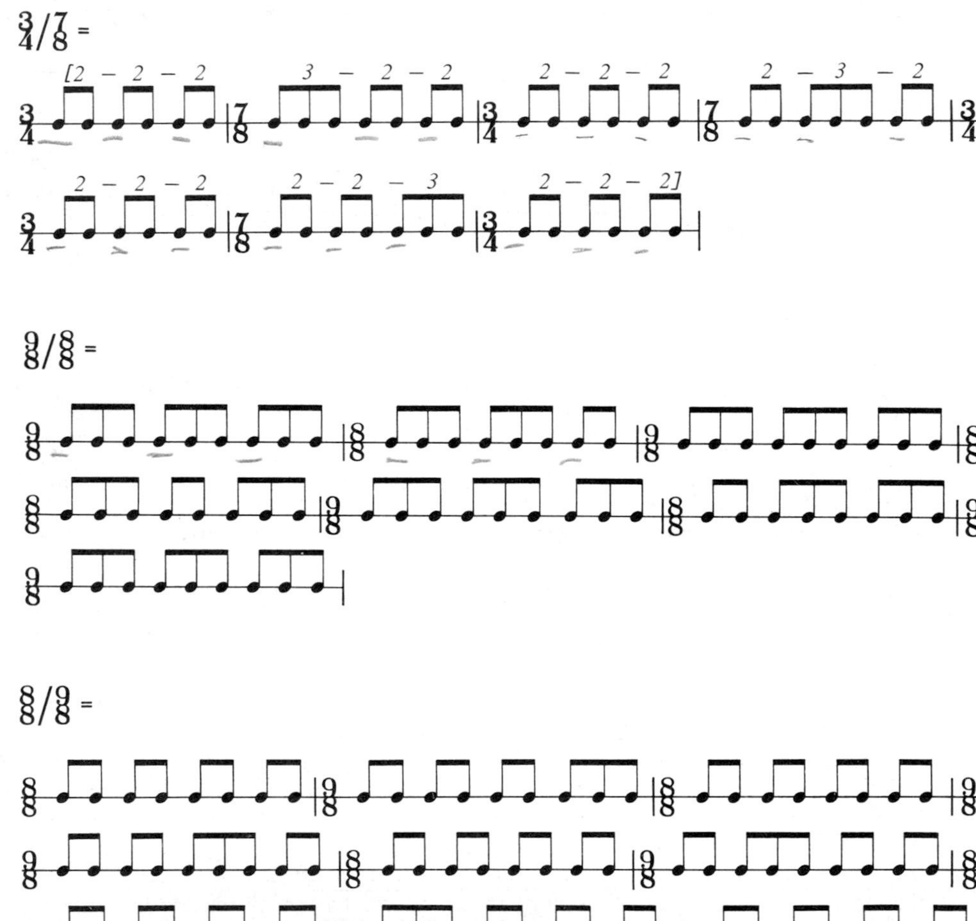

The excerpt in Figure 8-4 from *L'Histoire du soldat* ("The Soldier's Tale") is an example of music with changing beat lengths. The triangle and line symbols are sometimes used by conductors to designate beat groupings.

FIGURE 8-4
Igor Stravinsky, *L'Histoire du soldat* ("The Soldier's Tale").

Practice the exercise in Figure 8-5, *conducting each measure in one.* The length of the measures will change while the eighth-note pulse remains constant. Use a metronome, if possible, for the eighth-note pulse, MM160–208.

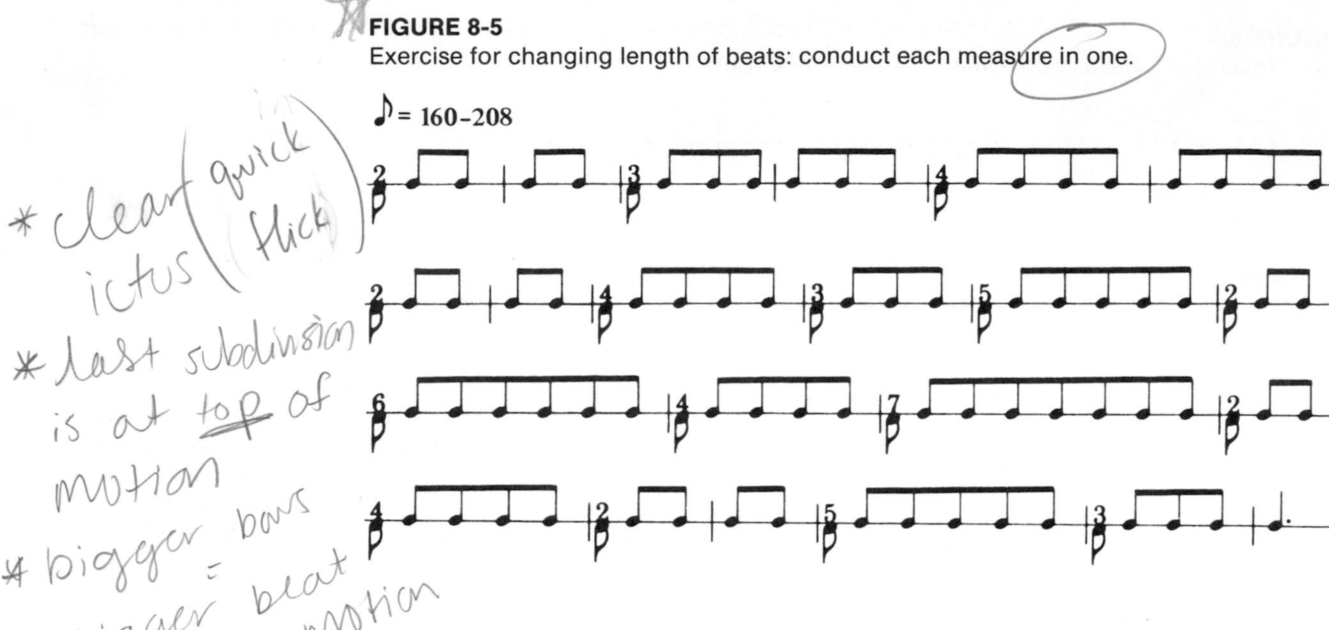

FIGURE 8-5
Exercise for changing length of beats: conduct each measure in one.

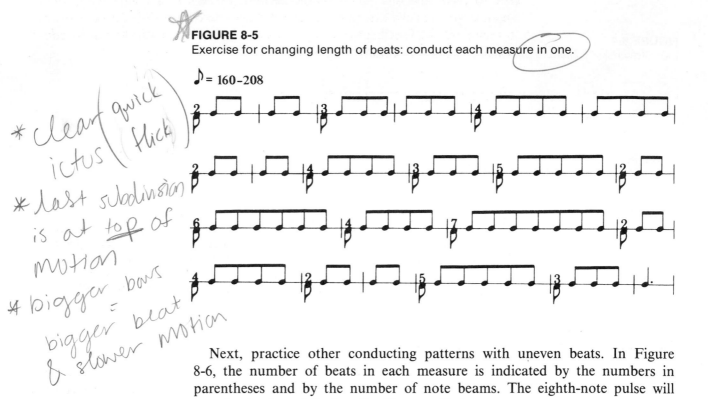

Next, practice other conducting patterns with uneven beats. In Figure 8-6, the number of beats in each measure is indicated by the numbers in parentheses and by the number of note beams. The eighth-note pulse will remain steady and the length of beats will change.

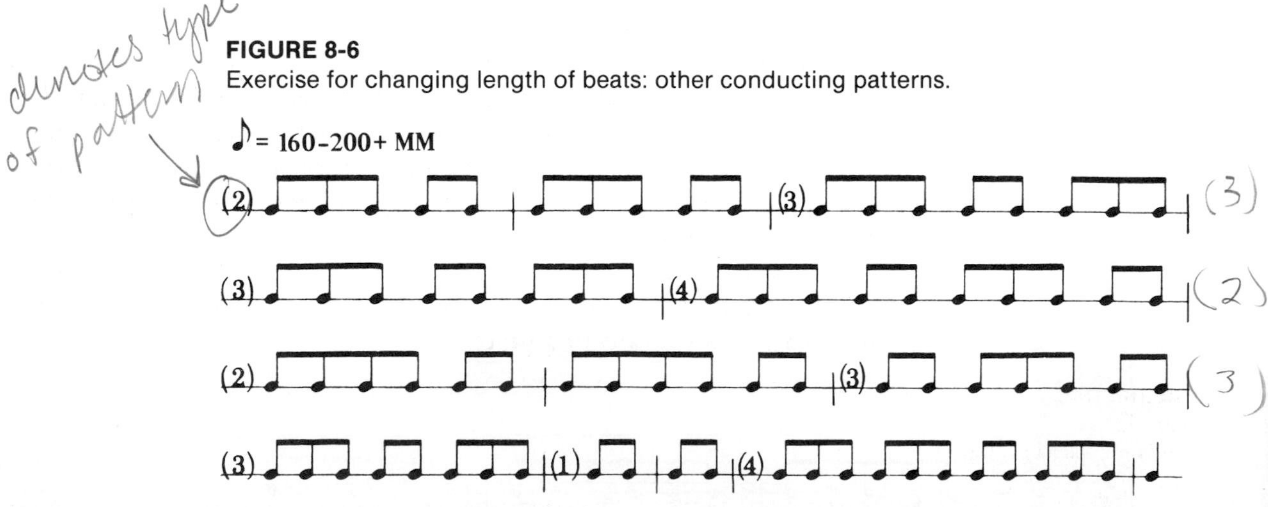

FIGURE 8-6
Exercise for changing length of beats: other conducting patterns.

Combining Symmetrical Patterns

Practice conducting the examples in Figure 8-7 by combining patterns. Be sure to place the first count of the second pattern on a higher plane than the first count of the first pattern. This should make it possible for performers to recognize the first beat in every measure. Seven-beat patterns can be conducted in the same manner (4 + 3 or 3 + 4).

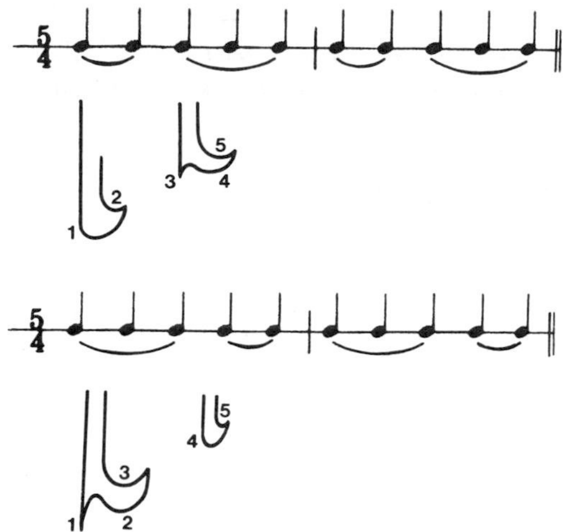

FIGURE 8-7
Consecutive two-beat and three-beat patterns. (*Note:* Although the patterns shown here are side by side for the sake of clarity, they are actually conducted in the same vertical plane.)

Choosing a Pattern: Rhythmic Focal Points

Choosing the most effective conducting pattern sometimes depends on analyzing rhythmic groupings, focal points in the rhythm, and the melodic structure, rather than simply conducting a large section in the indicated meter. Avoid the tendency to be drawn visually to the time signature for your patterns rather than to the shape of the melodic or rhythmic material.

A helpful exercise for learning to do this is writing out metrical and asymmetrical melodic lines with the bar lines removed. (See Figure 8-8.) Rebar the excerpt without time signatures and practice beat patterns based on the melodic material itself. When the class does this exercise, several versions of the rebarring will occur, depending on each student's perception of the rhythmic patterns.

An optional variation on this exercise is to write two or three melodic lines without bar lines and distribute them to other members of the class for barring and conducting practice.

FIGURE 8-8
Exercise:
rhythmic focal points.

AURAL ANALYSIS

Continue acting as designated listeners and observers (the procedure is described in Chapter 3). In addition to checking the correctness of the conducting and performance, focus on the expressive potential and subtleties of asymmetrical patterns.

ASSIGNMENT

In addition to practicing the exercises in the chapter, select excerpts for Chapter 8 in the Anthology for conducting and performing in class. Instruments can be added to, or substituted for, vocal parts.

PERFORMANCE EXCERPTS FOR CHAPTER 8

Section Three, pages 290–308

8-1 Persichetti, *Mass,* Kyrie
8-2 Mussorgsky, *Pictures at an Exhibition,* "Promenade"
8-3 Berger, *Six Madrigals,* "Harvester's Song"
8-4 Bernstein, *Mass,* "Almighty Father"
8-5 Makris, *Aegean Festival* Overture
8-6 Grainger, *Lincolnshire Posy,* "Rufford Park Poachers"
8-7 Orff, *Carmina Burana, Uf dem Anger* ("On the Green")

CHAPTER 9

SUSTAINING GESTURES

PATTERN MODIFICATION

CONDUCTING SUPERMETRIC PATTERNS

The conducting patterns that have been studied so far are based on the meter of the music. Sometimes, however, it is effective to depart briefly from metric conducting patterns in order to give emphasis to larger structural and expressive features of a composition. In this chapter, some of the logical possibilities will be discussed.

SUSTAINING GESTURES

It is often more effective to indicate a long note with one continuous motion than to conduct all the individual beats, because this will give a more accurate visual representation of the sound. Sample sustaining gestures are indicated by a double line in Figure 9-1. Use one continuous motion for each note that is longer than one beat in duration. The travel should be smooth to indicate a sustaining or supportive quality. The sustaining gesture can move in any direction, but it should finish in a location that will enable you to give the next beat in the correct direction.

FIGURE 9-1
Jean Baptiste Lully, *Au Clair de la lune* ("Lo, there in the moonlight").

Sustaining gestures can be used effectively for endings in which all performers have a long note indicated, and also to give emphasis to the melody or a supporting voice. Do not use sustaining gestures if the modification of the beat pattern may become confusing to the performers.

PATTERN MODIFICATION

Frequently, it is possible to depart from regular beat patterns to give increased emphasis to specific features of the music, particularly when the music has a regular and prominent pulse that the performers can maintain easily without constant attention from the conductor. Departing, carefully, from the beat pattern for a few beats or even a few measures can dramatically emphasize dynamic contours, rhythm patterns, melodic shapes, entrances, and other features. Complete beat patterns should be given, however, when the performers may need them.

The rhythm of melodic lines and motives can be emphasized by sustaining gestures. Figure 9-2 (opposite page) shows several examples of sustaining gestures. Practice these, concentrating on making a visual representation of the rhythms. Notice that the sustaining gestures can be used for groups of notes as well as for single notes. Sustaining gestures are indicated by wider lines and preparatory gestures by broken lines.

The examples in Figure 9-2 are not intended to suggest that all or even most of the changes should be included in any one interpretation. This would probably lead to overconducting a fairly simple and straightforward composition. They do show, however, that it is possible to avoid strict time beating and to emphasize or deemphasize specific aspects by altering beat patterns.

To depart from the beat pattern, you may need to make a deliberate effort at first. Conduct the vivace section of the excerpt from Haydn's Symphony No. 97 in the Anthology (Excerpt 9-3), using beat patterns for only the first few measures. Then conduct anything other than the beat pattern, showing entrances, releases, dynamic contours, focal points of phrases; use either hand alone or both hands together, or alternate hands. After practicing in this manner (with the ensemble), conduct the vivace section again, using beat patterns most of the time but departing from them to give increased emphasis to other aspects of the music.

CONDUCTING SUPERMETRIC PATTERNS

The rhythm of metric music is usually perceived on at least three planes simultaneously. Two of these planes are on the *metric level;* the upper one is the rhythm created by the grouping of beats into measures, and the lower one is the subdivision of beats. Rhythm patterns larger than a measure form a third plane of perception, the *supermetric level.* This is the rhythm created by patterns of strong and weak beats within phrases and sections and by the relative duration and emphasis of large sections.

The supermetric aspect of score analysis is seldom given sufficient attention; as a result, performances are frequently less musical and convincing than they might otherwise be. There are many instances in which it is possible to achieve a more effective interpretation by conducting supermetric patterns instead of metric patterns.

In the scherzo of his Symphony No. 9 in D Minor, Beethoven indicates that the music is in three-measure units (a supermetric pattern) and that each measure should be conducted as one beat of a three-beat pattern (see Figure 9-3 on page 114). He does this by indicating *Ritmo di tre battute* ("three-beat rhythm") and later indicates four-beat rhythm in the same manner. A continuous one-beat pattern would make the supermetric organization less clear.

FIGURE 9-2
Sustaining gestures for modified beat patterns:
Haydn, Symphony No. 97, first movement, vivace.

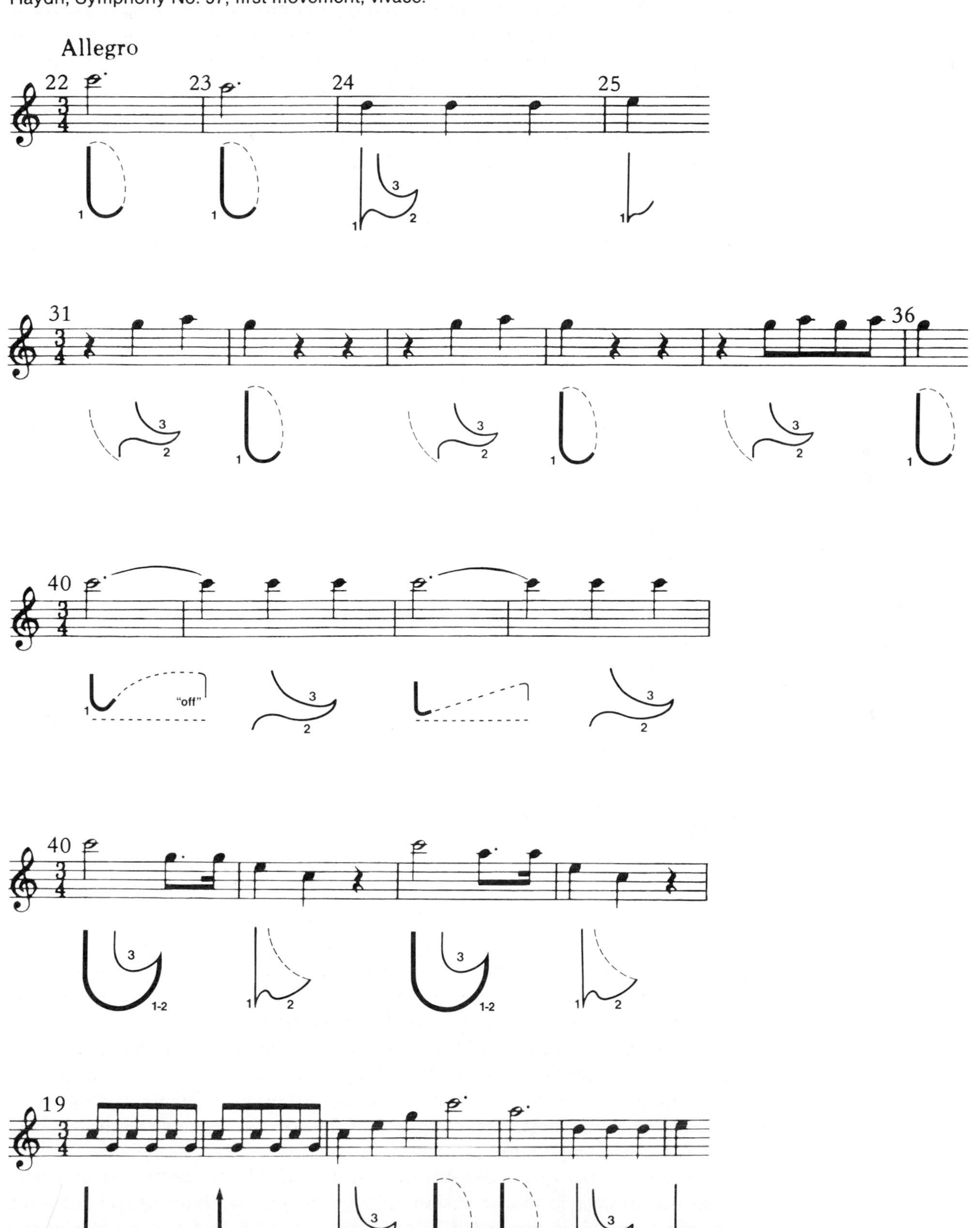

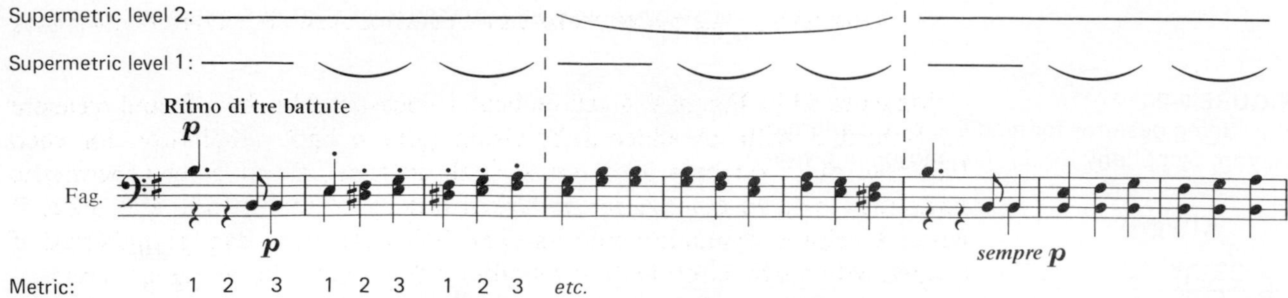

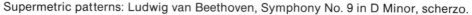

FIGURE 9-3
Supermetric patterns: Ludwig van Beethoven, Symphony No. 9 in D Minor, scherzo.

In Figure 9-3, the metric rhythm is indicated below the staff, and the supermetric rhythm is indicated by symbols above the staff. These symbols for supermetric rhythm, commonly used for analyzing the rhythm of poetry, have also been used by music theorists: — for a strong pulse and ⌣ for a lighter pulse. (Although there are other systems of indicating supermetric levels, this system lends itself particularly well to marking and reading scores.) Supermetric level 1 shows that the measures group into three-measure patterns. Supermetric level 2 shows that the second three-measure grouping has a lighter primary pulse than the first. Study this example carefully.

To conduct the excerpt in Figure 9-4, from the Overture to *Candide* by Leonard Bernstein, in supermetric units, conduct the seven-beat melody with the 3½-beat pattern in Figure 9-5. (See also Excerpt 9-6 in the Anthology.)

FIGURE 9-4
Leonard Bernstein, *Candide,* Overture.

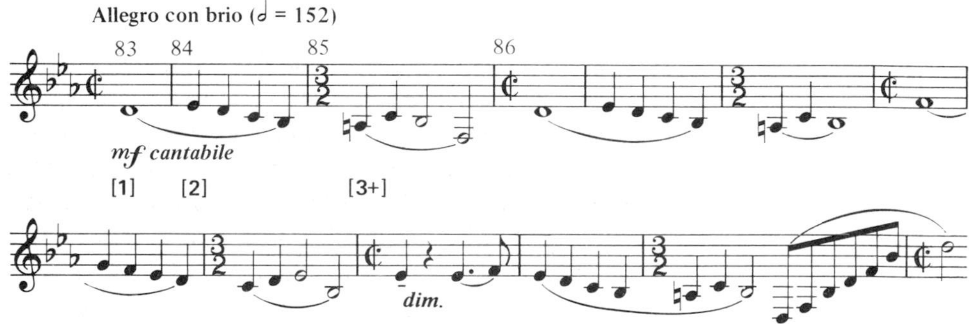

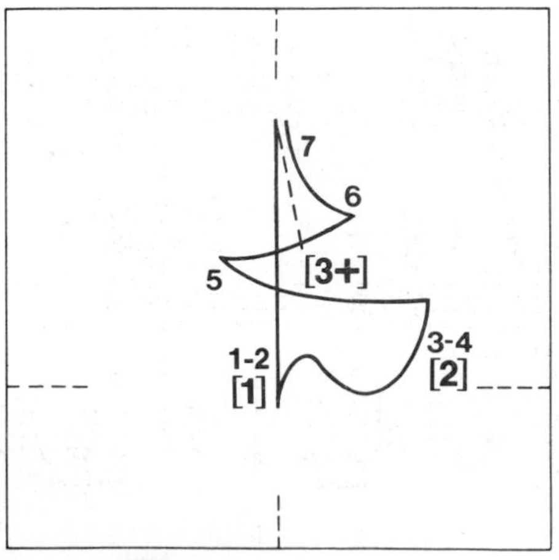

FIGURE 9-5
Three-and-a-half-beat supermetric pattern for *Candide.*

Measure 83 in Figure 9-4 will be beat 1, measure 84 is beat 2, and measure 85 is beat 3 with an added subdivision (give a light subdivision for each half-note pulse on beat 3 or use a single gesture). Conducting supermetric units may help to emphasize the lyrical quality of the melody and make it easier to shape dynamic contours. The half-note pulse can be indicated if desired with a light continuation-rebound subdivision. The decision to conduct either metric or supermetric patterns, however, is always a matter of individual preference.

Supermetric patterns are prominent in several parts of "Mars" in Gustav Holst's *The Planets.* Although these passages are often conducted entirely in metric units, it is possible to give more emphasis to large dynamic contours and improve ensemble quality by conducting supermetric units.

Practice the excerpt in Figure 9-6, conducting measures 1 and 2 with a *five*-beat pattern to emphasize the marcato style of the ostinato, and then shifting to an uneven *two*-beat pattern for measures 3–6 to emphasize the lyrical quality of the melodic line.

FIGURE 9-6
Gustav Holst, *The Planets,* "Mars."

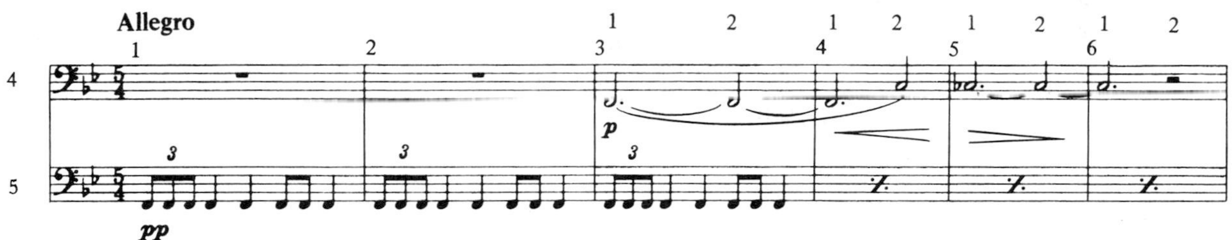

Before continuing with the following examples, study the score of "Mars" in the Anthology (Excerpt 9-5) to form a concept of the whole.

In measures 38–39 of "Mars," shown in Figure 9-7, conducting in $\frac{5}{4}$ will give emphasis to the cross-rhythms. Shifting to a $\frac{5}{2}$ pattern for these two measures (indicated by the numbers above the staff) will help to give more emphasis to the crescendo, as a result of the larger conducting strokes. A six pattern with a shortened second half can be used. A good case can be made for either metric or supermetric patterns here.

FIGURE 9-7
"Mars," measures 38 and 39.

In measures 43–65, the ostinato continues in $\frac{5}{4}$ while the melodic parts are in $\frac{5}{2}$, as shown in Figure 9-8 (with some exceptions, discussed below). The ostinato will continue with little or no attention, and the development of the music is entirely in the $\frac{5}{2}$ parts in this section. Conducting in $\frac{5}{2}$ (try a modified six pattern) will facilitate shaping the phrases and will be more helpful to the players. The melodic contour suggests a series of dynamic swells, with each phrase starting and ending softly.

FIGURE 9-8
"Mars," measures 43–46.

Measures 47–48 and 54–55 depart from the overall supermetric $\frac{5}{2}$ organization, but the rhythmic pulse of the melody is still in half notes (see Figure 9-9). These can be conducted as 2½-beat measures, using a three pattern with a shortened third beat. Measures 62 and 63 are also 2½-beat measures, with the second beat shortened (see Figure 9-10). A shortened three pattern can be used.

FIGURE 9-9
"Mars," measures 46–48.

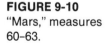

FIGURE 9-10
"Mars," measures 60–63.

Various systems can be used for marking supermetric patterns in the score. For example, the beats in each pattern can be indicated with either large numbers or a vertical line. A slash mark under the number or through the line can be used to indicate the shortened beats, as shown in Figures 9-9 and 9-10.

Under most conditions, a few words of explanation to the performers will be helpful. For example, in these sections of "Mars," the performers will understand more easily and have fewer problems if the following points are explained:

1 You will conduct in $\frac{5}{2}$ time in some parts of the $\frac{5}{4}$ sections, which will be much more helpful to most of the players.
2 Throughout most of these sections, those who need to focus on the quarter-note pulse for counting measures of rest can do so by listening to the ostinato; continuing the count by themselves; and realizing that when half-note units are being conducted, the beginning of their $\frac{5}{4}$ pattern will coincide with a conducting downbeat in every second measure.

Performers can mark wider bar lines to indicate supermetric units, but this usually will not be necessary.

Practice the excerpt from "Mars" in the Anthology, using both the suggested supermetric patterns and metric patterns only. Supermetric patterns can also be conducted with subdivisions. Shift into metric patterns to emphasize the rhythmic drive of the ostinato, and shift into supermetric patterns to emphasize the lyrical quality of the melody. Conduct the class and discuss the advantages and disadvantages of each approach. Remember also that "Mars" can be conducted entirely in metric units; the decision to use supermetric patterns is completely at the discretion of the conductor.

One of the problems of rehearsing and performing a work with a long ostinato section is maintaining the sanity of the ostinato players, especially when the section is played repeatedly in rehearsals. This problem will be even greater in a conducting class. In either situation, one solution is to do much of the rehearsing without the ostinato. In the conducting class, in which each person will want to have the fullest representation of the score, take turns playing the ostinato on the piano, percussion instruments, improvised percussion instruments, or any other instrument that can produce the correct pitch.

AURAL ANALYSIS

Continue the designated-listener and designated-observer procedures described in Chapter 3.

ASSIGNMENT

Practice the excerpts for Chapter 9 in the Anthology, finding appropriate places to use sustaining gestures, pattern modification, and supermetric patterns. Experiment with all possibilities and evaluate the results.

PERFORMANCE EXCERPTS FOR CHAPTER 9

Section 3, page 309-338

9-1 Lully, *Au Clair de la lune* ("Lo, there in the moonlight")
9-2 Rossini, Il Barbiere di Siviglia ("The Barber of Seville"), Overture
9-3 Haydn, Symphony No. 97, first movement
9-4 Grainger, *Lincolnshire Posy,* "Harkstow Grange"
9-5 Holst, *The Planets,* "Mars"
9-6 Bernstein, *Candide,* Overture

CHAPTER 10

PROGRAMMING AUDIENCE RAPPORT

ADMINISTRATIVE RESPONSIBILITIES

PROGRAMMING

Programming concerts is one of the conductor's most difficult tasks, but it is also one of the most enjoyable. Creating a concert program filled with music of the highest caliber that will inspire both performers and audience is one of the unique privileges and responsibilities of conducting.

Factors to Consider

Decisions about programming are a direct, personal reflection of each conductor's response to questions about several important factors:

- *Musical literature.* Does the quality and artistic level of the music programmed reflect the ever-changing current practices of music composition?
- *Personnel.* Does the programming challenge the performers' technique, interpretative capabilities, and capacity for artistic involvement? Is the music within the capability of the ensemble, given the practical limitations of the rehearsal schedule? Does it balance interpretative and technical demands?
- *Audience.* Will the programming raise the musical consciousness of the listeners rather than merely reflecting the most accessible common denominator of popular art? Is most of the program intellectually within reach of most of the audience?
- *Conductor.* Does the program challenge the conductor's own abilities and potential? Does it include some element of composition or performance practice not attempted in previous programs? Is each program a growth experience for the conductor's musical comprehension and conducting skills?

If the answer to any of these questions is negative, then a serious analysis of programming philosophy is in order.

The conductor must examine each and every composition under consideration and formulate a rationale for presenting it to both the performers and the audience. A broad range of the best repertoire should be programmed. Programming of popular music should be kept in balance with the rest of the repertoire, selecting the best of the genre and not exploiting its immediate appeal.

The music performed must challenge the performers to increase their comprehension of compositional techniques. If an ensemble performs very little music written later than the nineteenth century or the first decade of the twentieth century, the introduction of works from the second half of the twentieth century must be planned carefully so as not to overwhelm the performers with too many new instrumental or vocal techniques, harmonic variations, and rhythmic devices.

Seasonal Planning

Conductors should usually plan each season's programs at least 1 year in advance. The following points should be checked in the early stages of planning:

1 Begin by *summarizing the current season.* What worked well? Can you build on that in some way? What did not work well, and why? What should you have done but did not do? Make written notes and keep them on file.

2 Make a list of possible *sources of conflict for concert dates.* Check on religious holidays and other major artistic and entertainment events. If high school students are involved, check on the dates of SAT and ACT tests, semester and final examinations, and important extracurricular events such as basketball tournaments.

3 Consider what *main strengths of the ensemble* could be highlighted. What compositions would do this? What are the *weaknesses of the ensemble* that should not be overextended? Match the ensemble's increasing performance ability throughout the year with increasingly difficult music.

4 Consider what *special features* might be included in the season, such as soloists, guest conductors, commissioned works, and important anniversaries such as composers' birthdays and national holidays.

5 Make a tentative *concert calendar,* check it with everyone concerned, and then proceed to planning the specific details.

6 Establish a *balance of instrumentation requirements,* providing tutti ensemble writing versus lighter scoring, with sufficient solo opportunities for principal performers.

Program Types

Types of programs are as numerous as the conductor's imagination permits. Final decisions will always depend on musical and artistic taste; but here are some examples of several types of programming:

- *Historical perspective.* Program chronologically from earlier periods to the present. This is usually quite pleasing to an audience because it presents many different styles of composition and scoring. The performers will find the changes in performance styles and (sometimes) ensemble size challenging. This can become a monotonous routine, however, if other programming approaches are not used for variety. A variation on this technique contrasts works from two or more periods, such as Renaissance and contemporary or Renaissance and classical.

- *Nationalistic styles, period styles, one composer.* Program several works from one school of composers, such as English vocal music from the time of Elizabeth I, Viennese orchestral music of 1915–1925, or the wind ensemble music of Kurt Weill.
- *Soloists.* Soloists may play one lengthy composition or be featured more than once, with contrasting compositions, during the program.
- *Major compositions.* A symphony, suite, or choral work is usually the main part of such a program; the rest is constructed to highlight the featured composition.
- *Calendar events.* Music can be programmed to commemorate important birthdays, anniversaries, or other events.
- *Boston Pops-style concert.* In this format there are two intermissions, with each third of the concert a complete entity. It allows for the use of soloists, popular music in symphonic arrangements, and encores.
- *Prism concert.* Approximately 1 hour of music by numerous large and small ensembles and soloists, using theatrical staging and lighting. The transition from one composition to the next takes place without interruption or applause, creating a feeling of looking at different facets of music.

Length and Order of Programs

From beginning to end, a school program should ordinarily last about 90 minutes or less. This time can be increased somewhat for select audiences or for works that are certain to maintain a high level of attention. Professional programs usually do not exceed 2 hours in length.

The conductor should time each composition carefully and add a realistic amount of time for (1) pauses between movements and between compositions, (2) tuning, (3) intermissions, (4) changes in staging, and (5) applause. If the nonmusical time is not exceptionally long, about 60 to 70 minutes of actual music will result in a 90-minute program that includes a 15-minute intermission. The conductor should try not to overprogram. Although it is hard to eliminate some choices, save them for another program.

It is not possible to state any hard and fast rules for the order of programming, but the following guidelines are often helpful:

1. Start with a composition that is not hazardous for the performers and that will create a positive first impression.
2. Place the compositions that are most intellectually challenging for the audience on the first half of the program.
3. The last composition before intermission should make the audience want to return.
4. Consider potential endurance problems, espcially for brass players and string players.
5. Alternate compositions by volume, tempo, mode, and style.
6. End the program with a work which is sure to create a positive feeling in both the ensemble and the audience.

A checklist for program planning is given in Appendix 4.

AUDIENCE RAPPORT

Talking briefly with the audience about one or two special aspects of a program often adds a personal touch that can have a very positive effect on the responsiveness of the audience. This can be overdone, but there does seem to be a trend toward it among leading soloists and conductors. In addition to developing empathy with the audience, it may also put both you and the performers more at ease.

Take time to acknowledge applause graciously and with a smile. Remember to acknowledge soloists individually. If there are several soloists, it may be helpful to clip a note to the last page of the score as a reminder. After the soloists have been acknowledged, acknowledge the whole ensemble by shaking hands with the concertmaster or concertmistress and motioning for the ensemble to stand. A sweeping motion with the hand can direct the audience's applause to the ensemble. Leave the stage and be prepared to return for additional bows and acknowledgments.

ADMINISTRATIVE RESPONSIBILITIES

The conductor should plan each and every detail leading to the initial rehearsal before a public performance so that all support personnel will function properly. The most common lapse in planning is not providing sufficient "lead time" for each support person to fulfill his or her obligations.

In a professional conducting position and in some universities, much of the planning and organization discussed here is the responsibility of a paid staff. In most situations, however, the conductor will need to oversee much of this administrative work. The following checklists are provided to help with the numerous administrative details.

Prerehearsal Preparation

Musical preparation and score study have been discussed in Chapter 5. *Logistical preparation* begins with identifying and reviewing areas such as the following:

- Musical materials (from the library)
- Score preparation
- Parts preparation
- Personnel assignments
- Seating charts and additional forms

Musical Materials

Ensembles' music libraries range from those with a professional library staff to those with part-time student help or no help at all. Regardless of the conditions, however, several procedures are essential.

1 Use a logical, organized filing system with cross-references by composer and title. Be consistent in filing all necessary information such as publisher, copyright date, instrumentation, and timing. Computer software for filing and retrieving such information is currently in use in many libraries. Various physical filing systems, complete with file folders, envelopes, or boxes, are available for purchase.

2 Be sure that all materials are numbered. Check out and check in all materials each time they are used. Repair damaged score parts and replace lost parts.
3 Maintain a log of all performances for future programming reference. Record sources for rental materials in a separate file for future reference.
4 Have individual folders of music available 1 to 2 weeks before the initial rehearsal for performers to review and practice.

See also the music materials checklist in Appendix 5. A highly recommended text to assist in developing music libraries is *A Practical Guide to the Music Library* by Frank Byrne (listed in Appendix 8).

Score Preparation

1 Begin studying the score well in advance of rehearsals.
2 Mark your score with sufficient rehearsal numbers.
3 Identify long tacet or rest sections for players, to ensure proper cuing.
4 Check the score for proper edition and for translation of text.
5 Add bowings, phrasings, articulations.
6 Write in pronunciation guides for vocal music.

Parts Preparation

1 Check to be sure that there is a sufficient number of parts for the ensemble.
2 Order extra parts as necessary (do *not* make illegal photocopies).
3 Add sufficient rehearsal numbers in the parts. (It is sometimes instructive to have the players write in extra rehearsal numbers, because it helps them learn form, climactic points, and so on. This is also less time-consuming than doing it yourself.)
4 Add bowings, articulation marks, and phrasings.
5 Add text, translations, or pronunciation guides.

It is always helpful to examine the individual parts and compare them with your score. This provides insight into the thought processes of the performers as they view their individual voice lines or parts. And it is absolutely necessary when working with a condensed score, especially with a traditional "leader's" part, such as a first violin or solo cornet part.

A form such as the music materials checklist in Appendix 5 is a helpful organizational guide.

Personnel Assignments

Many ensembles use the traditional practice of establishing one seating assignment for each performer for the entire season, but others change assignments from one concert to the next and even from one composition to the next within a concert. The conductor who follows the latter practice will have many more details to handle in each concert period but will, in return, see a greater degree of satisfaction and development among the performers.

Sufficient "lead time" in establishing personnel assignments is important, since performers assigned to a solo position or a doubling instrument (such as piccolo, English horn, or E-flat clarinet) should have ample time to prepare for the first rehearsal. In addition, performers must be allowed sufficient time to study their individual parts for bowings, fingerings, foreign terms, difficult solo and section passages, and endurance problems. (Endurance—for the ensemble and for individuals—should be a major consideration in planning the program and assignments, as we noted above.)

Seating Charts and Additional Forms

Review the sample seating charts and additional forms in the Appendixes for organizing and checking administrative procedures.

Rehearsal Philosophy and Procedures

Each rehearsal period must be planned with consideration for every performer's development and with an overview of the entire rehearsal time span, from initial rehearsal to concert dress rehearsal. Following are useful planning aids.

1 Establish a long-term rehearsal plan. It should be flexible enough to be altered as needed as you progress toward the concert.

2 Plan the introduction of each new work. Know how the style of the work will fit into the current thinking of the ensemble. Present background and corollary information to make the new composition more meaningful. Build on the ensemble's past experiences without pedantic overteaching.

3 Plan a realistic goal for each rehearsal. Nothing is more demoralizing for performers than sitting through a sloppy, aimless rehearsal.

4 Plan the balance of tutti versus section rehearsing. Release those performers who are not needed, if possible. If many difficult solo passages are involved, establish a separate coaching schedule for each performer outside of the full ensemble's rehearsal time.

5 Plan rehearsal time with regard to any unusual circumstances, such as

- Holidays and vacations
- Soloists or guest conductors, who will arrive later in the time span and take up most of the time in final rehearsals
- Extramusical elements, such as lighting, technical effects, and amplification (especially with jazz ensembles)

6 Remember the elements of tension and release. Pace your rehearsal to produce moments of relaxation to balance periods of intense concentration.

7 Establish tuning procedures.

- Use a fixed-pitch instrument or a principal performer who has reference to an electronic tuner.
- Tune by sections so that players can hear their own pitch more easily. Aid younger players with tuning, but lead them to become responsible for their own pitch.
- Always establish and maintain silence in the rehearsal room when sections are tuning. (Players often complain that they cannot hear themselves.)
- In a choral rehearsal, after explaining the requirements for rehearsal, establish silence so that the accompanist can give pitches for the first entrance.

8 Vary the format of the rehearsal to hold the performers' interest.

9 Keep instructions short and to the point. One of the most common criticisms of conductors is that they talk too much.

10 Post a schedule for several days of rehearsals in a prominent place to enable performers to organize their time and efforts and pace themselves throughout the rehearsal. Try not to schedule the most strenuous passages for the end of a long, difficult rehearsal period.

11 Balance the rehearsal with musical variety, placing soft and subtle music in prominent positions throughout the time span. An entire rehearsal with too much loud music will usually have an adverse effect on the performers.

12 Avoid the use of speech mannerisms: "OK," "you know," "you see," "uh," "like," and so on. Repetition of these in a rehearsal is very annoying and distracts from the clarity of instructions.

13 Develop a rehearsal style to permit friendly, enjoyable relationships with performers while remaining firmly in charge of the rehearsal.

14 Be positive in your attitude on the podium, projecting strong leadership along with a feeling of sensitivity for the individual performers and their current level of ability. Ensembles cannot perform artistically in a state of fear. Although the conductor must be musically demanding, always challenging the musicianship of the performers, criticism of musical problems must be balanced with sincere praise and respect for each performer's accomplishments.

Rehearsal Evaluation

Videotapes or audiotapes of rehearsals should be made and analyzed on a regular basis. Conductors seldom have an opportunity to get objective, comprehensive evaluations of rehearsal procedures, so it is important to become systematic about making self-evaluations. Video equipment is ideal for this purpose, but a great deal can be learned by listening to an audiotape made with a portable cassette recorder.

Check the following in analyzing rehearsal tapes:

1 Are your verbal instructions clear and concise?

2 Are there any distracting speech mannerisms?

3 Is too much time spent talking?

4 Are you giving verbal explanations that you should be communicating visually?

5 Are you ignoring any aspects of the performance, such as intonation, balance, or phrasing?

6 Are you ignoring any of the performers? Some conductors, for example, rarely make any musically discriminating comments to the basses or percussion—a poor condition for the morale and musicianship of the performers.

7 Does the rehearsal progress in a logical manner and at a quick pace? Do you build and maintain a high level of concentration?

8 Are you giving instructions without degrading any of the performers?

9 Are you giving honest and sincere praise when it is warranted?

10 Did you follow the schedule you planned?

The usefulness of the tapes for analyzing the quality of performance and planning subsequent rehearsals depends very much on the quality of the recording. Even a tape with very limited fidelity, however, will often reveal problems overlooked in rehearsal. It is sometimes difficult to evaluate tone quality and balance, but most other aspects of performance—such as rhythmic accuracy, intonation, and tempo changes—can be evaluated with recordings of even moderate quality. Review your rehearsal tapes with a colleague and solicit sincere, honest reactions that will help you improve your technique and communication.

ASSIGNMENTS

1. Attend two concerts and analyze the programming decisions using the factors discussed in this chapter. Attach copies of the programs to your written analyses.
2. Analyze two rehearsals in which you are not involved as a performer, using the points in this chapter as a basis for evaluation. Consider using the form for evaluating conductors in Appendix 6.

SECTION TWO

SPECIAL TOPICS AND TECHNIQUES

CHAPTER 11

CONDUCTING ACCOMPANIMENTS

The conductor has special responsibilities and opportunities when conducting accompaniments. He or she must coordinate and balance the ensemble with the soloist at all times, responding to the slightest expressive nuance of the soloist. Most conductors find that accompanying a good soloist is both challenging and gratifying.

PREPARATION

In preparing for a performance, the solo part as well as the accompaniment must be studied thoroughly before rehearsals. The conductor and the soloist should meet before the first rehearsal to discuss all aspects of interpretation. At that time the soloist should also play or sing representative samples of major sections, in addition to passages that may present special problems, such as transitional areas, fermatas, caesuras, and those passages in which the interpretation may differ from the score.

A soloist may tend to give misleading indications of tempo when playing or singing without accompaniment. Therefore, it is usually advisable to provide a pianist to accompany the soloist at this prerehearsal session, or for the conductor to accompany at the piano. Any planned deviations in tempo, and any sections in which balance may be a special problem, should be carefully marked in the score. Even when advance planning has been thorough, however, the conductor should be prepared for the soloist to vary tempos and make other changes when performing with the ensemble. This may occur because playing with ensemble accompaniment inevitably sounds and feels different, and also because spontaneity—within reasonable bounds—is a proper and necessary aspect of musical artistry. The soloist should be accommodated as graciously as possible.

RHYTHMIC ENSEMBLE

When the conductor has studied the score with the soloist carefully and developed a feeling for the soloist's interpretation, it will be possible to anticipate tempo variations. Discrepancies in tempos between the soloist and the accompaniment will not be frequent or large and should be easy to deal with. If the conductor is not quick in responding to tempo variations, however, a whiplike effect may occur. For example, if an accelerando is not immediately detected, an abrupt, "catch-up" tempo will be necessary, which in turn will need adjustment again when rhythmic ensemble with the soloist is reestablished. Subtle changes can be made without preparatory gestures for the ensemble, but abrupt changes need preparatory gestures. For example, the ensemble could not follow a downbeat given earlier than expected unless the beat was given with a clear preparation.

Measures of rest for the ensemble should be indicated with only a very small downward motion at the beginning of each measure to assist the players in counting. Do not give all the beats in each measure. The indication at the start of a measure can be done with either hand, and with the hand close to the body in order to be less obtrusive. It is also an accepted practice (though not necessarily advisable), when more than four or five measures of rest occur, to give all the downbeats in quick succession, in a clear but nonexpressive manner, to show the number of measures of rest, and then to wait until the end of the rests to resume conducting. However, this is not as reliable as indicating each downbeat when it occurs.

If there is a very long rest for the ensemble, it is preferable to ask the players to mark in their parts the exact measure at which you will resume conducting. If this is done, it is not necessary to show downbeats or give any other indications during the rest. In this case, and at the end of a cadenza, raise your hand (or both hands) to the ready position several beats (probably six to eight, depending on the tempo) before the ensemble entrance to give the players sufficient time to get ready.

BALANCE

The balance between soloist and ensemble should vary, depending on their musical functions. In addition to presenting the main melodic material, the soloist may also play tutti with the entire ensemble, in duet with parts of the ensemble, or in accompaniment as the melodic line is played by the ensemble. The most frequent concern is to balance the large dynamic resources of the ensemble with the relatively smaller resources of the soloist in a manner that will support, but not cover, the soloist.

The problems of accompanying the soloist in dynamic changes are seldom given enough consideration. For instance, if the conductor does not provide sufficient support in a crescendo, the musical effect is less dramatic than it should be. On the other hand, the conductor must not overpower the soloist before the peak of the crescendo. Examples 1 to 9 below illustrate specific balance relationships and ways in which they are treated (effectively and otherwise) by conductors. The solo part is represented by the solid line, the accompaniment by the broken line, and the peak of the crescendo (when applicable) by an X.

1 *Long solo crescendo with narrowing balance gap.* When the balance gap is narrowed near the peak, the effect of the crescendo is intensified.

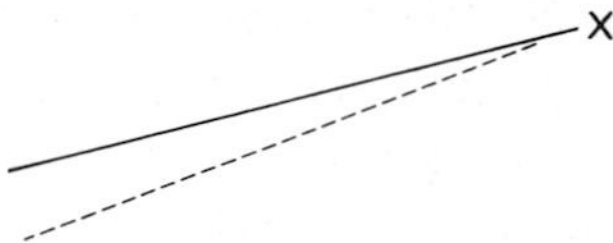

2 *Long solo crescendo with constant balance.* Here the balance relationship is maintained throughout. This is acceptable, but usually not as effective as example 1.

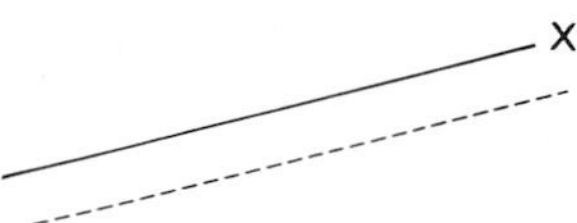

3 *Long solo crescendo with soloist covered briefly.* It is sometimes acceptable to cover the soloist very briefly at the end of a crescendo which leads to a tutti section because staying below the soloist may not allow a continuous dynamic increase to the tutti. The covering will not be noticed if it is very brief.

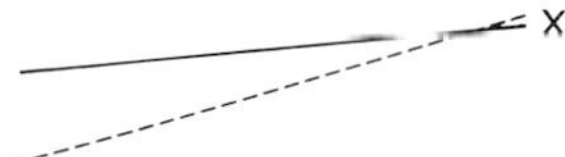

4 *Long solo crescendo without adequate support.* This is usually less dramatic and less convincing than it should be.

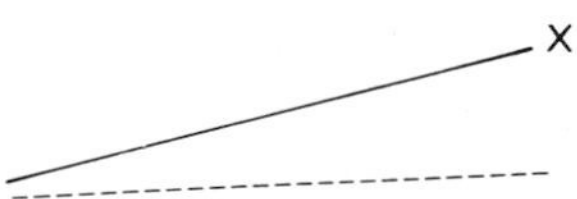

5 *Long solo crescendo with accompaniment inadequately controlled.* Here the accompaniment is not controlled and overwhelms the soloist.

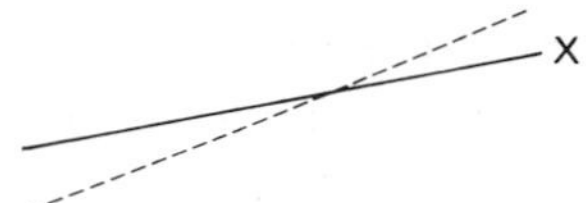

6 *Long solo decrescendo with widening balance gap.* Here the accompaniment leads the way and gives the soloist adequate room to make a full decrescendo. Widening the balance gap makes the decrescendo more effective.

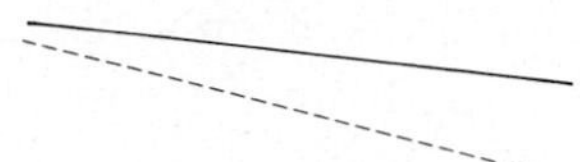

7 *Long solo decrescendo with constant balance.* Here the balance relationship is maintained throughout. This is acceptable, but example 6 is usually preferable.

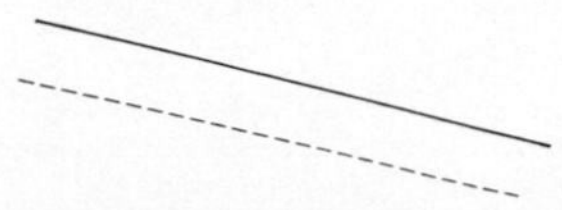

8 *Decrescendo with slow or late accompaniment.* Here the accompaniment decreases too slowly, too late, or both, limiting the dynamic range of the soloist or covering the soloist.

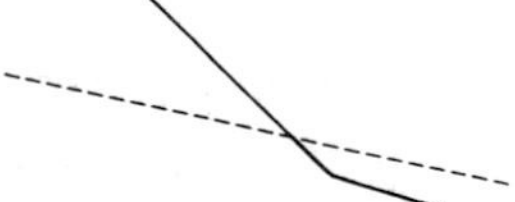

9 *Dynamic fluctuations by soloist with contour in accompaniment.* Here the soloist makes short dynamic changes while the accompaniment shapes the larger, underlying contour. This can be effective for a crescendo (as shown) or a decrescendo.

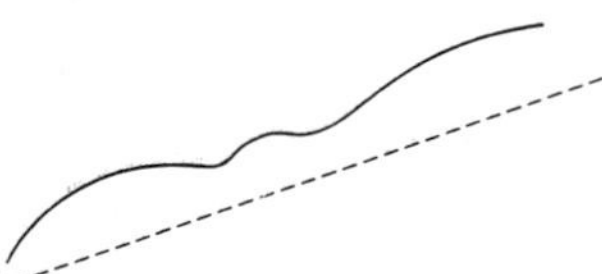

On the basis of the concept of balance illustrated in these examples, you can usually improve players' responsiveness by telling them that you will usually try to narrow the balance relationship on a crescendo and widen it on a diminuendo, and explaining why you choose to do so.

To avoid covering the soloist, it may also be necessary to make adjustments to the balance of the ensemble itself. High-pitched accompaniment parts, or instrumental voices in the tessitura of a solo instrument, or sustained parts tend to cover the solo instrument or voice and may need to be deemphasized in relation to lower-pitched or more rhythmic parts. In supporting a solo flutist in a crescendo, for example, it may be necessary to emphasize lower or more rhythmic parts while slightly limiting the support of similar upper-voice parts—all within the bounds of maintaining musical relationships in the accompaniment itself. If all else fails, it may be necessary to reduce the number of players or make other small adjustments in scoring and dynamics. Making these adjustments does intrude somewhat into the territory of the composer or arranger, but the conductor has the final responsibility and should feel justified in making small changes that improve the performance without seriously altering the composer's intended musical effect.

CRISIS SITUATIONS

Accompanying a soloist who may omit beats because of nervousness or technical problems or has a memory lapse and skips large sections is a grim experience—one that conductors should be prepared for.

In concert performances, playing solos from memory with an ensemble accompaniment should be undertaken only by very experienced and secure performers, who have already performed frequently from memory. But even the most experienced soloists sometimes have problems that require quick and decisive action by the conductor, and the conductor should decide in advance on techniques to be used in dealing with specific kinds of problems. The procedures that follow are effective for some of the more common problems. They are also applicable to solos in musical theater (see Chapter 13) and in opera.

- *If the soloist omits a beat or two,* reestablish coordination at the beginning of the next measure. Give a prominent preparatory gesture and downbeat, possibly with both hands. If some of the players miss this, repeat it in the next measure.
- *If the soloist skips more than a measure,* try to coordinate the ensemble with the soloist at the next prominent entrance, rehearsal letter, or new section. Hold the left hand in the attention position to indicate that a major entrance is coming and establish intense eye contact with the ensemble. Make the cue so reassuring that the players will enter despite the fact that it is earlier or later than expected. Facial expression and mouthed directions can also be helpful.
- *If the soloist is seriously disoriented but takes the lead anyway,* it may be necessary to mouth or say aloud an approaching rehearsal letter to the soloist and recoordinate at that point.
- It may be necessary to *skip ahead to a tutti section or orchestral interlude,* which will give the soloist a chance to get ready for a fresh start. Mouth or say aloud the rehearsal letter several times and then give a very decisive preparatory gesture and downbeat for the new section.
- When no other solution is possible, it may be necessary to *stop both soloist and ensemble* and designate a starting point.

Of the remedies listed above, the first and sometimes the second can usually be accomplished with only slight distraction, but the others may not prevent a major distraction and embarrassment—which brings us back to our earlier point: the conductor must be ready to make instant adjustments.

ASSIGNMENT

Practice the excerpts for Chapter 11 in the Anthology, substituting other instruments in the solo part if necessary. Use piano with other instruments for the ensemble part.

PERFORMANCE EXCERPTS FOR CHAPTER 11

Section Three, pages 339-358

11-1 Handel, *Messiah,* "Behold, I tell you a mystery" (recitative for bass) and "The trumpet shall sound" (air for bass)

11-2 Mozart, Concerto for Flute and Orchestra in D Major, second movement

11-3 Mozart, *Die Zauberflöte* ("The Magic Flute"), recitative

11-4 Rimsky-Korsakoff, *Scheherazade,* opening

11-5 Traditional, "Sometimes I Feel Like a Motherless Child"

CHAPTER 12

CONTEMPORARY MUSIC

During the second half of the twentieth century, the music world has seen the introduction of many new forms of notation and rhythmic experimentation. Primary among these innovations is *aleatoric composition*—composition "by chance" or through organized improvisation.

CONTEMPORARY SCORES

Notation

Iconic Notation

Much of the new melodic notation is *iconic;* that is, the notational symbols look like the sounds they represent. Thus a long tone is represented by a long symbol, the rising or falling of a melodic line may be indicated by a wavy line, and so on.* Duration of a sound is represented by the horizontal length of the notation symbol, and pitch is indicated by the shape and location of the symbol.

The iconic rhythmic notation in contemporary music is usually called *proportional notation,* referring to the relative size of the symbols and spacing. Duration may be approximate, subject to the performers' or the conductor's interpretation of the symbol's relationship to other symbols or to a specific unit of measure, such as a steady pulse of minutes and seconds.

Contemporary Notational Symbols

Figure 12-1 (on the following pages) shows some of the notational symbols that are commonly used in contemporary music, and particularly in aleatoric music.

*An *icon* is a symbol that looks like whatever it stands for. Traditional rhythmic notation is not iconic—that is, a whole note does not look longer than a quarter note.

FIGURE 12-1
Glossary of common contemporary notational symbols.

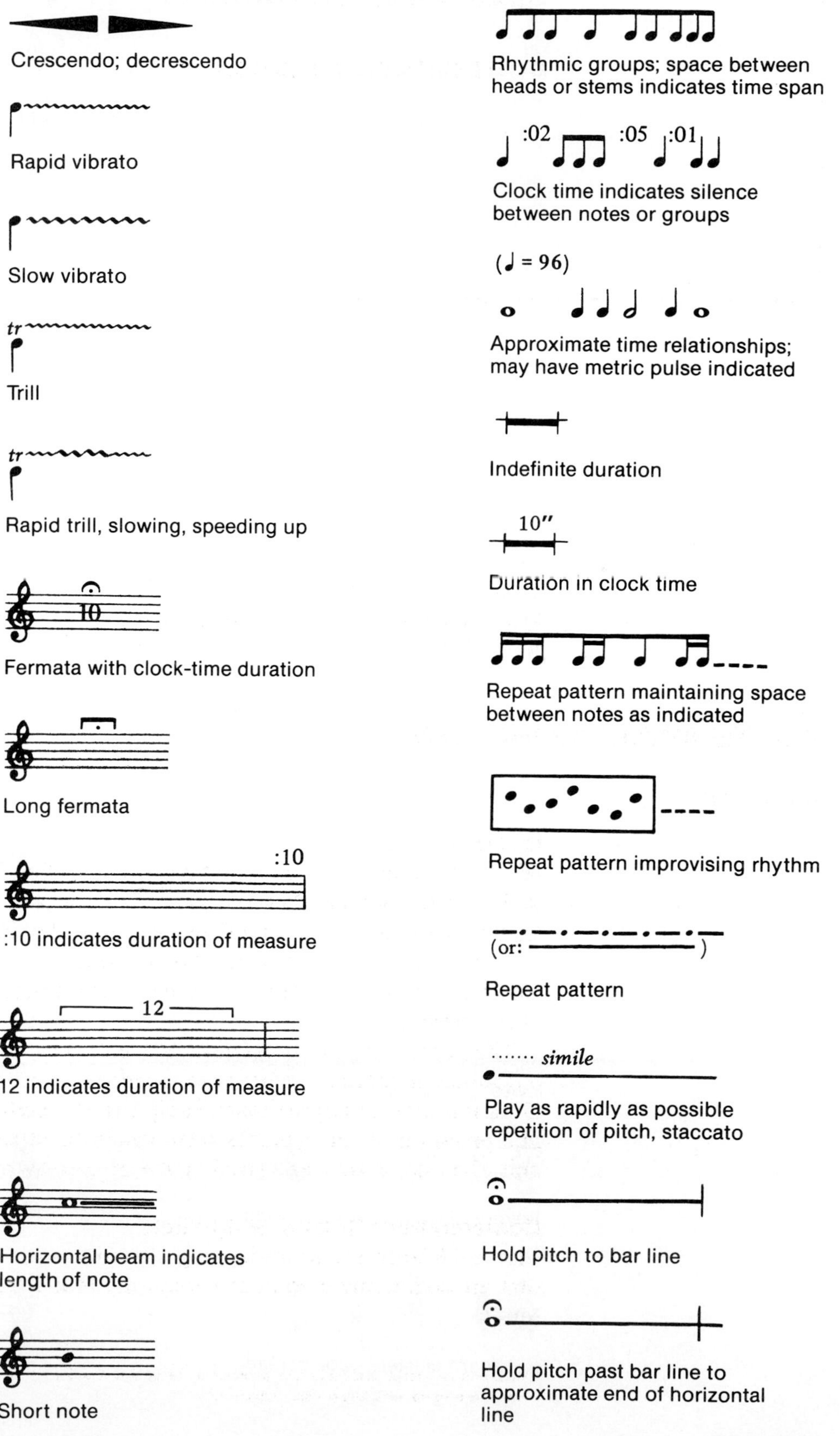
Crescendo; decrescendo
Rapid vibrato
Slow vibrato
tr
Trill
tr
Rapid trill, slowing, speeding up
10
Fermata with clock-time duration
Long fermata
:10
:10 indicates duration of measure
12
12 indicates duration of measure
Horizontal beam indicates length of note
Short note
Rhythmic groups; space between heads or stems indicates time span
:02 :05 :01
Clock time indicates silence between notes or groups
(♩ = 96)
Approximate time relationships; may have metric pulse indicated
Indefinite duration
10″
Duration in clock time
Repeat pattern maintaining space between notes as indicated
Repeat pattern improvising rhythm
(or:)
Repeat pattern
simile
Play as rapidly as possible repetition of pitch, staccato
Hold pitch to bar line
Hold pitch past bar line to approximate end of horizontal line

(Continued)

FIGURE 12-1
(Continued)

Approximate pitch notation—play high, in staff, or low as indicated

Highest possible pitch—on some instruments such as piano, xylophone, etc., pitch is fixed; on others, pitch depends upon ability and development of individual performer

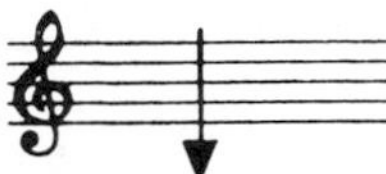
Lowest possible pitch—same rationale as above applies to pitch to be produced

Cluster—frequently exact pitches will be given with exact instrument assignment

Section or keyboard cluster of highest possible pitches

Section or keyboard cluster of lowest possible pitches

Keyboard cluster—narrow width

Keyboard cluster—wide spread

Repeat notes in box until duration of horizontal line

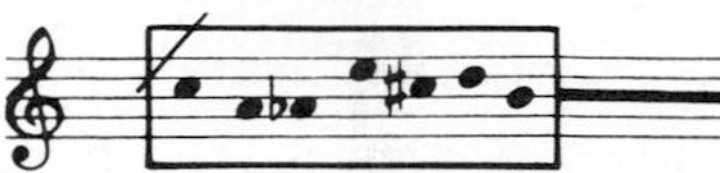
As above—but as fast as possible

Play a melodic line following the contour of the wavy line

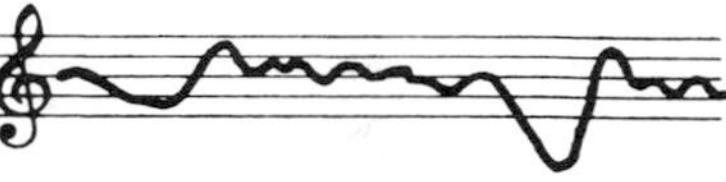
As above

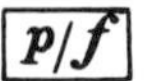

Free choice of dynamic level

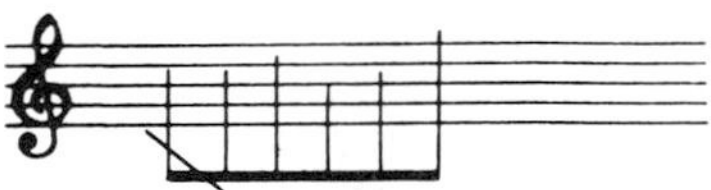
\ Indicates "as fast as possible"

Legato line, length of note indicated by note head

Accelerando, ritard

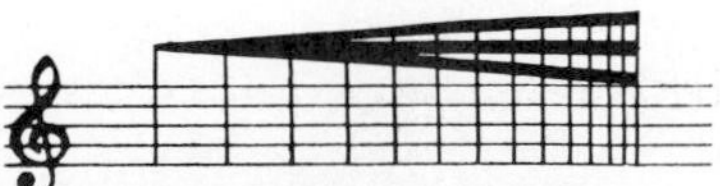
Free accelerando

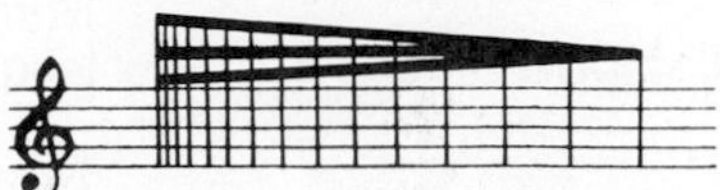
Free ritard

French Scores

Many contemporary composers prefer French-style scores in which parts with extended rests and empty staves are not shown. Scores with large blank spaces of various shapes and sizes may look complicated to those who are unfamiliar with them, but they are actually much easier to read, since they give a clearer visual representation of the music. (See Figure 12-2.)

FIGURE 12-2
Krzysztof Penderecki, *Stabat mater* ("The mother was standing").

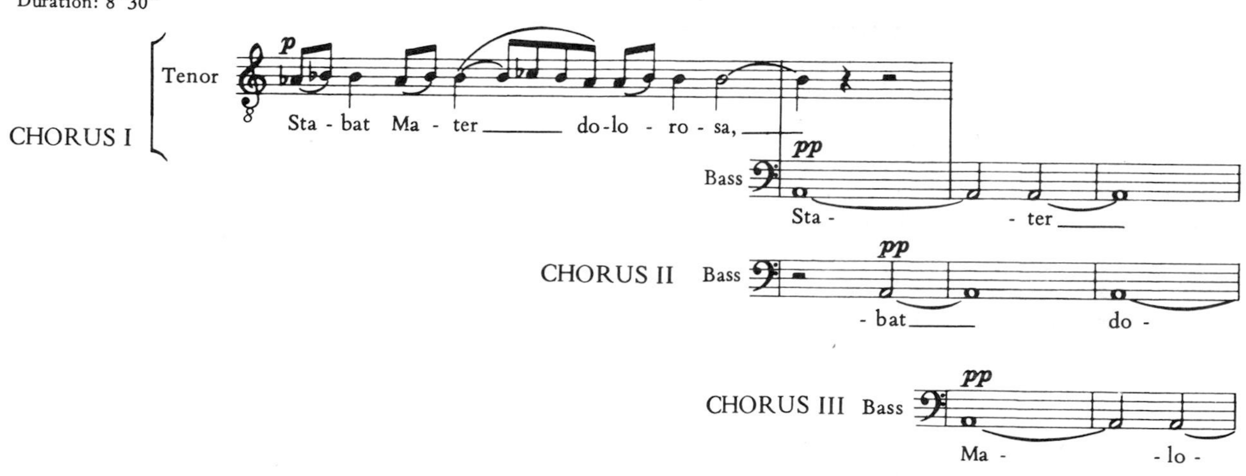

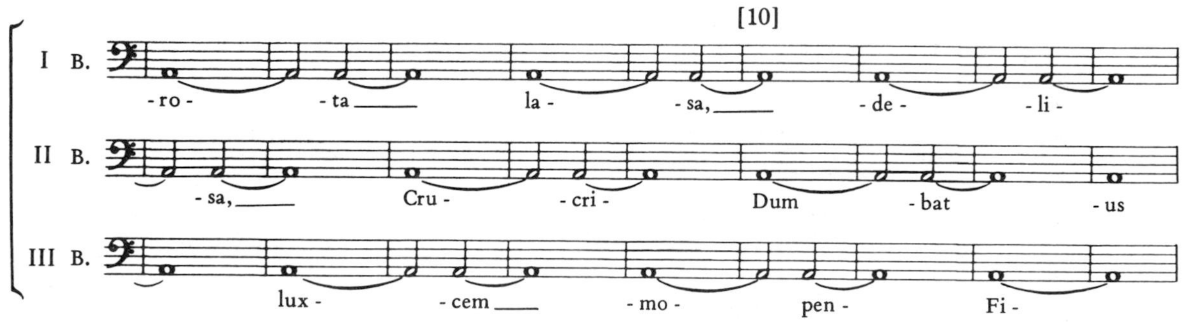

Individual Performance Parts

The individual part for each performer or section may now be in score form, in complete section voice parts, or in traditional-style individual voice parts.

Explanatory Keys

Most contemporary compositions contain elements foreign to traditional practices, either in performance requirements or in notation. To ensure an accurate reproduction of the score requirements, many composers prepare a *key,* or explanatory section, at the beginning of the score to explain exactly how each notational marking is to be interpreted.

FIGURE 12-3
Hans Werner Henze, *Aria de la folía española* ("Fantasia on the Spanish 'Folly' "), explanatory key. (Note: A *folía*—"folly"—is a Spanish carnival dance.)

zeichenerklärung / explanation of symbols

N = normale spielweise
normal playing

= gehaltene töne (ligatur)
tied notes (ligatura)

+ = pizzicato (horn: bouché)

= Bartok - pizzicato

= flatterzunge
flutter tongue

= vom normalton einen viertelton aufsteigen und zum normalton zurückkehren
rising to one quarter tone above and returning to the normal note

= halb mit dem bogenholz, halb mit dem bogenhaar auf die saiten klopfen, während die linke hand die vorgeschriebenen töne greift
tap on strings, half with bow-stick and half with hair of bow whilst left hand stops given notes

= wiederholung der noten ab [und freie rhythmische gestaltung
repeat notes from [and free rhythmic interpretation

= moderato

= bewegt
agitated

= so schnell als möglich
as fast as possible

= crescendo/decrescendo

= atempause
short caesura

= kurzer halt
very short halt

= kurze fermate
short fermata

= mittlere Fermate
medium length fermata

△ ▲ = rechter unterarm auf den weißen bzw. schwarzen tasten
right forearm on the white, respectively black keys

▽ ▼ = linker unterarm auf den weißen bzw. schwarzen tasten
left forearm on the white, respectively black keys

△ ▲ = rechte hand auf den weißen bzw. schwarzen tasten
right hand on the white, respectively black keys

▽ ▼ = linke hand auf den weißen bzw. schwarzen tasten
left hand on the white, respectively black keys

○ ● = mit der faust auf den weißen bzw. schwarzen tasten
with fist on the white, respectively black keys

= beliebige töne auf weißen bzw. schwarzen tasten
freely chosen notes on white, respectively black keys

▲ = höchster ton auf dem instrument
the highest tone on the instrument

= clusters

N.B. graphische zeichen werden frei gedeutet.
the graphic signs are to be freely interpreted.

Items covered in an explanatory key may include the following:

- Realization of *alea* or improvisatory symbols
- Temporal instructions about proportional or nontraditional rhythmic devices
- Stage actions for works that involve theater performance
- Physical arrangement of instrumentalists or vocalists onstage or in the auditorium
- Exact instrumentation and doubling of percussion section parts
- Score information—whether score is in C or transposed

The conductor must become familiar with each indication and be sure that each performer has the same information and understands each instruction.

Figure 12-3 on the opposite page shows an example of an explanatory key.

PERFORMANCE TECHNIQUES

The most important element in the successful performance of contemporary music is a logical study procedure combined with practice of the gestures required. The conductor who has accumulated knowledge of traditional music practices will find that these techniques can easily be transferred to the performance of aleatoric or proportional music.

Frequently, however, a conductor will approach a new score with a sense of helplessness, a feeling that the notational symbols are undecipherable and thus unteachable to a traditionally minded ensemble. The following points may be of assistance:

1 Instrumentalists and vocalists are seldom required to perform in a manner totally foreign to their traditional training or experience.

2 Although new instruments may be introduced or new methods of playing traditional instruments may be required, the same diligent score study and rehearsal procedure will work for contemporary music as well as for traditional music. You must expect that the same items that were new to you as you began your study process will also create doubt among the individual performers as they begin rehearsals.

3 Coordination between performers in contemporary music often depends entirely on the conductor, since there will be no "binding" elements such as a traditional melodic line (with sequential answers and countermelodies) or a supporting harmonic progression.

4 Fear of the unknown is a normal human emotion; the conductor must be aware that performers may fear embarrassment because of their lack of knowledge and experience in contemporary techniques. Once the performers learn the techniques involved and realize that they will not be subjected to personal or musical embarrassment, they will progress quickly.

5 In this music, performers who normally are section players may become individual performers with their own line and responsibilities; thus the conductor may need to encourage more projection of sound combined with increased conviction of purpose.

6 The conductor must constantly convey positive thinking and confidence during rehearsal and discourage premature negative aesthetic judgments.

7 Invite the composer to attend rehearsals whenever possible. He or she may not always be certain that everything written in the score is actually playable or know the most satisfactory way to achieve a particular effect. The conductor can assist the composer by having performers demonstrate various possibilities on each instrument, joining actively in the creative process. The reward will be a more satisfying rehearsal and performance experience.

CONDUCTING TECHNIQUES

Most contemporary compositions retain the use of traditional bar lines as a temporal dividing system, but the activity between bar lines may be released from traditional rhythmic division. Effective physical communication may well be based on the following practices:

1. Use the right hand for all bar-line downbeats (beat 1) or major subdivisions within bar lines.
2. Use the left hand in a downward, lateral, or cuing motion for secondary entrances. (RH, LH, and arrows are frequently placed in scores to show the use of each hand and the direction of the motion.)
3. Many proportional scores use areas of duration measured in minutes and seconds. Use a watch or maintain a pulse of ♩ = 60 MM to measure the time required.
4. Number each entrance within a measure to aid those performing from their separate parts. (Each part may have numbered entrances as well. Always check your score against the parts so that you will know what assistance the performers will expect from you.)
5. Most conductors use the fingers of one hand to indicate the rotation of entrances within each measure. If the composer has labeled the entrances A-B-C-D and so on, change this to 1-2-3-4. If the numbers run above five (the limit on one hand), place a subdividing line in the measure at that point and begin again on 1.
6. The composer's directions are sometimes incomplete or unclear. If you discover that the performers have difficulty determining their actual position within a given measure or following cued entrances, make as many subdivisions as necessary and devise a directing scheme for clear communication.
7. Maintain a feeling of support for the rhythmic flow. Many compositions begin to sound choppy and lack a sense of continuity if some element of support is not present.
8. Reflect subito or extreme changes of dynamics, tensions, accents, or releases of tension with appropriate physical gestures. The performers and the audience do not have the visual impact of the continuing traditional conducting pattern as a guide. Also, the visual impact of well-planned gestures heightens the performers' and audience's involvement in the performance.
9. Encourage the performers to make the most of each event in the score, both in technical execution and in style.
10. Above all, show the performers that you are well prepared and committed to the performance.

LOGISTICAL CONSIDERATIONS

Contemporary compositions often have unusual logistical requirements, such as the use of nonstandard equipment or special arrangements onstage or in the auditorium. Here are some examples.

- Compositions using *prerecorded tape* require extra technical equipment and staff, with the tape line fed both to house speakers and speakers onstage for the performers. In addition, a separate track may be fed to the conductor and performers to serve as a "click track"—a rhythmic pulse prerecorded to establish an exact tempo. This track is fed into a headset and requires time and experience to assimilate.
- Many contemporary works involve *stage movement* by the performers and frequently place performers away from the stage, out in the auditorium or balcony. Careful practice will lead to tight ensemble performances despite the distribution and varying acoustic effects. Practice all the parts onstage first, and then disperse the ensemble to its various locations.
- A piece may involve *dancers* in addition to the musical ensemble, placing new demands on the physical confines of the stage area. Always consult with the choreographer and dancers before rehearsal of such compositions to ascertain the feasibility of dance and to solve any problems.
- *Movement within the ensemble,* such as is used in "choralography" (choreography for a choral group) and in jazz and swing choirs, requires an understanding of the symbols and techniques used by the composer. As with compositions involving physical dispersal, always rehearse the musical portion of the composition first until it is secure before adding elements of dislocation or movement, which will place added demands on the performers.
- *Narrators or actors* may be used with speech amplified or unamplified. A good balance between speech and music must be established.
- Special *stage lighting* can be very effective if it is well conceived and well executed. The audience should not sense an effort to apply special lighting to mood or dynamic changes—the lighting should be an integral part of the performance. Thus, it is always necessary to include a separate lighting or technical rehearsal before the ensemble dress rehearsal, and then to leave sufficient time in the dress rehearsal to rerun light cues if necessary.
- *Slide and film projection* is a frequent addition to contemporary programs. All the precautions listed above regarding feasibility, proper equipment, staff, and adequate rehearsal also apply here.

ALEATORIC PRACTICE EXERCISES

Conduct the class in performing these single-line exercises on the following pages.

1 In the four measures in Figure 12-4, the right hand (RH) is used for the primary downbeat (↓) of each measure plus a secondary downbeat in measure 4. The left hand (LH) gives an entrance with a downward motion slightly off to the left side. Count the duration in seconds silently as you give each cue.

FIGURE 12-4
Aleatoric practice exercises: exercise 1.

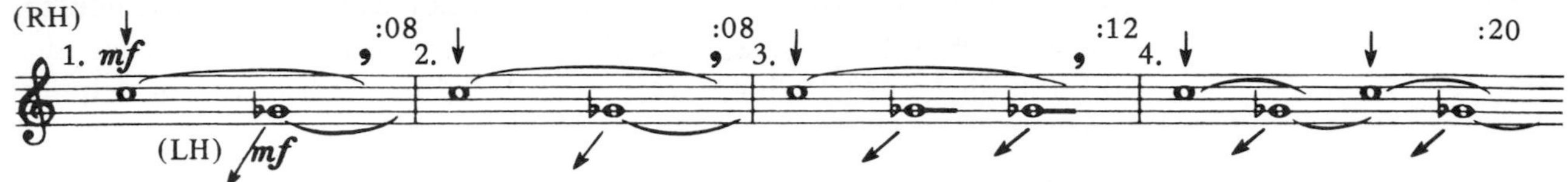

2 Dynamic contrasts and changes, Figure 12-5. RH: After giving the initial cue in measures 1, 2, and 3, give dynamic increases and decreases in traditional fashion by raising and lowering of the hand. LH: Give the cued entrances with the suggested dynamic markings and accents.

FIGURE 12-5
Exercise 2.

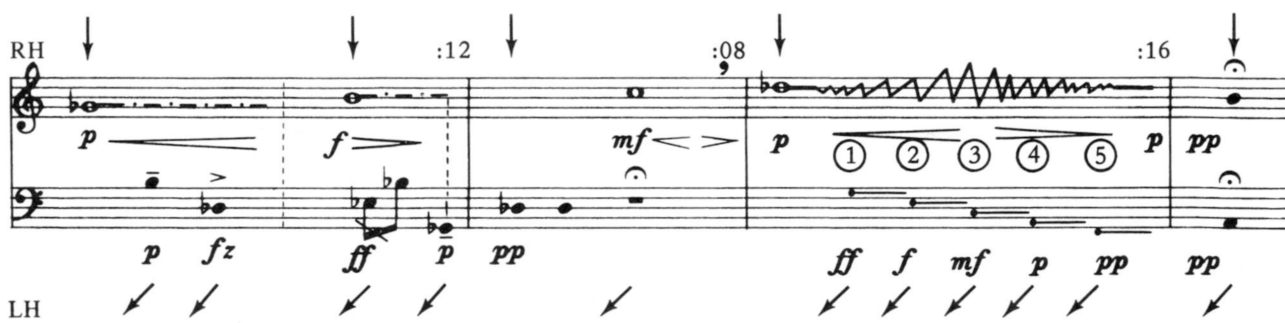

3 Carefully proportion the length of each measure in Figure 12-6 within the given time span; cue each entrance. (RH will still give the beginning of each measure.)

FIGURE 12-6
Exercise 3.

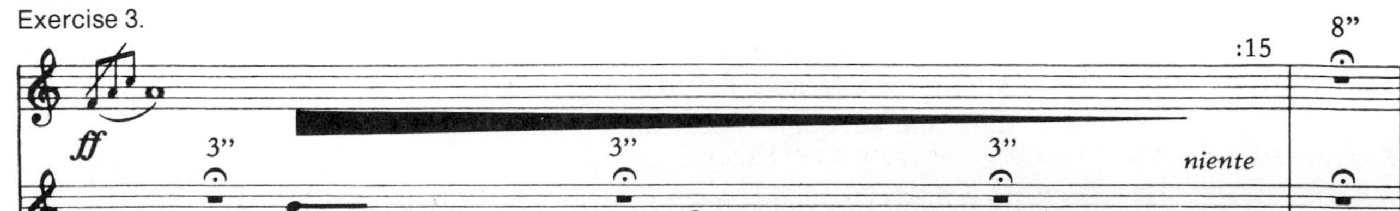

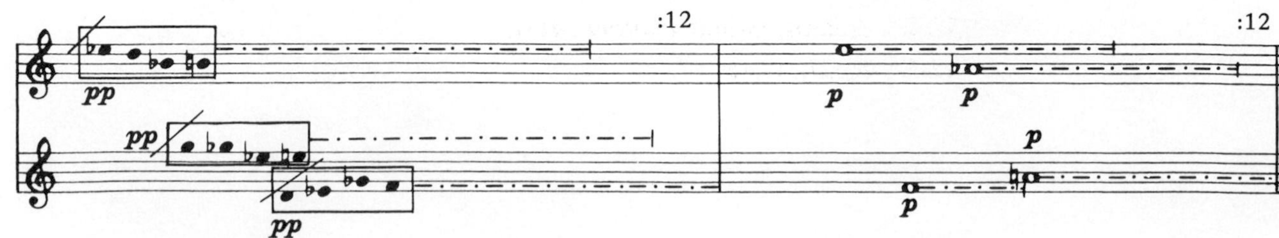

4 Clock diagram, Figure 12-7: RH is extended straight upward. Begin a slow motion simulating the sweep of a second hand. Maintain a steady movement. Each complete rotation will last 60 seconds. Use different dynamics for each event. Performer may enter unassisted, or LH may be used to cue events.

FIGURE 12-7
Exercise 4.

ASSIGNMENTS

1 Conduct the class in performing *Signposts* (Excerpt 12-3) and the instrumental étude (Excerpt 12-1) in the Anthology.

2 Analyze the conducting and performance requirements indicated on the title page of *and the mountains rising nowhere* (Excerpt 12-4 in the Anthology).

PERFORMANCE EXCERPTS FOR CHAPTER 12

Section Three, pages 359-371

12-1 Hunsberger, Étude
12-2 Grainger, *Lincolnshire Posy,* "Lord Melbourne"
12-3 Hemberg, *Signposts,* "Signpost I"
12-4 Schwantner, *and the mountains rising nowhere*
12-5 Adams, *Grand Pianola Music*
12-6 Reich, Octet

CHAPTER 13

MUSICAL THEATER

The problems involved in conducting musical theater are basically the same as those in opera—an accompanying ensemble in a pit area; singers moving on all areas of the stage; a chorus not always in a good sight line with the podium or even in a good location for aural projection; dancers; lighting cues; and set changes. Once the lights dim and the overture begins, the conductor is in charge of the performance and thus must be conversant with the stage director's thinking and procedures, the technical director's requirements, and the stage manager's function in set changes. This chapter describes some of the typical conducting materials and procedures.

SCORE AND SCRIPT

In musical theater, a *score* consisting of piano plus solo staff is usually used. (See Chapter 5 for a discussion of the condensed score.) The conductor may mark in cues, both sung and spoken, plus instrumental or choral entrances and exits. You should always work also with a complete copy of the *script,* into which you can add notes about staging and cues. Partial cues are given in the score but are usually too sketchy to rely on for adequate orchestral preparation.

Scores for Broadway musicals are published in the form in which they were used in the early stages of rehearsal and performance. As later performances continue with changes of cast, these original scores are often altered to provide better keys for the singers. Examples of other changes that might occur include lengthening or shortening the music to cover a set change, or shortening a dance sequence for dancers who are not capable of sustaining interest in a long segment.

Each local company performing a show must assume that the original score and production book are guides that may need to be modified for the unique resources and limitations of each production. Do not hesitate to make revisions when necessary, but always remember that when alterations are made in staging or technical procedure, the conductor must be part of all decisions—since the conductor must make corresponding changes in the musical score to fit the new staging.

A written list of all changes, such as cuts, holds, vamps, repeats, and reprises (see below), should be presented to the players. Always mark any such changes clearly in the score (in dark, soft pencil); never leave anything to your memory for recall during rehearsal or performance.

Above all else, both score and script must be learned thoroughly before rehearsals begin.

CONDUCTING TECHNIQUES AND PROCEDURES

The conductor should analyze each *singer* and his or her melodic and rhythmic idiosyncracies. Before rehearsals with the orchestra, rehearse with the singers individually until they are well prepared. Try to anticipate and prevent problems, but know the score well, so that you can deal with any if they do occur.

The conductor works closely with the *stage director*. The stage director's primary concerns are the acting and the general impression created by everyone onstage, while the conductor's responsibility is the musical requirements of both the singers and the score.

The *stage manager* and the conductor also work closely, to establish lines of communication in the event of a physical mishap backstage. A stuck curtain, a missed lighting cue, or a missed entrance must be covered by the conductor when possible.

The conductor may arrange a set of *hand signals with the orchestra* to cover any such emergency or deviation from the normal flow of the show. Hand signals might indicate the following directions:

- Repeat a section again or continuously.
- Omit the repeat.
- Vamp till ready. (A *vamp* is a short section—usually one, two, or more measures—that can be repeated indefinitely.)
- Go back to the beginning.
- Add a fermata and hold until ready.
- Quick cut-off; segue to next tune.
- End at the next cadence.

Such cues are usually given with the left hand. A raised fist is commonly used for an indication to move ahead at the end of a repeated section. Holding the hand horizontally in front of the body with the index finger extended frequently means "go ahead, no repeat." A circular motion with the hand usually indicates repetition of a section. Always give special emphasis to the downbeat when proceeding into a new section following a fermata or vamp repeat. All these signals should be done unobtrusively so as not to reveal to the audience that anything is amiss.

All scene changes during each act should ordinarily be covered with music, and the score usually provides *reprises*—repeated sections—for this purpose. If the reprise music is too short, the conductor should go back in the score to find a longer section that can be modified and used as a reprise. Usually the previous song or dance will work. If the reprise music is too long, it should fade as the curtain opens. Do not delay the curtain until the end of reprise.

The *balance* between soloists or chorus and orchestra is frequently a problem, especially in an auditorium without a submerged pit. The conductor must control the volume of the orchestra at all times. If the stage sound is being amplified, the conductor may use a headset to double-check the volume and balance in the auditorium. This is critical when performing outdoors, as at a summer festival, where the stage and orchestra sound will probably be amplified. If the orchestra volume is too great for the stage volume, add mutes to the brass or strings and alter the scoring if necessary. Carpeting can be added to the pit area to dampen the sound.

The *conducting style* must be clear and concise at all times. Remember that many different people located all over the stage and pit area will be depending on you for cues and directions.

"Anatevka," in *Fiddler on the Roof* (Figure 13-1 on the following pages), illustrates a typical piano-conductor score. Measure 1 is a repeated vamp which is performed until Golde is ready to make her entrance. At rehearsal number 14, the entire cast joins in.

ASSIGNMENT

Conduct "June Is Busting Out All Over" (Excerpt 13-1 in the Anthology).

PERFORMANCE EXCERPT FOR CHAPTER 13

Section Three, pages 372–377 **13-1** Rodgers and Hammerstein, *Carousel,* Act I, finale.

FIGURE 13-1
Jerry Bock (music) and Sheldon Harnick (lyrics), *Fiddler on the Roof,* "Anatevka."

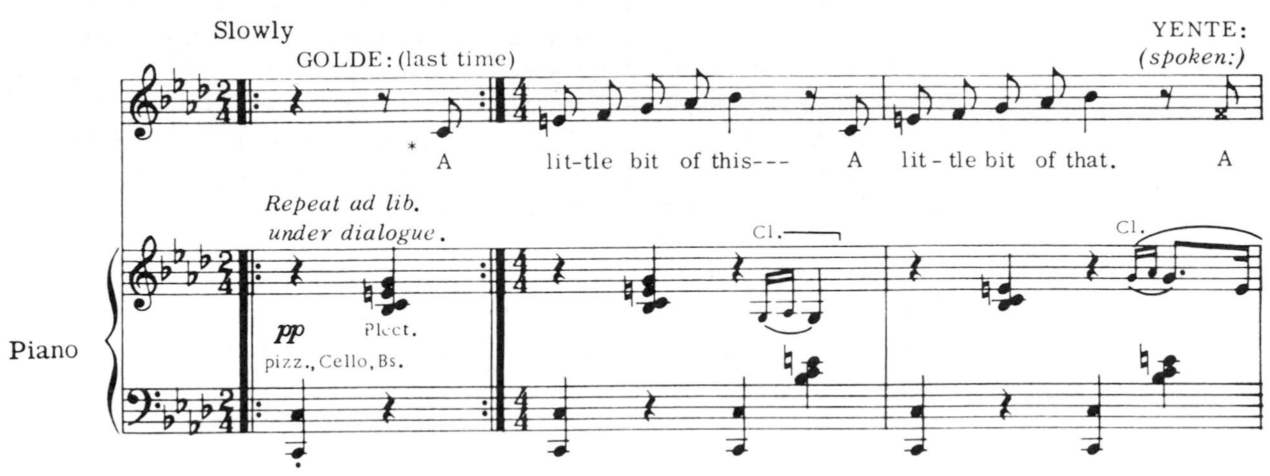

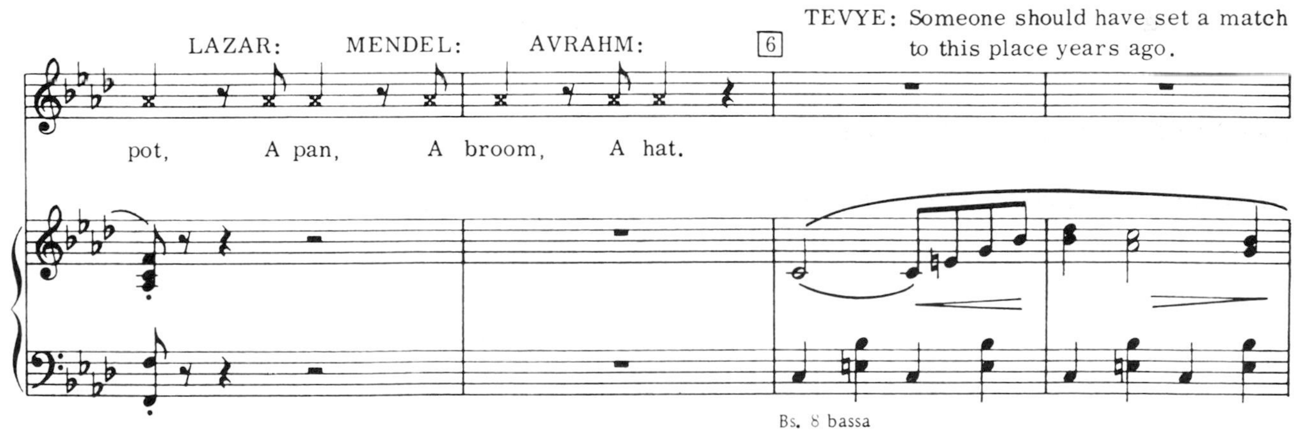

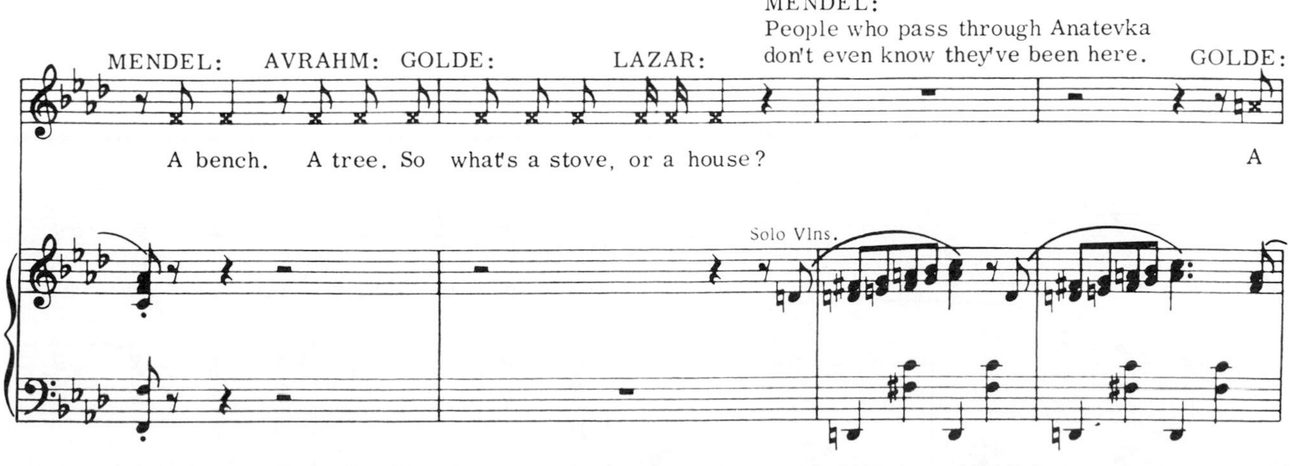

(Continued)

* This entire number is sung an octave lower in the New York production.

FIGURE 13-1
(Continued)

FIGURE 13-1
(Continued)

(Continued)

FIGURE 13-1
(Continued)

Tum-ble down, work-a-day An-a-tev-ka, Dear lit-tle
Str.
rall.
49
Allargando
GOLDE: Eh---it's just a place.
vil-lage, lit-tle town of mine.
ten.
Acc.
rit.
pp
Fl. Solo
MENDEL: Our forefathers...etc.
TEVYE: Maybe that's why we always wear our hats.
[Change of Scene]
f Str., Plect.
Acc.
SHPRINTZE: Where will we live in America?...etc.
Acc.
rit.
fade
pp

CHAPTER 14

THE JAZZ ENSEMBLE

Every conductor should be aware of performance practices and rehearsal procedures for ensembles that play jazz or popular music (rock, Latin, salsa, rap, and so on) and traditional ensembles playing compositions influenced by such music. In this chapter we will consider jazz ensembles as a representative type.

Many of the skills of rehearsing and conducting traditional ensembles also apply to jazz ensembles—so they should not be a totally foreign medium. The primary difference between leading a traditional concert ensemble and leading a jazz ensemble is that the leader *conducts* the former but *directs* the latter. This does not imply that the jazz ensemble director does not need to know traditional conducting techniques; rather, it means that most of the conductor's time in front of the ensemble will be spent cuing, highlighting entrances, offering gestures to reflect interpretative moods, or giving dynamic indications—*without* a continuous beat pattern. Yet contemporary jazz ensembles and choirs still base their standards of performance, tone production, and balance on comparable classical standards.

THE RHYTHM SECTION

The rhythm section, which consists of keyboard, bass, guitar, and trap set, plus extra percussion, is normally responsible for the continual rhythmic pulse, or *time.* The director is responsible for the steadiness of the time and the musical manner in which the rhythm section provides a foundation for the other instrumental sections. The director usually works more closely than the conductor of a traditional ensemble with each member of the section to continually increase each player's musical awareness of the rest of the ensemble.

FIGURE 14-1
Manny Albam, *Pennies for Evan,* rhythm section score.

The rhythm section also needs guidance in the interpretation of individual written parts. Jazz has an *aural tradition,* and most techniques and performance styles have been passed on through generations of jazz musicians. The typical jazz piano part and bass part consist of only chord symbols and melodic cues. Occasionally, however, bass parts are written out to provide a constant, stable bass voice rather than permitting an improvisatory feeling, which might interfere with specific harmonic-rhythmic patterns in the brass and saxophones.

The drum part will usually be quite sketchy, providing only rhythmic highlights, solo sections, ensemble entrances, and similar cues. The drummer is a focal point in most rhythm sections and may have a tendency to overplay that role without considering the keyboard, bass, and guitar players. The director must constantly balance the efforts and mold a musical unit from the three or more independent musicians. Figure 14-1 (opposite page) shows a typical rhythm section score.

JAZZ STYLE

The aural tradition of jazz has given rise to the question of how to determine style, depth, and length of accents, and balance of voices within each section. The jazz composer or arranger has usually been on the scene as a bandleader or performer, and thus is able to focus the ensemble's efforts toward a satisfactory rendition during rehearsal and performance, with little preserved stylistic or technical information other than an occasional recording. Listening to recordings and live performances and studying books on jazz performance are essential. The books by Rick Lawn and Rayburn Wright listed in the bibliography (Appendix 8) should be used as primary sources of information. The score-study process described in Chapter 5 should be adapted for works in the jazz medium. Compare your analysis with professional recordings for performance style and then apply your knowledge in actually rehearsing an ensemble.

Jazz rhythms often are not played as notated. For example, consecutive eighth notes and dotted-eighth rhythms are usually played with a $\frac{12}{8}$ feeling at moderate to fast tempos. Eighth notes are played evenly in rock styles.

JAZZ ARTICULATIONS

Vocal jazz is the realization through vocal sounds of instrumental articulations and embellishments. It has grown from individual "scat" singers to vocal jazz ensembles, which may also incorporate body movements and actual choreography. Because many prominent jazz ensembles sing through their parts in rehearsal, the director should become familiar with the use of descriptive vocal sounds that imitate instrumental techniques and should practice singing jazz-oriented lines with vocal inflections. *Conduction Blues* in the Anthology (Excerpt 14-1) shows the use of a vocalized line in a jazz exposition.

Figure 14-2 (on the following page) shows common jazz articulations and alterations.

FIGURE 14-2
Jazz articulations and alterations.

TONGUING, ACCENTS

Heavy accent:
Hold full value

Heavy accent:
Less than full value

Staccato:
Short, not necessarily heavy attack

Heavy staccato:
Short as possible, heavy attack

Legato tongue (tenuto):
Hold full value

TONE ALTERATIONS

Du-wah:
Closed-open. *Du* is a tone muffled by the hand over the bell or a harmon mute plunger; may also be closed throat-open throat.

Ghost tone:
½ value, definite pitch or very deadened tone—indefinite pitch, example within melodic line

Doo - n - doo - dot

PITCH ALTERATIONS

Bend (on note):
Attack note, dip in pitch and return within rhythmic note value

Bend (before note):
Dip in pitch on previous note just before attack

Doit:
Establish pitch, slide (gliss) upward one or more steps

Short gliss (up):
Slide into note—½ valve or lipped

Long gliss (up):
Same but more notes from below

Short gliss (down):
Same with fewer notes in drop

Long gliss (down):
Same with more notes in drop

Rip or lift—short:
Fingered, chromatic or diatonic from interval below

Rip or lift—long:
Same from larger interval below

Spill or falloff—short:
Fingered or lip drop from pitch, chromatic or diatonic, quick

Spill or falloff—long:
Same over larger interval; may have length or duration specified

Lip trill:
Harmonic series trill, lip controlled

Shake:
Horn is shaken to produce wider deviation in harmonic series

CONDUCTING TECHNIQUES

Traditional conducting patterns and techniques may be used when necessary to provide ensemble stability in areas of rhythmic deviation—ritards, fermatas, slow recitative-style passages, or any area where a definite beat is not evident or might help. In other situations, where the rhythm section is providing the steady time, the director should refrain from traditional patterns, instead providing downward or sideward cue strokes to heighten the impact of accents or entrances.

The director indicates the rotation of soloists in improvisatory or "ride" sections and counts down measures (4-3-2-1) for section entrances following lengthy sections of improvisation—especially drum solos, during which an inventive performer's improvisation may depart from a definite sense of the beat. The director can reestablish the beat and bring the ensemble back in with common hand signals (see Chapter 13).

Each individual section—saxophone, trumpet, trombone—follows its lead player in interpretation and also in adjusting for blend and balance. The director should support the lead players in this responsibility. Instructions that change the style set by the lead player should not be given in a manner that will erode the lead player's own confidence or the section's confidence in him or her. A director who is an experienced, competent jazz performer might contribute an occasional solo to become still more a part of the ensemble performance.

Many ensembles get caught up in the excitement of performing fast, rhythmic music and lose their sense of perspective with regard to dynamic levels and contrast. Directors must constantly be on guard against the tendency to play too loudly, which often leads to other problems, such as uncontrolled tones, poor balance, and lack of precision.

Tape-recording and playback during rehearsals are well worth the necessary time and effort. Commercial recordings of the same repertoire can also be played to improve concepts of style.

ASSIGNMENTS

1 Write a short jazz melody with vocal syllables for unison singing by the class. Add a rhythm section to help provide a feeling of the time (pulse) and the harmonic background possibilities.

2 *Conduction Blues* (Excerpt 14-1 in the Anthology) was written by Rayburn Wright for performance in conducting classes. Study and prepare this piece for performance in class. Read the instructions included with the score. Sing through the melodic line first with a neutral syllable such as *du* or *tah.* Then try singing the vocal syllables printed under the staff.

3 Practice *Pennies for Evan* by Manny Albam (Excerpt 14-2 in the Anthology).

PERFORMANCE EXCERPTS FOR CHAPTER 14

Section Three, pages 378-383

14-1 Wright, *Conduction Blues*

14-2 Albam, *Pennies for Evan*

SECTION THREE

ANTHOLOGY: MUSICAL EXCERPTS FOR CLASS PERFORMANCE

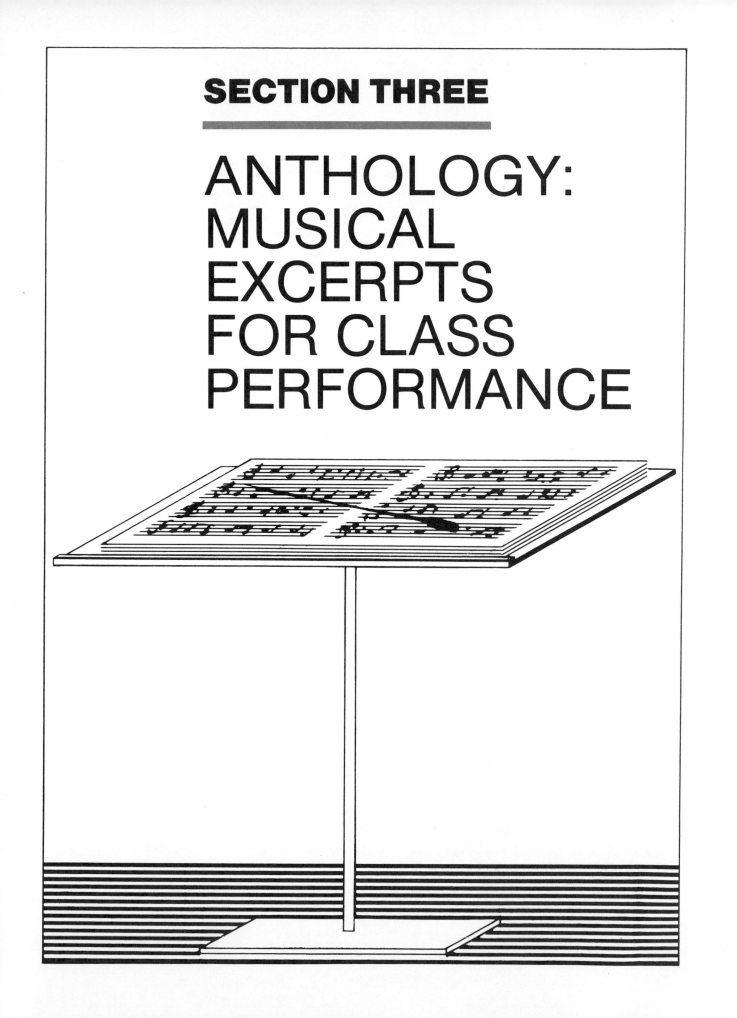

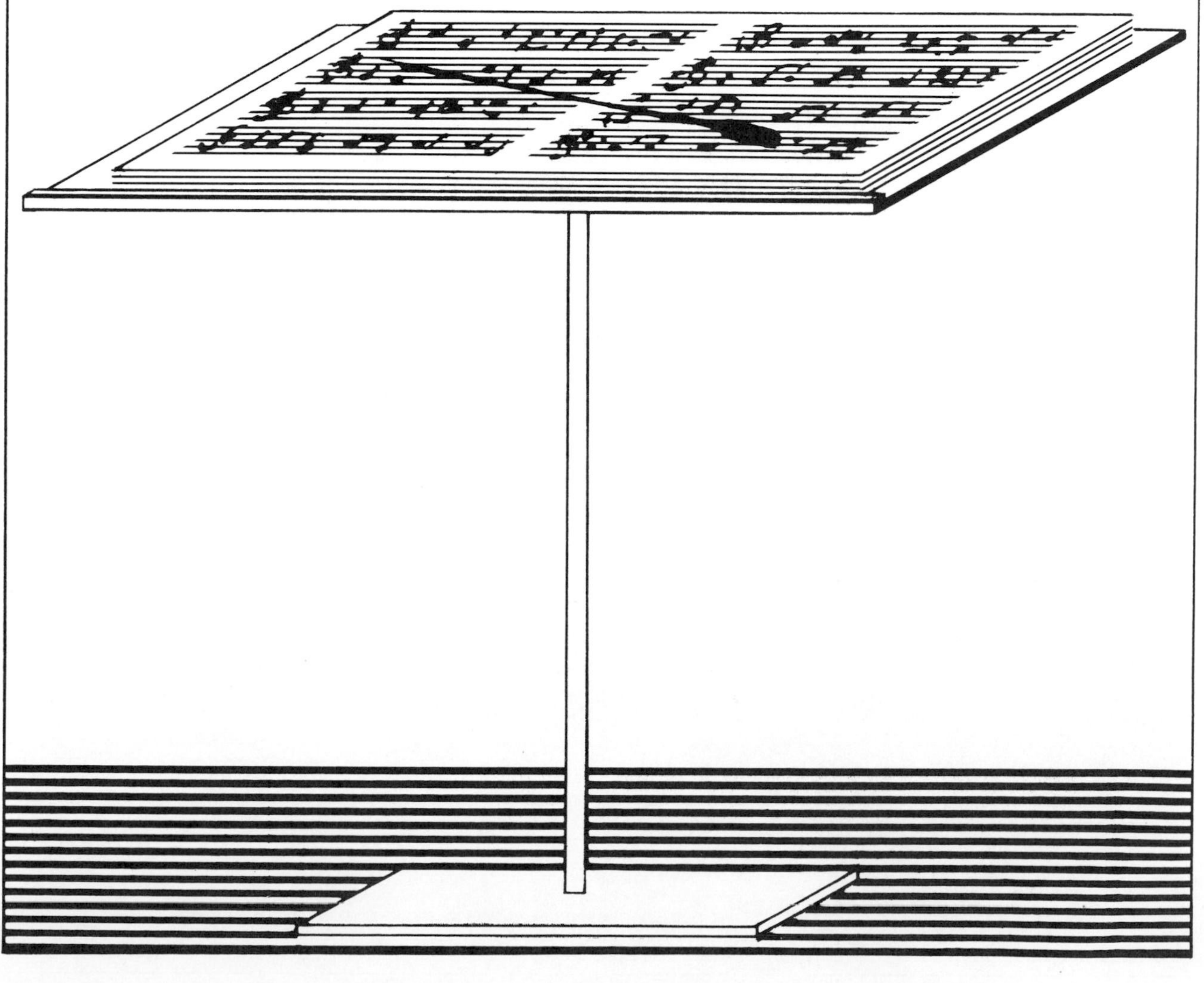

OVERVIEW

The excerpts in Section Three have been selected and arranged for performance by random voices and instruments. Excerpts for Chapters 1, 2, and 3 are to be sung or played in unison with piano accompaniment; if instruments are used, the instrumentalists should read the concert-pitch melody line and transpose as necessary. For the remaining chapters, transposed parts are provided for instrumentalists.

Perform as many of the excerpts as possible. Vocal parts can be played on instruments, and instrumental parts can be sung on a neutral syllable by vocalists. After practicing the excerpt for a given chapter, look for related excerpts in other chapters, for additional practice.

Following is a list of the performance excerpts for each chapter, with page numbers in parentheses. Note that because of the nature of Chapter 10, no specific excerpts are listed for it.

EXCERPTS FOR CHAPTER 1

EXCERPTS FOR CHAPTER 2

EXCERPTS FOR CHAPTER 3

EXCERPTS FOR CHAPTER 4

EXCERPT FOR CHAPTER 5

EXCERPTS FOR CHAPTER 6

6-1 Strauss, Serenade, Op. 7 (226)
6-2 Berlioz, *Roman Carnival* Overture (229)
6-3 Jacob, *William Byrd Suite,* Pavana (230)
6-4 Rimsky-Korsakov, *Scheherazade,* third movement (234)
6-5 Purcell, "In these delightful, pleasant groves" (236)
6-6 Traditional, "The Riddle" (239)
6-7 Handel, *Royal Fireworks Music, La Paix* ("Peace") (242)
6-8 Mozart, Symphony No. 36, second movement (245)
6-9 Tchaikovsky, Symphony No. 4, second movement (248)
6-10 Irish tune, "My Gentle Harp" (250)

EXCERPTS FOR CHAPTER 7

7-1 Schubert, Symphony No. 8, first movement (253)
7-2 Rossini, *L'Italiana in Algeri* ("The Italian Girl in Algiers"), Overture (254)
7-3 Holst, "I Love My Love" (257)
7-4 Traditional, "Shenandoah" (260)
7-5 Kodály, *Hegyi Éjszakák* ("Mountain Nights") (262)
7-6 Traditional, "Seekin' for a City" (264)
7-7 Holst, Second Suite in F, "Song of the Blacksmith" (267)
7-8 Elgar, *Enigma* Variations (268)
7-9 Delibes, *Coppélia* (271)
7-10 Haydn, Symphony No. 104 *(London),* first movement (279)
7-11 Schubert, Mass in F *(Deutsche Messe)* ("German Mass") (285)

EXCERPTS FOR CHAPTER 8

8-1 Persichetti, *Mass,* Kyrie (290)
8-2 Mussorgsky, *Pictures at an Exhibition,* "Promenade" (292)
8-3 Berger, *Six Madrigals,* "Harvester's Song" (296)
8-4 Bernstein, *Mass,* "Almighty Father" (298)
8-5 Makris, *Aegean Festival* Overture (300)
8-6 Grainger, *Lincolnshire Posy,* "Rufford Park Poachers" (307)
8-7 Orff, *Carmina Burana, Uf dem Anger* ("On the Green") (308)

EXCERPTS FOR CHAPTER 9

9-1 Lully, *Au Clair de la lune* ("Lo, there in the moonlight") (309)

9-2 Rossini, *Il Barbiere di Siviglia* ("The Barber of Seville"), Overture (312)

9-3 Haydn, Symphony No. 97, first movement (316)

9-4 Grainger, *Lincolnshire Posy,* "Harkstow Grange" (324)

9-5 Holst, *The Planets,* "Mars" (326)

9-6 Bernstein, *Candide,* Overture (334)

Note: As mentioned above, there are no specific performance excerpts for Chapter 10.

EXCERPTS FOR CHAPTER 11

11-1 Handel, *Messiah,* "Behold, I tell you a mystery" (recitative for bass) and "The trumpet shall sound" (air for bass) (339)

11-2 Mozart, Concerto for Flute and Orchestra in D Major, second movement (346)

11-3 Mozart, *Die Zauberflöte* ("The Magic Flute"), recitative (353)

11-4 Rimsky-Korsakoff, *Scheherazade,* opening (354)

11-5 Traditional, "Sometimes I Feel Like a Motherless Child" (356)

EXCERPTS FOR CHAPTER 12

12-1 Hunsberger, Étude (360)

12-2 Grainger, *Lincolnshire Posy,* "Lord Melbourne" (363)

12-3 Hemberg, *Signposts,* "Signpost I" (364)

12-4 Schwantner, *and the mountains rising nowhere* (367)

12-5 Adams, *Grand Pianola Music* (368)

12-6 Reich, Octet (371)

EXCERPT FOR CHAPTER 13

13-1 Rodgers and Hammerstein, *Carousel,* Act I, finale (373)

EXCERPTS FOR CHAPTER 14

14-1 Wright, *Conduction Blues* (379)

14-2 Albam, *Pennies for Evan* (382)

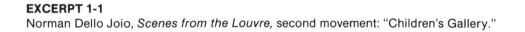

EXCERPTS FOR CHAPTER 1

EXCERPT 1-1
Norman Dello Joio, *Scenes from the Louvre,* second movement: "Children's Gallery."

EXCERPT 1-2

Traditional, "Aura Lee," verse 3 and refrain. Accompaniment arranged by Donald Hunsberger.

Moderato ♩= 104
mf
When the mis - tle - toe was green, midst the win - ter snows,
sun - shine in thy face was seen, kiss - ing lips of rose
Aur - a Lee, Aur - a Lee, take my gold - en ring.
Love and light re - turn with thee, and swal - lows with the spring.

EXCERPT 1-3
Howard Hanson, *Chorale and Alleluia.*

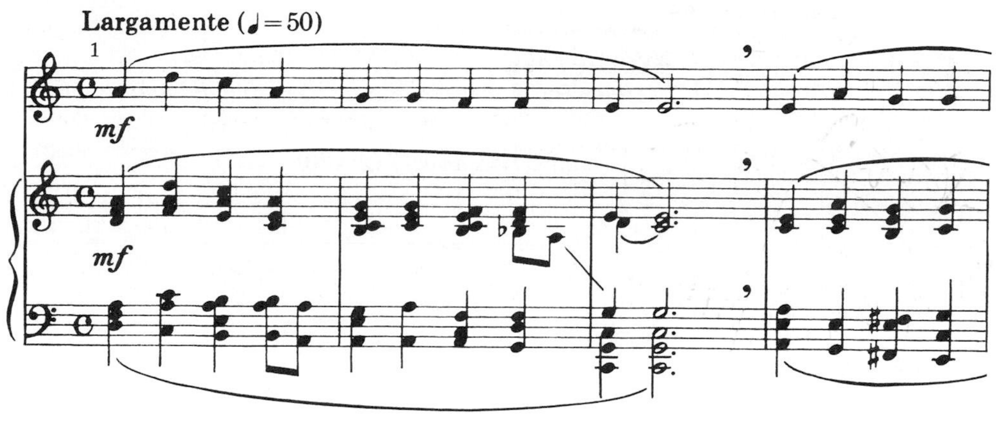

In Excerpt 1-4, by Ravel, the accompanying figure marked ♩♩♩♩ should be performed lightly and somewhat detached to contrast with the legato melodic line.

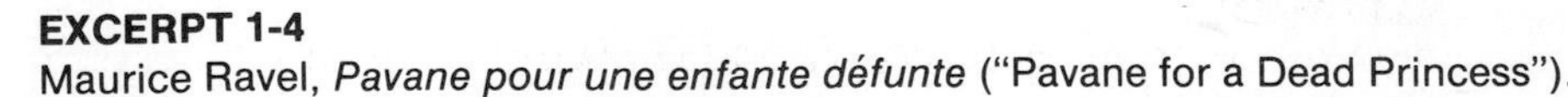

EXCERPT 1-4

Maurice Ravel, *Pavane pour une enfante défunte* ("Pavane for a Dead Princess").

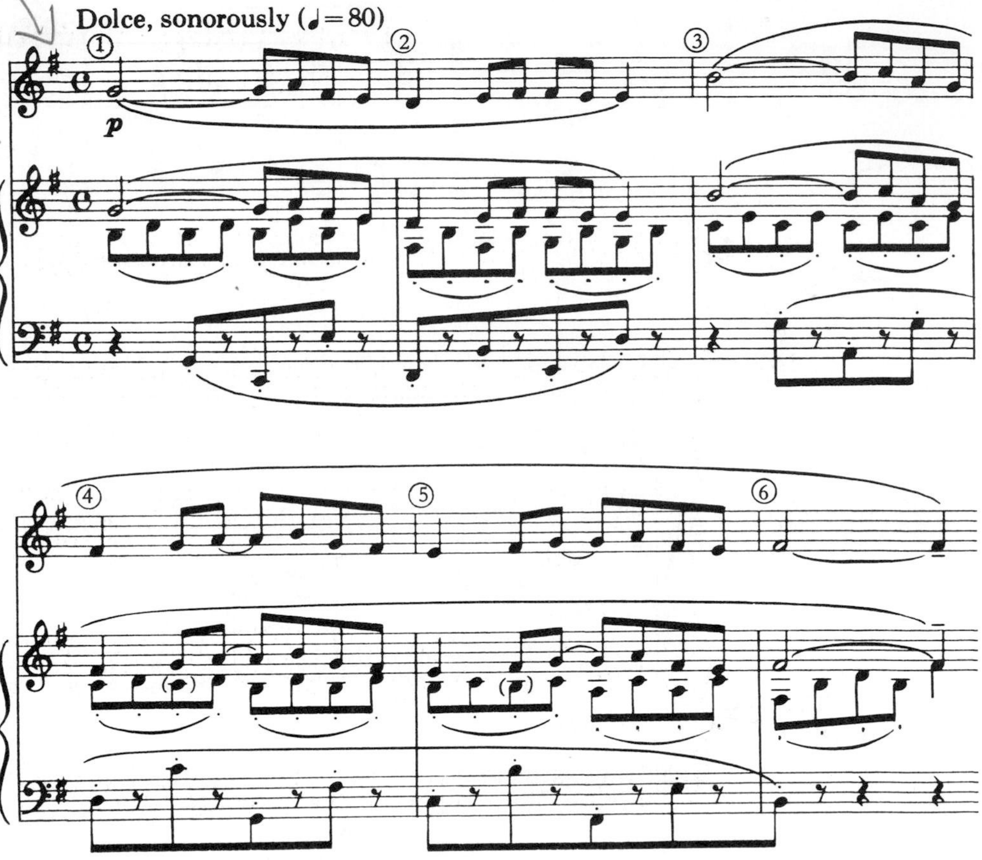

Dolce, sonorously (♩ = 80)

p

Divide the class into three equal ensembles for Excerpt 1-5 (*Dona nobis pacem*). Perform the round three times, with each ensemble singing line (1), line (2), and line (3) in succession.

EXCERPT 1-5
Anonymous, *Dona nobis pacem* ("Give Us Peace"), a round.
Accompaniment arranged by Myrtha B. Licht.

EXCERPT 1-6
Antonin Dvořák, Symphony No. 9, fourth movement.

EXCERPT 1-7
Carl Maria von Weber, *Der Freischütz* ("The Freeshooter"), Overture.

- think: "first sound"
prepatory
- phrasing (Dvorak)

EXCERPT 1-8
John Philip Sousa, *Semper Fidelis* March.

1.
2.
ff
fff

EXCERPTS FOR CHAPTER 2

"Chester" (Excerpt 2-1) may be conducted with a two-beat pattern or a four-beat pattern. The following note is given by the editor: "To achieve greater variety, the tenor and soprano parts are reversed in verses 1, 3, and 5. In verses 2 and 4, all voices remain in their original positions."

EXCERPT 2-1

William Billings, "Chester." From *The New England Psalm-Singer* (1770) and *The Singing Master's Assistant* (1778), edited by Oliver Daniel.

clank her gall - ing chains. We fear them not. we
broke, their lines were forc'd, Their ships were shat - ter'd
ren - der to the Lord? Loud Hal-le - lu - iahs
clank her gall - ing chains. We fear them not, we
broke, their lines were forc'd, Their ships were shat - ter'd
ren - der to the Lord? Loud Hal-le - lu - iahs

Fine
trust in God, New Eng-land's God for - ev - er reigns.
in our sight, Or swift-ly driv - en from our Coast.
let us sing, And praise His name on ev - 'ry Chord.
trust in God, New Eng-land's God for - ev - er reigns.
in our sight, Or swift-ly driv - en from our Coast.
let us sing, And praise His name on ev - 'ry Chord.
Fine

EXCERPT 2-2

Richard Wagner, *Lohengrin,* "Elsa's Procession to the Cathedral."
Original key is E major.

EXCERPT 2-3

Robert Schumann, Concerto for Piano, first movement.

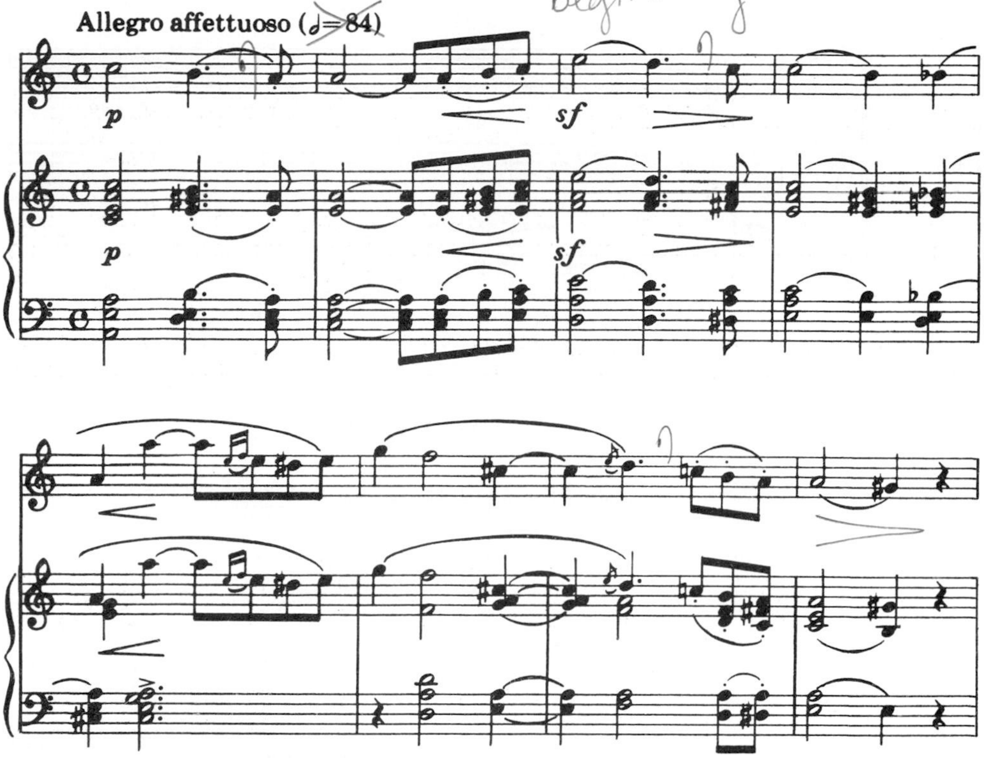

Allegro affettuoso (𝅗𝅥=84)

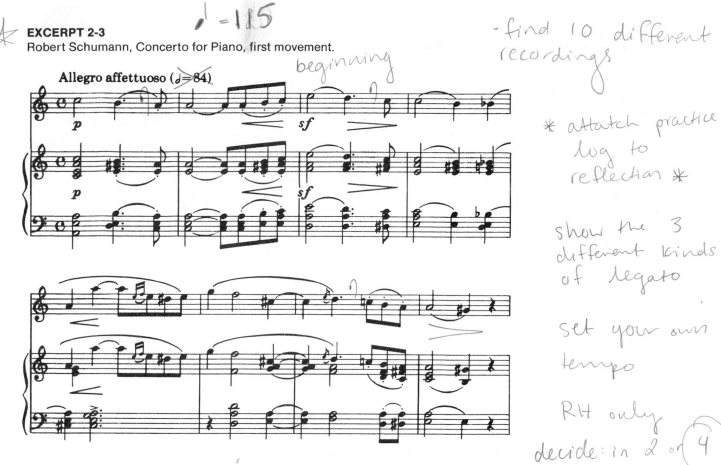

EXCERPT 2-4

Gordon Jacob, *William Byrd Suite,* "The Earle of Oxford's March."

EXCERPT 2-5

Randall Thompson, *The Peaceable Kingdom,* "Say ye to the righteous."

pp
p
Say ye to the right-eous, it shall be well with him: for
the right-eous, it shall be well with him: for
they shall eat the fruit of their do - ings.

Excerpt 2-6, by Orlando di Lasso, may be conducted with a two-beat pattern or a four-beat pattern, depending on the tempo. Note that the tenor voice sounds down an octave.

EXCERPT 2-6

Orlando di Lasso, *Matona, mia cara* ("Matona, lovely maiden"), four-part vocal score.
English version by William Alexander Barrett; edited by H. Clough-Leighter.

EXCERPT 2-7

"What Shall We Do with the Drunken Sailor," arranged by Alice Parker and Robert Shaw.

This Shanty has been recorded by the Robert Shaw Chorale in RCA Victor Album LM 2551. Approximate duration 2:48

EXCERPT 2-8
Béla Bartók, "Enchanting Song."

Enchanting Song

Old Hungarian Poem
English translation by
NANCY BUSH

BÉLA BARTÓK

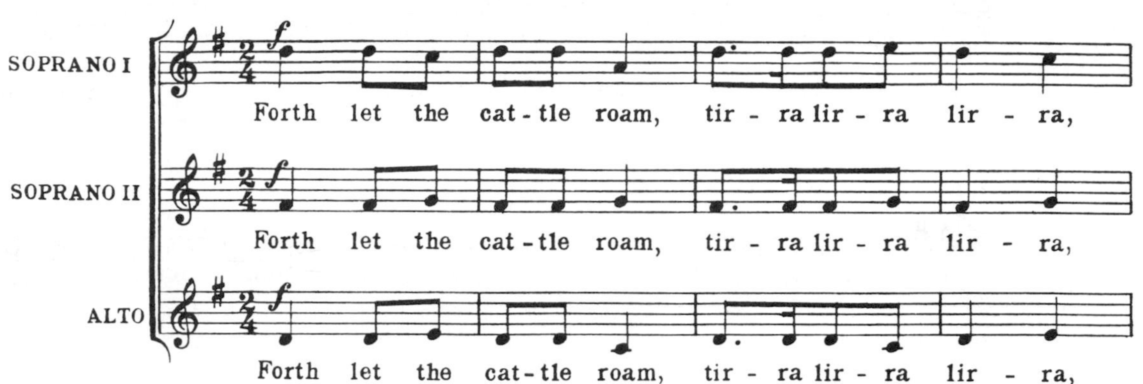

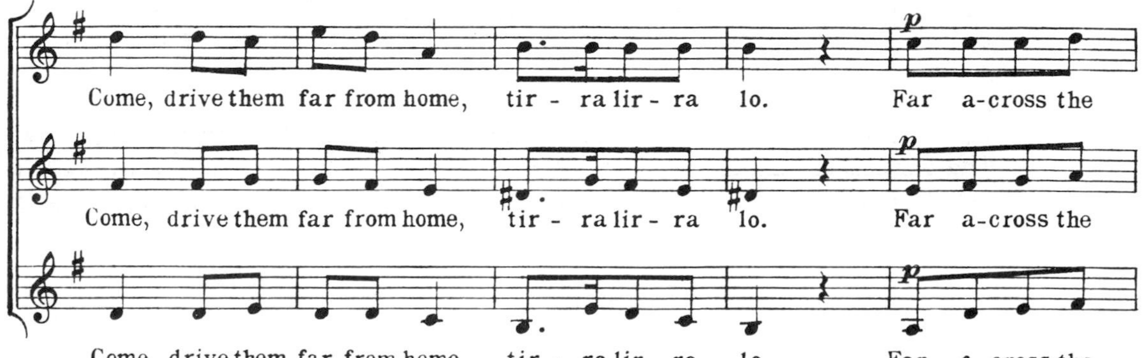

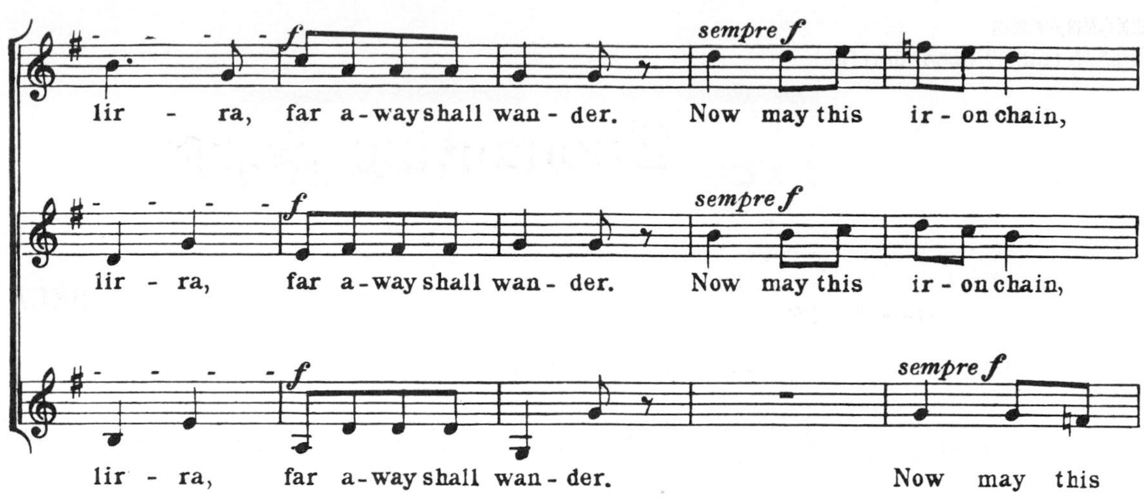
f
sempre f
lir - ra, far a-way shall wan-der. Now may this ir - on chain,
f
sempre f
lir - ra, far a-way shall wan - der. Now may this ir - on chain,
f
sempre f
lir - ra, far a-way shall wan-der. Now may this

tir - ra lir- ra, lir - ra, Bring them safe-ly home a-gain, tir- ra lir- ra
tir - ra lir- ra, lir - ra, Bring them safe-ly home a - gain, tir- ra lir- ra
ir - on chain, tir-ra lir-ra lir - ra, Bring them safe- ly home a-gain,

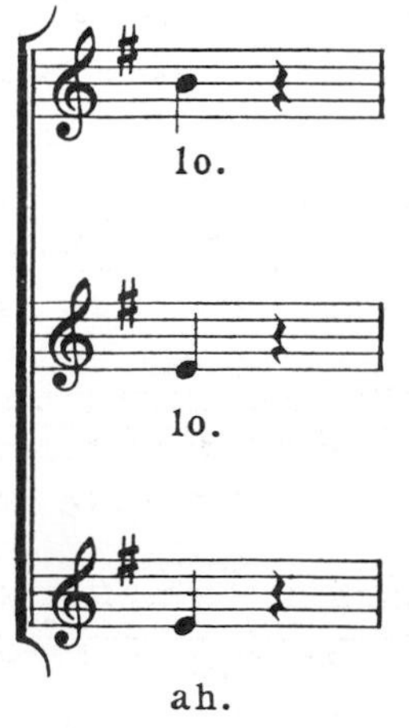
lo.
lo.
ah.

EXCERPTS FOR CHAPTER 3

EXCERPT 3-1
Emil Waldteufel, *España* Waltz.

EXCERPT 3-2
Léo Delibes, *Coppélia,* Waltz.

Excerpt 3-3, Morley's "Sing we and chant it," may be conducted with a three-beat pattern or a one-beat pattern. Note that it has been transposed down a major third.

EXCERPT 3-3
Thomas Morley, "Sing we and chant it."

EXCERPT 3-4
Percy Grainger, *Lincolnshire Posy,* "The Lost Lady Found."

EXCERPT 3-5

Johann Strauss, *Blue Danube* Waltz.

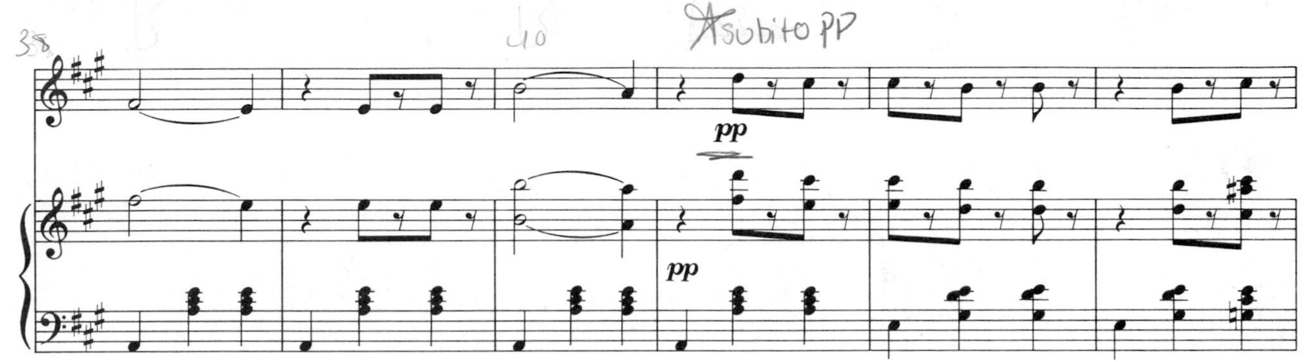

Patterns
1) 3)
2)

Tips

* anticipate problem spots
* know the score
* find out what distracts you from the music

- conducting gestures
- nerves
- uncomfortable from looking at ensemble
- knowing the score
- anticipate ensemble problems

* switch between 1 pattern & 3 pattern
* contrast between page 1 & 2
* show dynamics (possibly w/ LH)

EXCERPT 3-6
Peter Ilych Tchaikovsky, *The Sleeping Beauty, Thornrose* Waltz.

EXCERPT 3-7

Jacques Offenbach, *Orphée aux enfers* ("Orpheus in the Underworld"), Overture.

EXCERPTS FOR CHAPTER 4

EXCERPT 4-1

(a) Gordon Jacob, *Old Wine in New Bottles,* "Early One Morning." Cuing.

EXCERPT 4-1
(a) "Early One Morning" (continued).

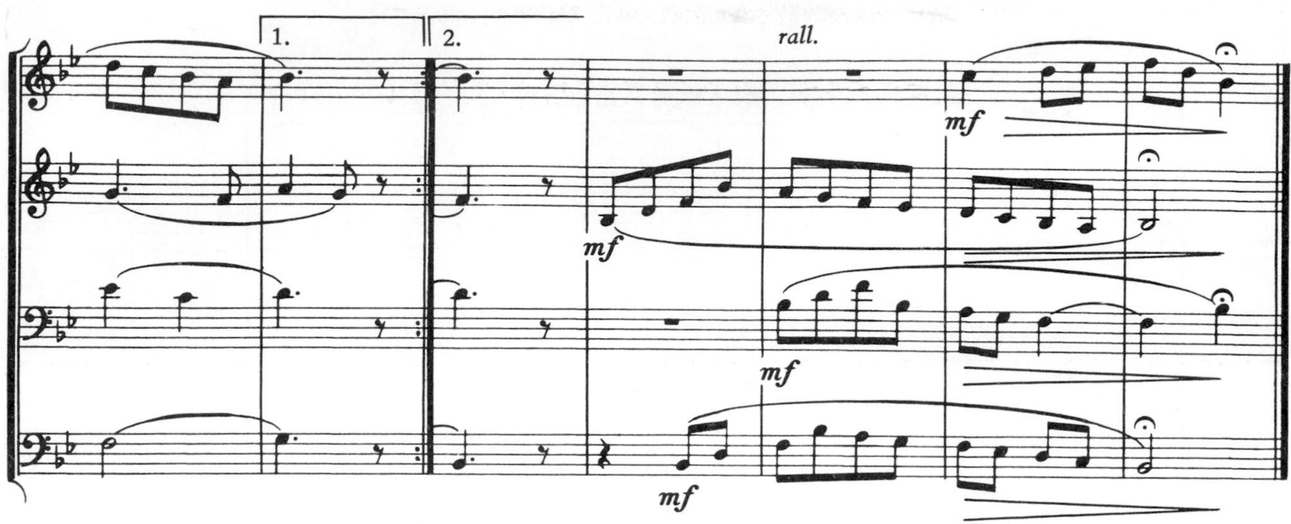

EXCERPT 4-1
(b) "Early One Morning," transposed parts.

Voice 1, B♭ transposition
Allegretto

p pp tr p
2 1. 2. 2
p rall. mf

Voice 2, B♭ transposition
Allegretto

p p pp tr p
tr 1. 2.
pp p mf rall.

Voice 3, E♭ transposition
Allegretto

p p pp p
1. 2.
p p mf rall.

EXCERPT 4-2

(a) Giovanni Gabrieli, *Sacrae symphoniae, Canzon septimi toni à 8* ("Sacred Symphonies, Canzona on the Seventh Tone for Eight Voices").

𝅗𝅥 = 84

1

2

3

4

R.H.

f

L.H.

f

A

Piano 4 hands

B

1

2

3

4

f

A

R.H.

f

B

1
2
3
4
A
B
L.H.

1
2
3
4
A
B

EXCERPT 4-2
(b) *Canzon septimi toni à 8,* transposed parts.

EXCERPT 4-3
Ludwig van Beethoven, Symphony No. 5, fourth movement.

EXCERPT 4-4
William Billings, *Three Fuguing Tunes,* "When Jesus Wept." Edited by William Schuman.

EXCERPT 4-5

George Frideric Handel, *Messiah*, "And the glory of the Lord."

Isaiah xl: 5

Allegro

SOPRANO

ALTO

TENOR

BASS

Allegro (♩ = 112)

f

Soprano: And the glo - ry, the glo-ry of the

Alto: *mf* And the glo - ry, the glo-ry of the Lord, the glo-ry of the

Tenor: *f* And the glo - ry, the glo-ry of the

Bass: *f* And the glo - ry, the glo-ry of the

mf

f

*) According to the original score.

(Continued)

EXCERPT 4-5

"And the glory of the Lord" (continued).

glo - ry, the glo-ry of the Lord shall be re - veal - ed,
glo - ry, the glo-ry of the Lord shall be re-veal - ed,
glo - ry, the glo-ry of the Lord shall be re-veal - ed,
glo - ry, the glo-ry of the Lord shall be re-veal - ed,

EXCERPT 4-6

Daniel Pinkham, *Christmas Eve,* setting of a poem by Robert Hillyer (1895–1961), for four-part chorus of mixed voices, a cappella. Entrance on beat 4 and beat 2; crescendo and decrescendo; ending.

long the paths, There is no oth - er sound. So
cold it is the road - side trees Snap in the rig - id

(Continued)

EXCERPT 4-6
Christmas Eve (continued).

Meno mosso
pp cresc.
25
rich drink in the hall. The Vir - gin and the Ho - ly
Meno mosso
pp
cresc.
Child Lie shiv - er - ing in a stall.
f
p
pp

The following note is appended to the music for "Don't Leave Me!" (Excerpt 4-7): "The original version of these choruses was an a cappella version; later an orchestral accompaniment was added. The piano reduction of the latter has merely been added to the present edition for rehearsal purposes when preparing the choir for a performance with orchestra. It is the composer's intention that performances should take place either a cappella or with orchestra, but not with piano."

EXCERPT 4-7

Béla Bartók, "Don't Leave Me!" Translation by Elizabeth Herzog. Cues; ending.

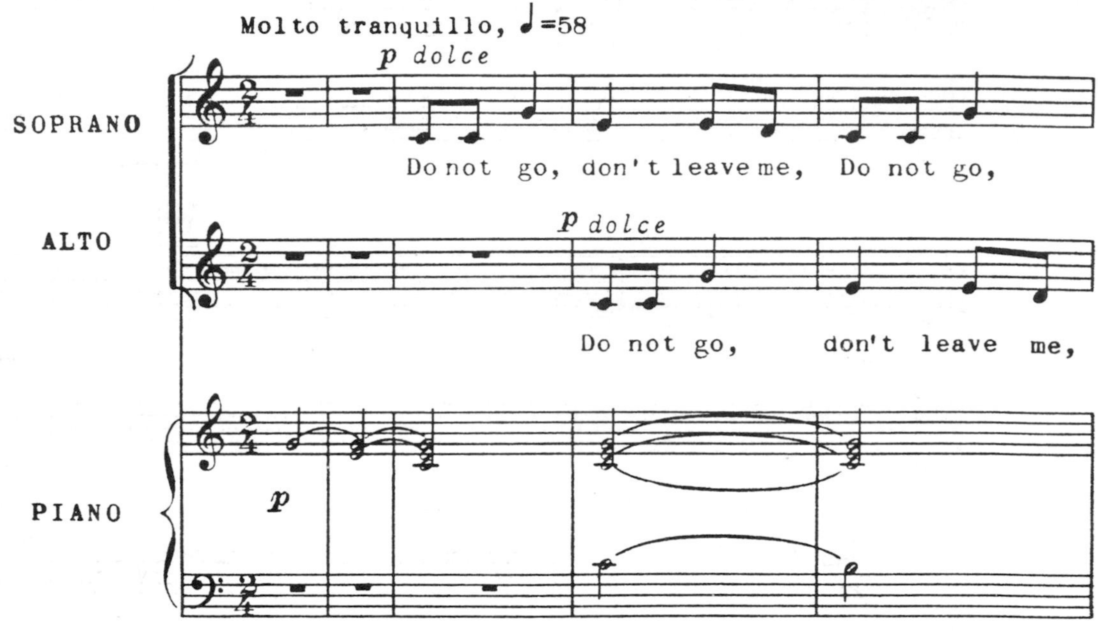

pp
pon me, For if you go from me Grief will be u–
pp
Grief will be u – pon me, For if you go from me
mp
17
pon me. With a soul sad for you,
mp
Grief will be u – pon me. With a soul
mp
With a heart lost for you How could I, how could I
sad for you, With a heart lost for you How could I,

(Continued)

EXCERPT 4-7
"Don't Leave Me!" (continued).

38
pp
You will come, come to me,
pp
al - ways, You will come, come to me,
pp
p
Più mosso, ♩=84
p
Stay with me for al - ways, Stay with me for al - ways,
p
Stay with me for al - ways, Stay with me for
mp
poco allarg. - - - -
Stay with me for al - ways, Live with me for al- ways.
al - ways, Stay with me for al-ways, Live with me for al - ways.
p
Duration: ca 1' 36"

EXCERPT 4-8

Anonymous, *N'ia gaire que auvit* ("A Long, Long Time Ago"), fifteenth-century French carol. Arranged by Gregg Smith for four-part chorus of mixed voices with two treble soloists, a cappella; English version by Alicia Smith. Entrance on beat 3; cues.

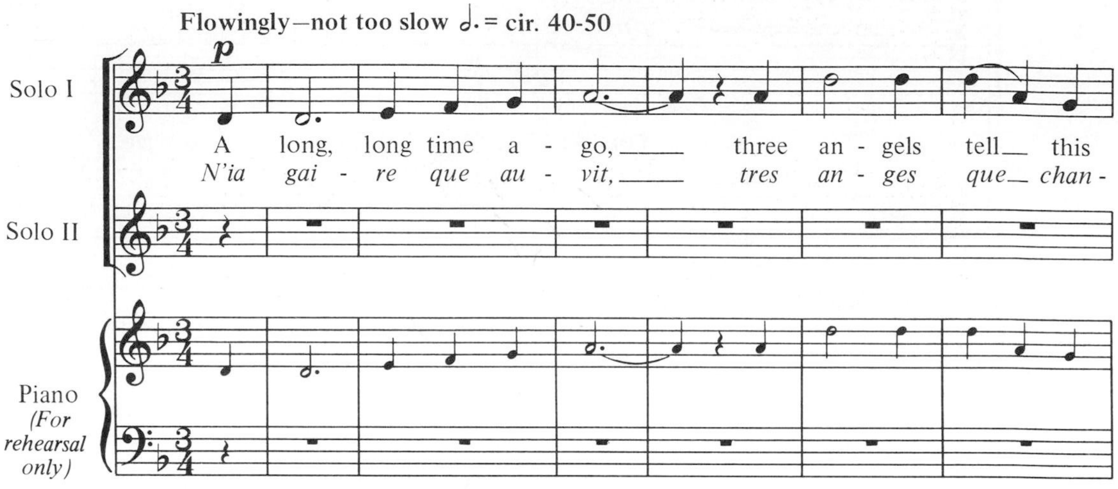

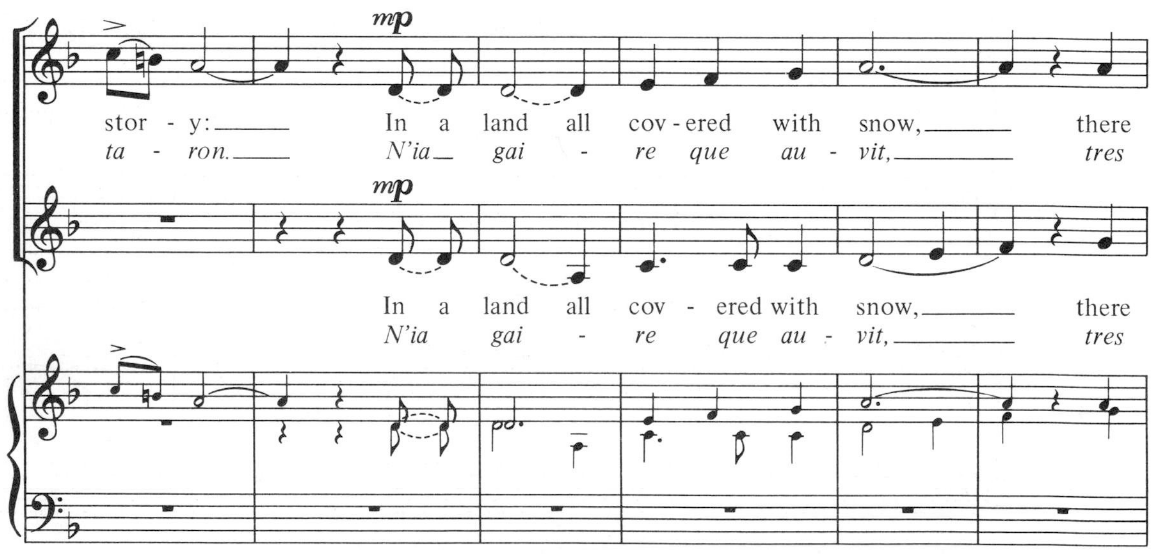

came a night of glo - ry. There in a low - ly
an - ges que chan - ta - ron. Chan - ta - ron qu'e - ra
came a night of glo - - ry. There in a
an - ges que chan - ta - - ron, Chan - ta - ron

man - ger, for - sa - ken and for - lorn,
nueg, vi - roun la miet ja nueg.
low - ly man - ger, for - sa - ken and for - lorn,
qu'e - ra nueg, vi - roun la miet ja nueg.

In Excerpt 4-9, "Sleep Little One," *Lu lu lu* etc. are to be performed with a steady unaccented tone.

EXCERPT 4-9
Ron Nelson, "Sleep Little One."

Sleep lit-tle one dream of good things, of good things, of good things.
Sleep lit-tle one dream of good things, of good things, of good things.
Sleep lit-tle one and dream of good things, good things, of good things.
mf
Snow flakes are gent-ly fall - ing and an-gels call - ing so soft - ly,
mf
Snow flakes are gent-ly fall - ing and an-gels call - ing so soft - ly,
mf
Snow flakes are gent-ly fall - ing an-gels call - ing soft - ly,
mp

EXCERPT 4-10

Thomas Moore, "The Minstrel Boy" (Irish tune, "The Moreen"), arranged by Alice Parker for four-part chorus of mixed voices with harp or piano accompaniment. Entrance on beat 4.

Approximate duration: 2:48

10
f marc.
wild harp slung __ be - hind him; "Land of song!" said the war - rior bard, Though
wild harp slung be - hind __ him; "Land of song!" said the war - rior bard, Though
wild harp slung be - hind him; "Land of song!" said the war - rior bard, Though
wild harp slung be - hind him; "Land of song!" said the war - rior bard, Though
mf

15
all the world be - trays __ thee, One sword at least _ thy _ rights shall guard, One _
all the world be - trays thee, One _ sword at least thy rights shall guard, One
all the world be - trays __ thee, One _ sword at least thy _ rights shall guard, One
all the world be - trays __ thee, One _ sword _ at least thy rights shall guard, One

(Continued)

EXCERPT 4-10
"The Minstrel Boy" (continued).

EXCERPT FOR CHAPTER 5

Following is an example of the beginning of phase 2 of score study analysis—as described in Chapter 5—for the performance excerpt, "Swansea Town."

Formal Design and Melodic Development

For this part of the score analysis, you should investigate the musical character of each main section, noting particularly those aspects that will be major interpretative factors. Here is a sample description of "Swansea Town."

- *Measures 1-24.* The general character is robust and marchlike. The change from unison writing to part writing at measure 16 creates a major expressive event. The entrance of each voice part must be clearly defined.
- *Measures 25-48.* Melodically similar to the opening section. Four-part choral style. The same style of rhythm and articulation should be maintained.
- *Measures 48-49.* Transition to next major contrasting section. Pay special attention to changes in tempo and dynamics.
- *Measures 50-66.* Frequently, a major contrasting section is set in a new key and may even use new melodic material; this example, however, is an exception on both counts. The key and the melodic material do not change; nevertheless, this section is obviously intended to provide contrast to the previous sections and to the final section. The following changes should be clearly projected: (a) tempo change; (b) dynamic change; (c) unison melodic line with contrasting accompaniment; (d) use of tone painting (crescendos and decrescendos) in the accompaniment.
- *Measures 64-66.* The transition back to the opening style should develop a sense of anticipation. This anticipation may be heightened through a very clean break in measure 66, giving more impact to the beginning of the next section. The final notes in measure 66 introduce the new section to follow and should be in the tempo and style of tempo I (even though the actual printed tempo indication does not occur until the beginning of measure 67).

- *Measures 67–90.* Similar to the second section of the composition, since both are full SATB writing; however, certain important changes are made to make this section the most brilliant passage so far: (a) the extreme contrast to the section preceding measure 67; (b) higher dynamic level; (c) higher tessitura; (d) divisi part writing; (e) doubled melodic line in the tenor and bass voices (reminiscent of opening section) with harmony in soprano and alto voices.
- *Measures 80–90.* The composition now has great momentum, and the abruptness of this tempo change may be difficult to control. (When you practice conducting this passage, sing one of the voice lines until you are able to achieve a musically convincing feeling.)

Harmonic Organization

The illustration below shows the harmonic background underlying each statement of melodic line A of "Swansea Town."

Now examine the harmonic background for the three remaining sections of the verse, and then the harmonic background for the refrain. How do they differ? What was Holst attempting to develop throughout the composition? How does the text relate to the harmonic background?

Rhythmic Development

Examine the various sections for rhythmic variations. Does the basic tempo change during the work? Does any variation deviate from the straightforward statement of the unison beginning? What type of audience response can be created by the rhythmic development?

Textural and Thematic Organization

The text setting and thematic organization are as follows:

- *Verse 1.* A, measures 1–8; A^1, measures 9–16
- *Refrain.* B, measures 17–24
- *Verse 2.* A, measures 25–32; A^1, measures 33–40
- *Refrain.* B, measures 41–49
- *Verse 3.* A, measures 50–57; A^1, measures 58–66 (one-measure extension)
- *No refrain.*
- *Verse 4.* A, measures 66–74; A^1, measures 75–82
- *Coda.* A^1, measures 83–90

Notice that each section—verse, refrain, or coda—ends with essentially the same four-measure melodic material.

"Swansea Town" appears on the following pages.

EXCERPT 5-1
Gustav Holst (arranger), *Five Folksongs,* "Swansea Town."

G. SCHIRMER SECULAR CHORUSES FOR MIXED VOICES No. 8097

To C. K. S. and the ORIANA.

Swansea Town.

HAMPSHIRE FOLK-SONG
Collected by G. B. GARDINER.
Arranged for Mixed Voices by
GUSTAV HOLST.

Old_
Old_ Swan-
still I live in hopes to see old Swan-sea Town once more. Old Swan-sea
still I live in hopes to see old Swan-sea Town once more. Old
17
Swan-sea Town once more, fine girl, you're the girl that I a-dore, But
sea Town once more, fine girl, you're the girl that I a-dore, But
Town once more, fine girl, you're the girl that I a-dore, But
Swan-sea Town once more, fine girl, you're the girl that I a-dore, But
still I live in hopes to see old Swan-sea Town once more. Oh! it's
still I live in hopes to see old Swan-sea Town once more. Oh! it's
still I live in hopes to see old Swan-sea Town once more. Oh! it's
still I live in hopes to see old Swan-sea Town once more. Oh! it's

(Continued)

EXCERPT 5-1
"Swansea Town" (continued).

still I live in hopes to see old Swan-sea Town once more. old
still I live in hopes to see old Swan-sea Town, old Swan-
still I live in hopes to see old Swan-sea Town, old Swan-sea
still I live in hopes to see old Swan-sea Town once more. old
41
Swan-sea Town once more, fine girl, you're the girl that I a-dore, But
-sea Town once more, fine girl, you're the girl that I a-dore, But
Town once more, fine girl, you're the girl that I a-dore, But
Swan-sea Town once more, fine girl, you're the girl that I a-dore, But
48 Più mosso.
still I live in hopes to see old Swan-sea Town once more. Oh
still I live in hopes to see old Swan-sea Town once more.
still I live in hopes to see old Swan-sea Town once more.
still I live in hopes to see old Swan-sea Town once more. (hum with closed lips)
Più mosso.
dim.

(Continued)

EXCERPT 5-1
"Swansea Town" (continued).

58
good old ship she is toss'd aft, our rigg-ing is all tore, But still I live in
hope to see Old_ Swan-sea Town once more. Oh it's
cresc.
lips open
Oh it's
cresc.
lips open
Oh it's
cresc.
lips open
Oh it's
ff
cresc.
ff

(Continued)

EXCERPT 5-1

"Swansea Town" (continued).

when our mon - ey is all gone we'll go to sea for
when our mon - ey is all gone we'll go to sea for
when our mon - ey is all gone we'll go to sea for more. Old
when our mon - ey is all gone we'll go to sea for more. Old
83
rall.
more. Old Swan - sea Town once more, fine girls, we'll make this tav - ern roar; And
more. Old Swan - sea Town once more, fine girls, we'll make this tav - ern roar; And
Swan - sea Town once more, fine girls, we'll make this tav - ern roar; And
Swan - sea Town once more, fine girls, we'll make this tav - ern roar; And
rall.
Lento.
when our mon - ey is all gone we'll go to sea for more.
when our mon - ey is all gone we'll go, we'll go to sea for more.
when our mon - ey is all gone we'll go, we'll go to sea for more.
when our mon - ey is all gone we'll go, to sea for more.
Lento.

EXCERPTS FOR CHAPTER 6

EXCERPT 6-1

(a) Richard Strauss, Serenade, Op. 7.

EXCERPT 6-1
(a) Serenade (continued).

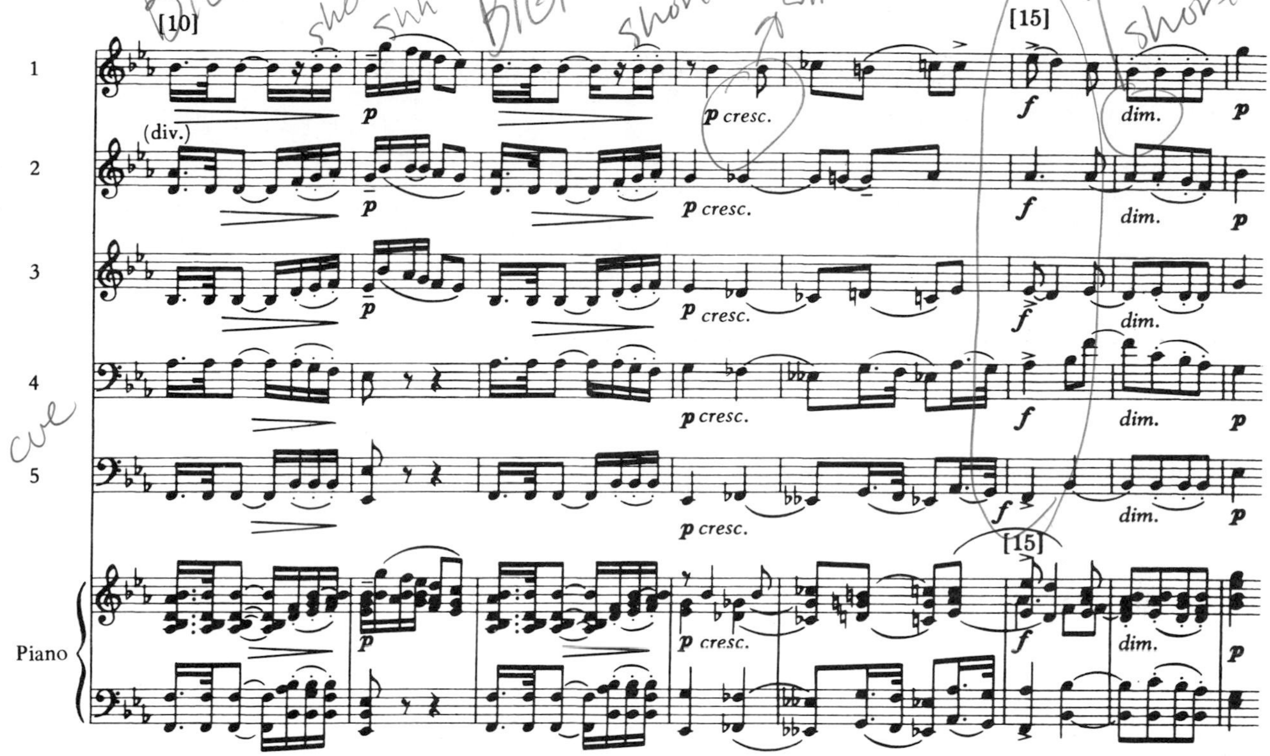

[10]
[15]
1
2
3
4
5
Piano
(div.)
p
p cresc.
f
dim.
p

EXCERPT 6-1
(b) Serenade, transposed parts.

Voice 1, B♭ transposition

Andante ♪= 56
[5]
[10]
[15]
p
p cresc.
f
dim.
p

Voice 2, B♭ transposition

Andante ♪= 56
[5]
[10]
[15]
p
p cresc.
dim.

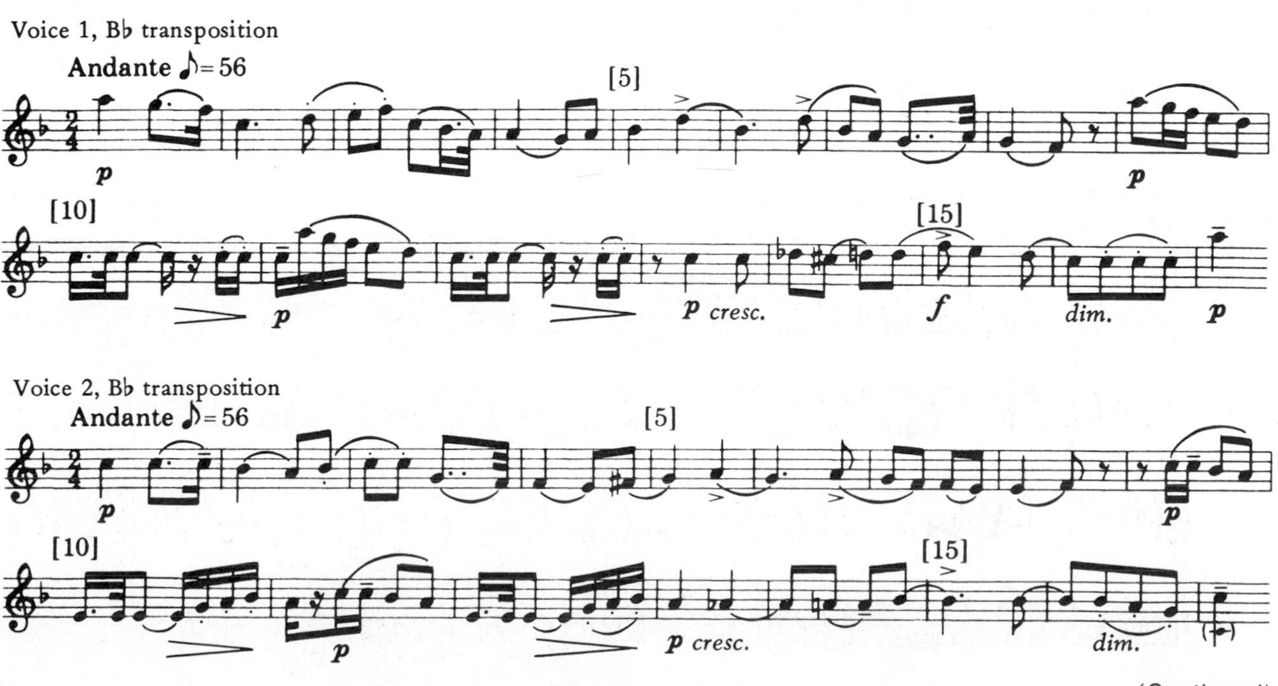

(Continued)

EXCERPT 6-1
(b) Serenade, transposed parts (continued).

In the *Roman Carnival* Overture (Excerpt 6-2), note the dashed-line slur: many conductors use this to indicate large phrasing sections when short phrasing slurs are shown in the score. The accompaniment at number 2 is pizzicato strings; achieve a similar staccato style.

EXCERPT 6-2
Hector Berlioz, *Roman Carnival* Overture.

EXCERPT 6-3

(a) Gordon Jacob, *William Byrd Suite,* Pavana.

1
ben sostenuto e legato
cresc.
p
p
p
p
1
p ben sostenuto e legato
cresc.
dim.
f
f
f
f
pp
pp
pp
pp
f
dim.
pp

EXCERPT 6-3
(b) Pavana, transposed parts.

Voice 1, B♭ transposition

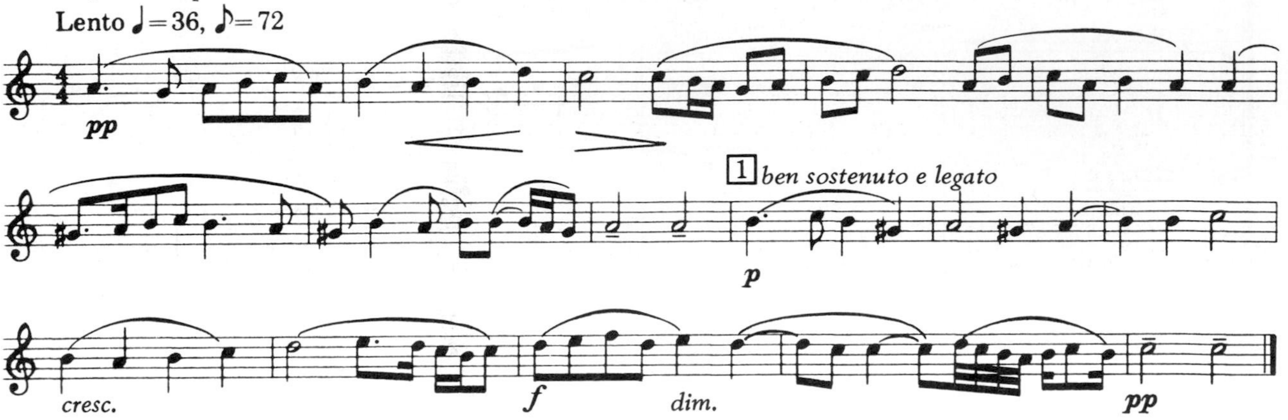

Lento ♩=36, ♪=72
pp
1 ben sostenuto e legato
p
cresc.
f
dim.
pp

Voice 2, B♭ transposition

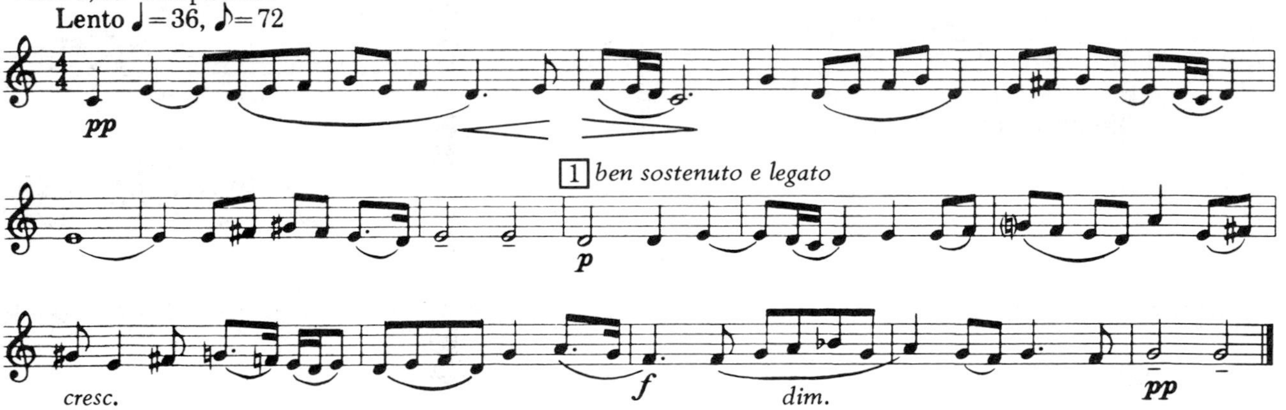

Lento ♩=36, ♪=72
pp
1 ben sostenuto e legato
p
cresc.
f
dim.
pp

Voice 2, F transposition

Lento ♩=36, ♪=72
pp
1 ben sostenuto e legato
p
cresc.
f
dim.
pp

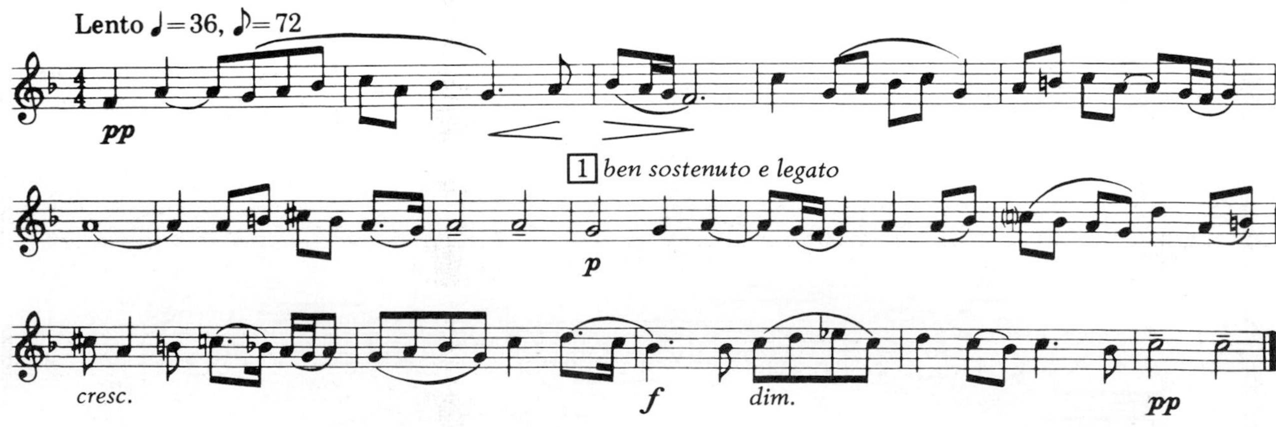

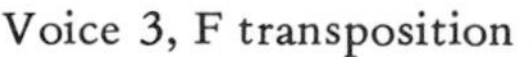

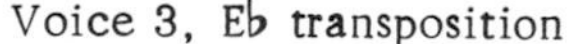

Voice 3, E♭ transposition

EXCERPT 6-4
(a) Nikolai Rimsky-Korsakov, *Scheherazade,* third movement.

EXCERPT 6-4

(b) *Scheherazade,* third movement, transposed parts.

EXCERPT 6-5
Henry Purcell, "In these delightful, pleasant groves."

cel - e - brate, let us cel - e - brate our hap - py, hap - py loves; In
cel - e - brate, let us cel - e - brate our hap - py, hap - py loves; In
cel - e - brate, let us cel - e - brate our hap - py, hap - py loves; In
cel - e - brate, let us cel - e - brate our hap - py, hap - py loves; In
f
these de - light - ful, pleas - ant groves, In these de - light - ful,
these de - light - ful, pleas - ant groves, In these de - light - ful,
these de - light - ful, pleas - ant groves, In these de - light - ful,
these de - light - ful, pleas - ant groves, In these de - light - ful,
mf

(Continued)

EXCERPT 6-5

"In these delightful, pleasant groves" (continued).

In Excerpt 6-6, "The Riddle," at the asterisk, the arranger has noted: "Open lips slightly, if necessary, because of high register!"

EXCERPT 6-6
Traditional, "The Riddle," arranged by Gregg Smith.

The Riddle

For Four-Part Chorus of Mixed Voices and Solo
a cappella

Traditional
Arranged by Gregg Smith

Slowly and freely

Solo

Oo Oo Oo

(For rehearsal only)

Oo

SOPRANO

ALTO

TENOR

BASS

Hmm

(Continued)

EXCERPT 6-6
"The Riddle" (continued).

has no_ bone; I gave my love a ring_ that has no end; I
poco
Hmm
*Hmm
*Hmm_
Hmm
Hmm
Hmm_
Hmm
Hmm
Hmm
Hmm
Hmm_

poco rit.
gave my love a ba-by with no cry-en!_
div.
Hmm
Hmm
Hmm
Hmm

EXCERPT 6-7

(a) George Frideric Handel, *Royal Fireworks Music,* third movement: *La Paix* ("Peace").

EXCERPT 6-7
(a) *Royal Fireworks Music* (continued).

EXCERPT 6-7
(b) *Royal Fireworks Music,* transposed parts.

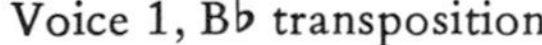

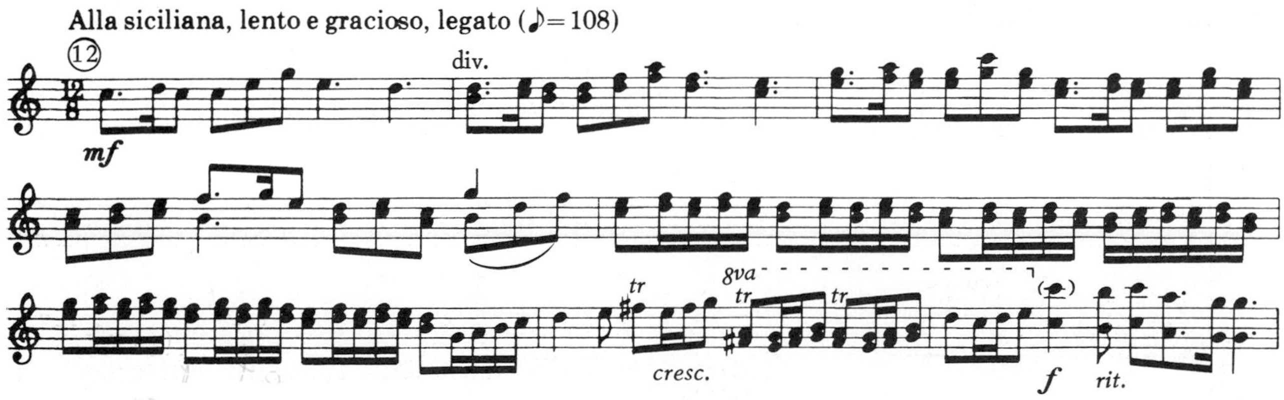

(Continued)

EXCERPT 6-7

(b) *Royal Fireworks Music,* transposed parts (continued).

Voice 2, B♭ transposition

Voice 2, E♭ transposition

Voice 3, E♭ transposition

cue beginning of phrases & nuances

EXCERPT 6-8

(a) Wolfgang Amadeus Mozart, Symphony No. 36, second movement.

(Continued)

EXCERPT 6-8

(a) Symphony No. 36 (continued).

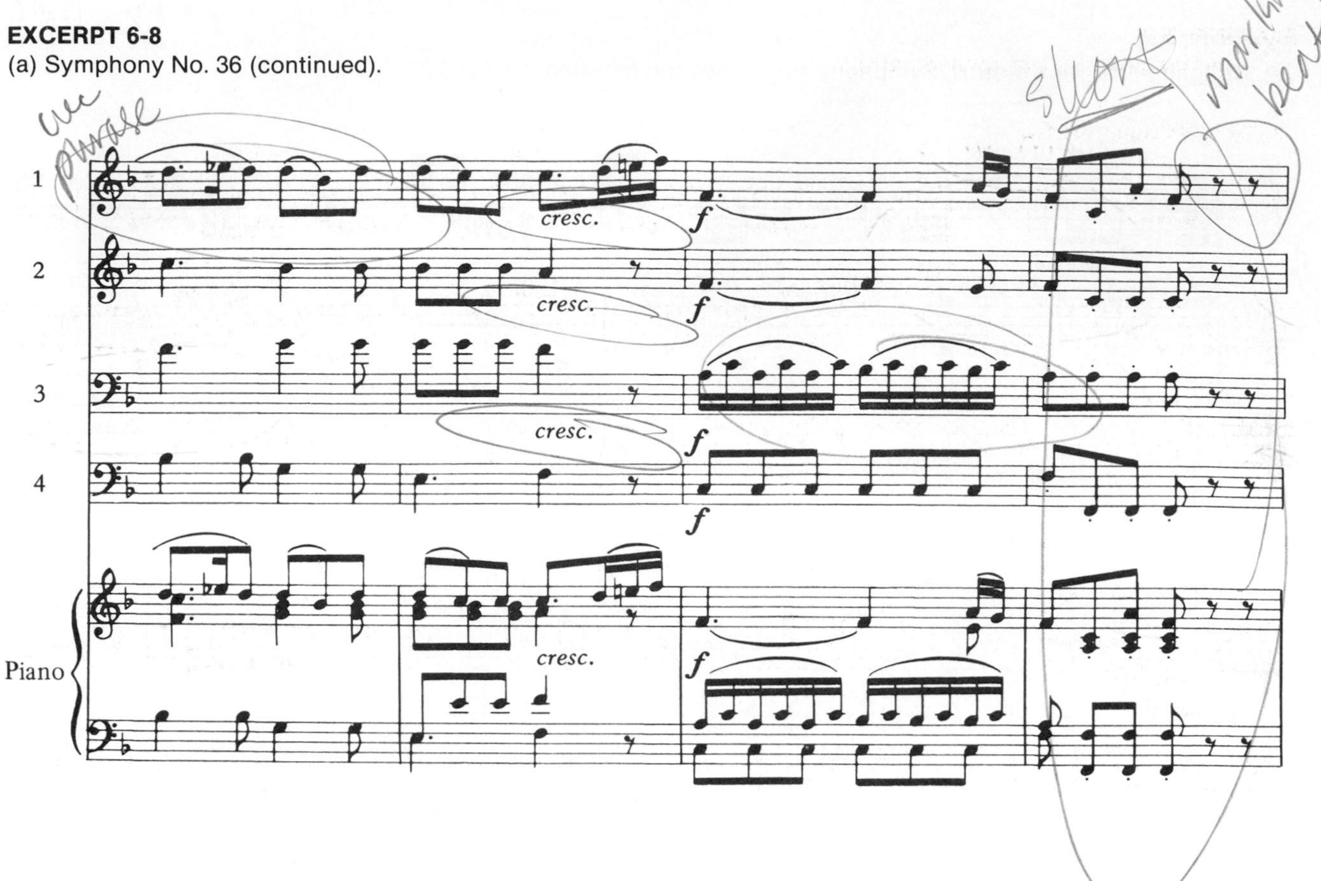

EXCERPT 6-8

(b) Symphony No. 36, transposed parts.

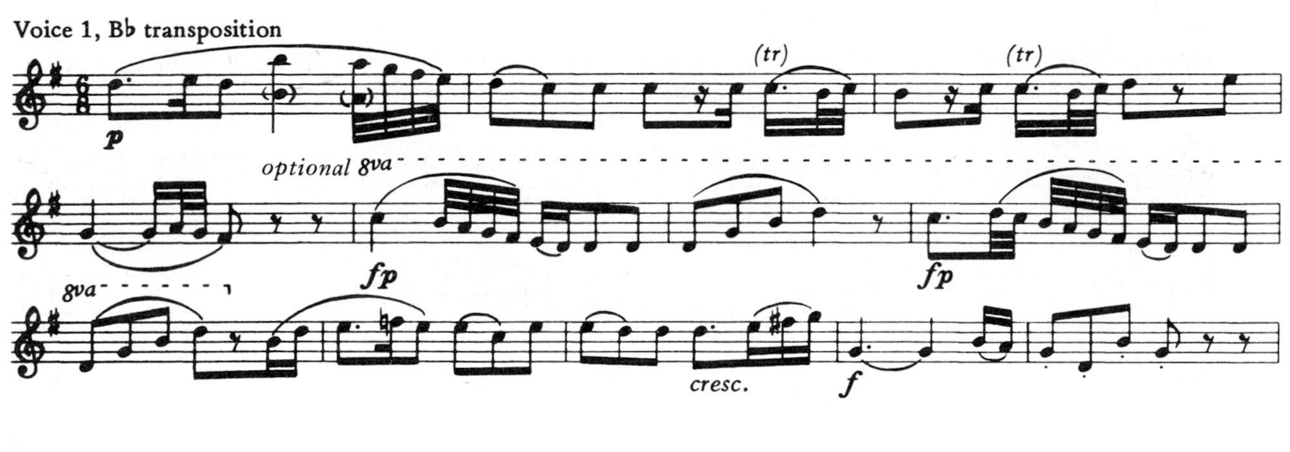

In Excerpt 6-9, from Tchaikovsky's Fourth Symphony, keyboard plays voices 2, 3, and 4.

EXCERPT 6-9

(a) Peter Ilych Tchaikovsky, Symphony No. 4, second movement.

EXCERPT 6-9
(b) Symphony No. 4, transposed parts.

EXCERPT 6-10
Thomas Moore, "My Gentle Harp" (Irish tune "Londonderry Air").
Arranged by Alice Parker for four-part chorus of mixed voices with harp or piano accompaniment.

My Gentle Harp

For Four-Part Chorus of Mixed Voices
with Harp or Piano Accompaniment

Approximate duration: 3:20

tears we meet_ a - gain. Yet, e- ven then, while Peace_was_ sing- ing Her hal-cyon
tears we meet a - gain. Yet, e-ven then, while Peace_was sing - ing Her hal-cyon
tears we meet a - gain. Yet, e- ven then, while Peace was sing - ing Her hal-cyon
tears we meet a - gain. Yet, e-ven then, while Peace was_ sing - ing Her hal-cyon

song o'er land_ and_ sea, Though joy and hope to oth- ers_ bring - ing, She on-ly
song o'er land_ and sea,_ Though joy and hope to oth - ers bring - ing, She on-ly
song o'er land and sea, Though joy and hope to oth - ers bring - ing, She on-ly
song o'er land and_ sea, Though joy and hope to oth - ers bring - ing, She on-ly

(Continued)

EXCERPT 6-10
"My Gentle Harp" (continued).

EXCERPTS FOR CHAPTER 7

EXCERPT 7-1
Franz Schubert, Symphony No. 8, first movement.

EXCERPT 7-2

Gioacchino Rossini, *L'Italiana in Algeri* ("The Italian Girl in Algiers"), Overture.

cresc.
simile
sf
cresc.
simile
sf

p
p
p
p

Allegro
p
sf
sf
Allegro
p
sf
sf

(Continued)

EXCERPT 7-2
L'Italiana in Algeri (continued).

EXCERPT 7-3
Cornish folk song, "I Love My Love." Collected by G. B. Gardiner and arranged for mixed voices by Gustav Holst. The piece is dedicated "To C. K. S. and the Oriana."

To C. K. S. and the ORIANA.

I love my love.

CORNISH FOLKSONG
collected by G. B. GARDINER.

Arranged for Mixed Voices by
G. T. HOLST.

(Continued)

EXCERPT 7-3
"I Love My Love" (continued).

with her hands, and thus re - pli - ed she: "I love my love be - cause I know my
with her hands, and thus re - pli - ed she: (closed lips)
with her hands, and thus re - pli - ed she: (closed lips)
with her hands, and thus re - pli - ed she: (closed lips)
mf
love loves me! 2.O cru - el were his par-ents who sent my love to sea, And
2.O cru - el were his par - ents who sent my love to sea, And
2.O cru - el were his par-ents who sent my love to sea, And
2.O cru - el were his par - ents who sent my love to sea, And
cru - el was the ship that bore my love from me; Yet I love his par - ents
cru - el was the ship that bore my love from me; Yet I love his par - ents
cru - el was the ship that bore my love from me; Yet I love his par - ents
cru - el was the ship that bore my love from me; Yet I love his par - ents

since they're his al - though they've ruin-ed me: I love my love be - cause I know my
since they're his al - though they've ruin-ed me: (closed lips)
since they're his al - though they've ruin-ed me:" (closed lips)
since they're his al - though they've ruin-ed me:" (closed lips)
love loves me!"

EXCERPT 7-4
Traditional, "Shenandoah," arranged for mixed voices by G. Schroth.

hear you, Way hay, we're bound a - way, 'Cross the
poco rit.
mp
wide Mis - sou - ri. Hum or ah
poco rit.
mp

EXCERPT 7-5
Zoltán Kodály, *Hegyi Éjszakák* ("Mountain Nights"), for four-part women's voices.

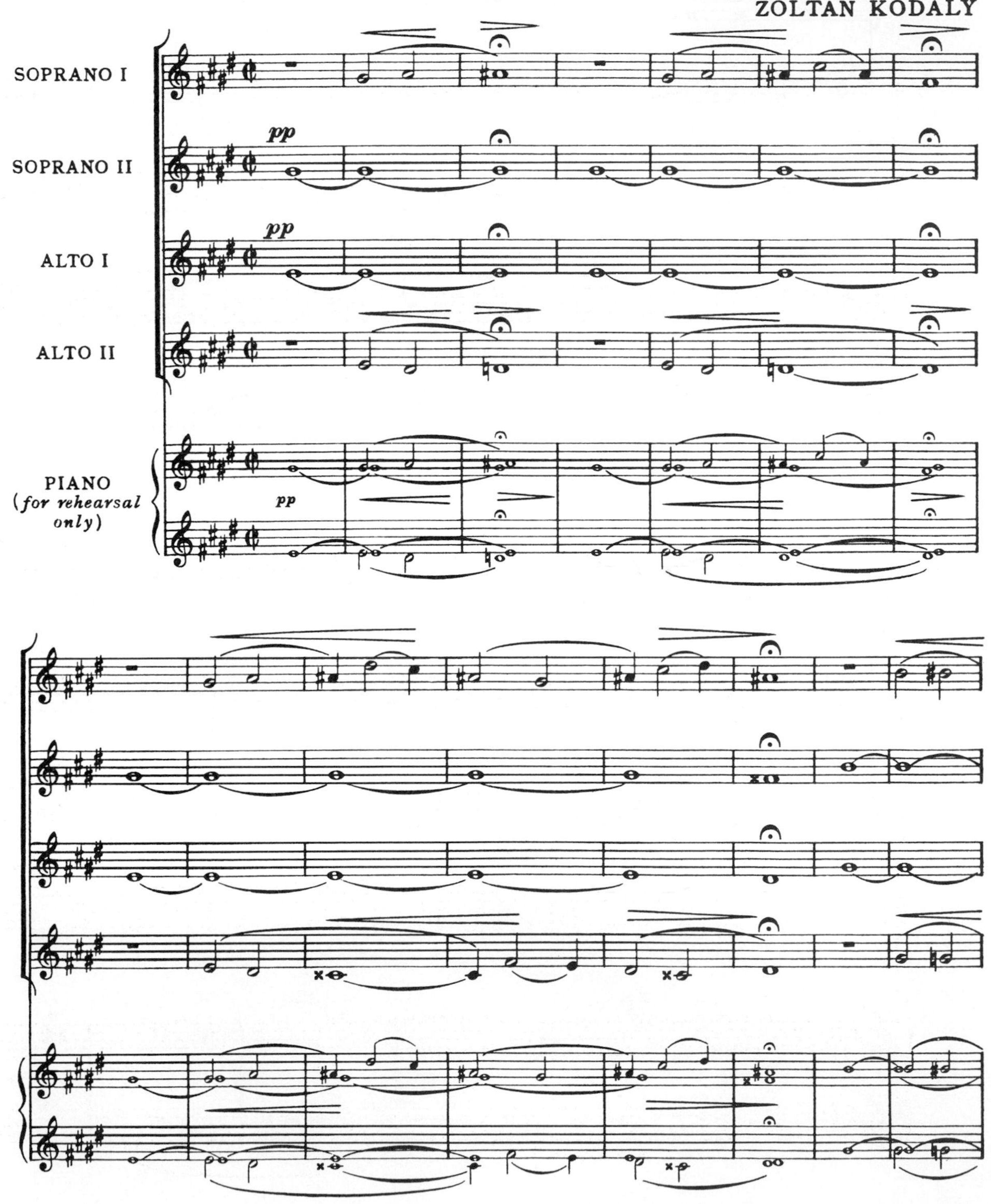

cresc.
cresc.
cresc.
f
f
f
f

EXCERPT 7-6

Traditional spiritual, "Seekin' for a City," arranged by Alice Parker for four-part chorus of mixed voices with baritone (or contralto) solo, a cappella.

15 47
King - dom, Hal - le - lu! Lawd, I don't feel
sor - row, Hal - le - lu!
lu, Hal - le - lu! I don't, I don't feel
lu, Hal - le - lu! Don't feel
20 52
no - ways tir - ed, Chil - der - en, oh, glo - ry, Hal - le -
no - ways tir - ed, Chil - der - en, glo - ry, Hal - le -
no - ways tir - ed, Oh, glo - ry, Hal - le -
25 57
lu - jah! For I hope to shout glo - ry when dis world is on
lu - jah! Hope to shout glo - ry, A -
lu - jah! Hope to shout glo - ry, A -

(Continued)

EXCERPT 7-6
"Seekin' for a City" (continued).

(30) (62)

1

fi - ah, Chil-der-en, Oh, glo - ry, Hal - le - lu!

p

men. Oh, glo - ry, Hal - le - lu!

p

men. Oh, glo - ry, Hal - le - lu!

(65)

2

lu!

lu! Lawd, I hope to shout glo - ry, glo - ry,

f

lu! Lawd, I hope to shout, when dis world is on

lu! Lawd, I hope to shout glo - ry, glo - ry,

f

lu! Lawd, I hope to shout, when dis world is on

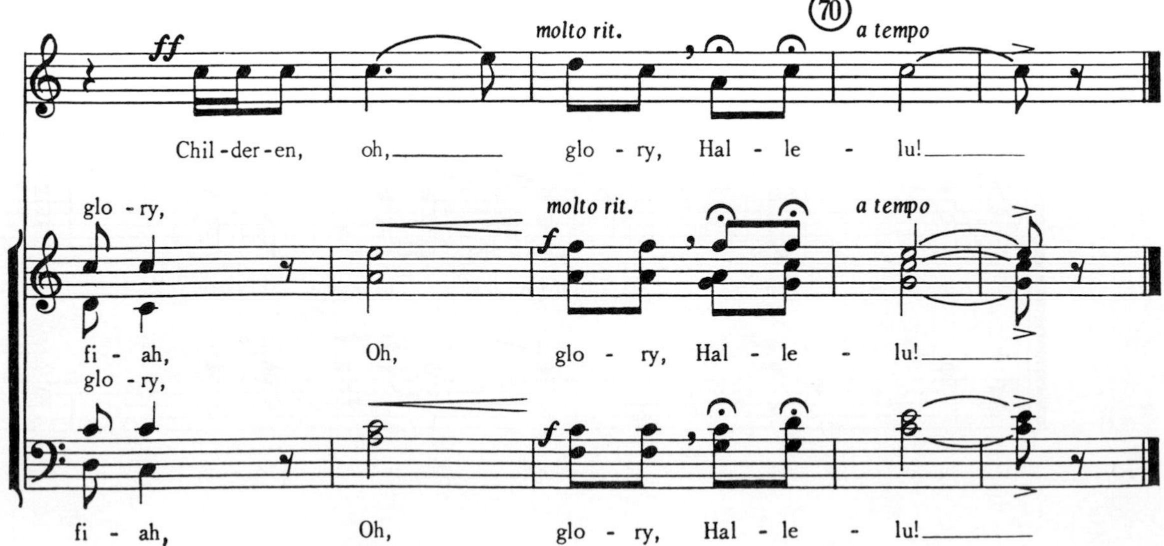

EXCERPT 7-7
Gustav Holst, Second Suite in F, "Song of the Blacksmith."

EXCERPT 7-8

(a) Edward Elgar, *Enigma* Variations, Op. 36.

EXCERPT 7-8
(a) *Enigma* Variations (continued).

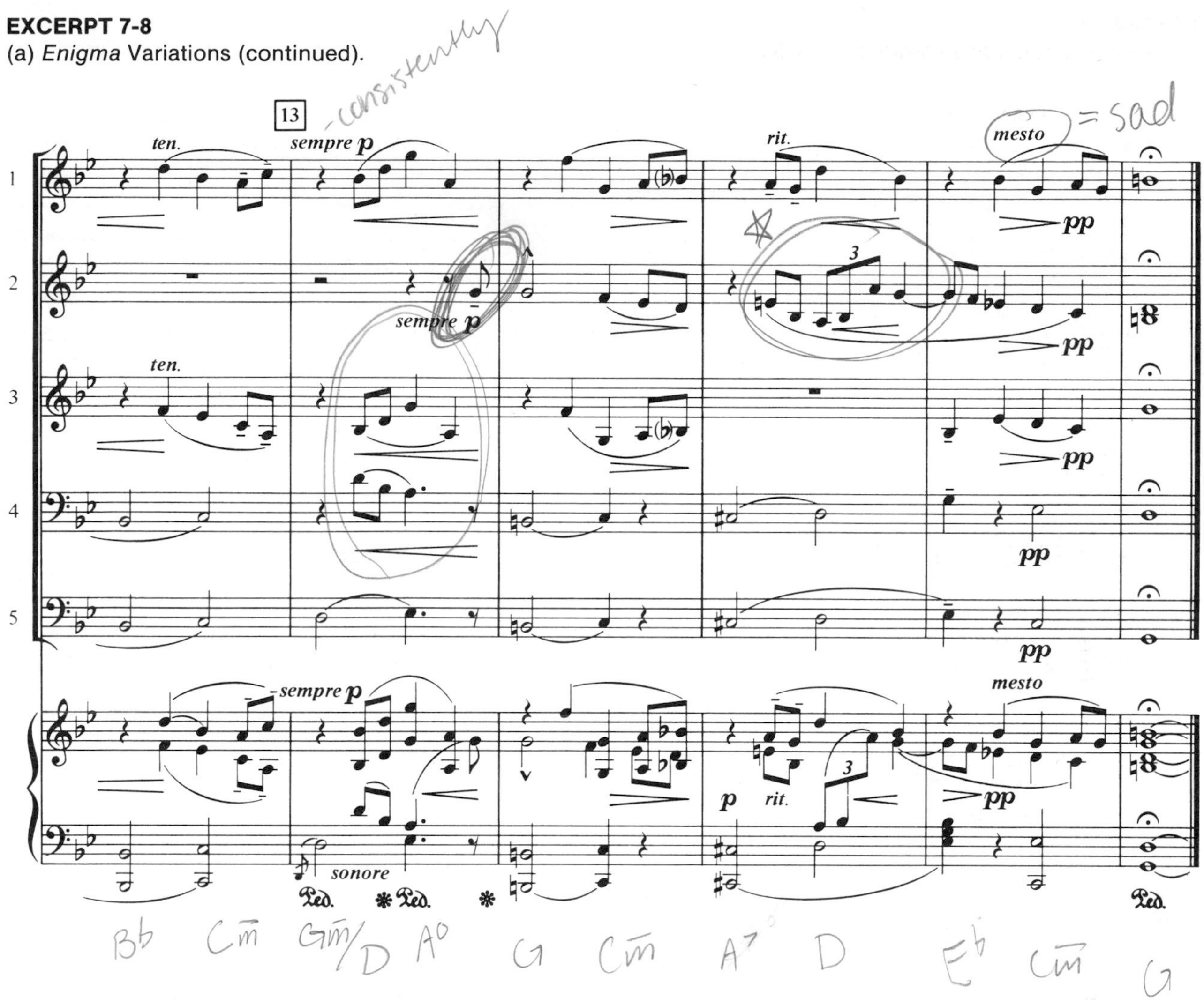

EXCERPT 7-8
(b) *Enigma* Variations, transposed parts.

(Continued)

EXCERPT 7-8

(b) *Enigma* Variations, transposed parts (continued).

In Excerpt 7-9, *Coppélia,* do the following. (1) Make cutoff: set new tempo for allegretto. (2) Use cutoff as downbeat of new tempo for allegretto.

EXCERPT 7-9
(a) Léo Delibes, *Coppélia.*

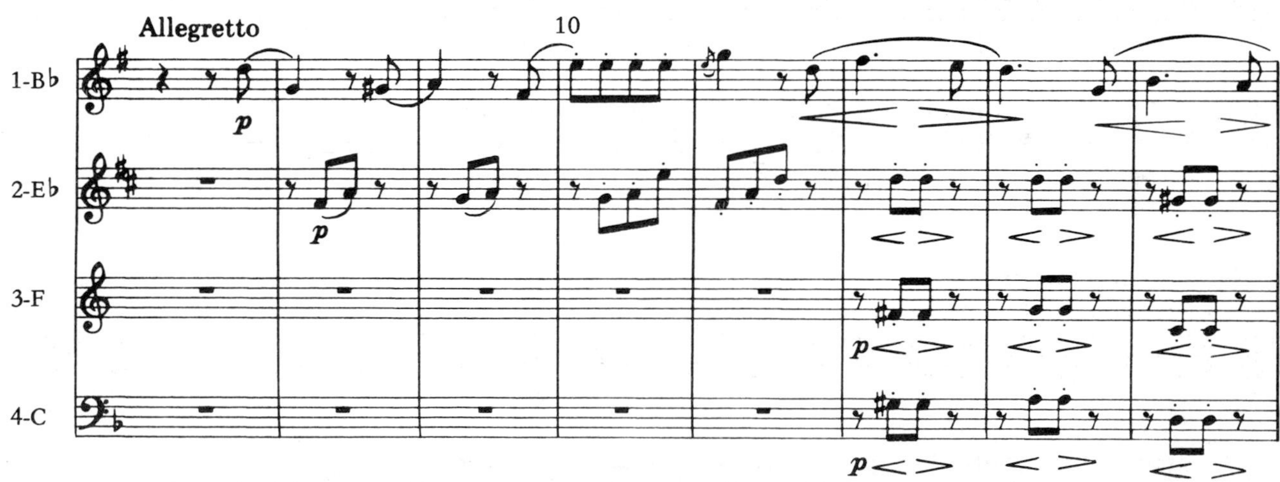

(Continued)

EXCERPT 7-9
(a) *Coppélia* (continued).

a tempo
50
1-B♭
2-E♭
3-F
4-C
p
p
p

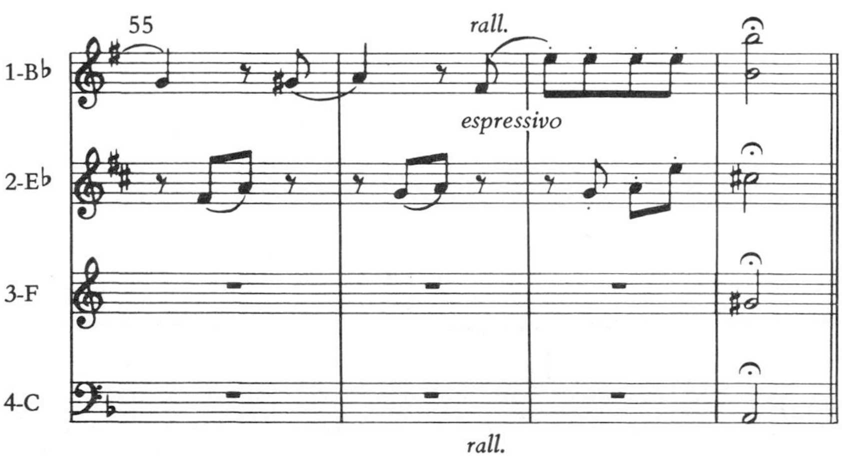

EXCERPT 7-9

(b) *Coppélia*, transposed parts.

Voice 2, C transposition
Moderato
Allegretto
10
15
20
poco rall.
a tempo
25
30
35
40
molto rall.
molto rall.
45
a tempo
50
55
rall.
espressivo
Voice 3, C transposition
Moderato
Allegretto
5
15
4
20
poco rall.
a tempo
2
30
2
35
40
molto rall.
2
a tempo
4
55
rall.
3
espressivo

(Continued)

EXCERPT 7-9
(b) *Coppélia,* transposed parts (continued).

In the piano part for *Coppélia* (Excerpt 7-9*c*), the notation in the measure marked with the asterisk is very confusing. We feel that the composer's intention was to have the lower voice finish the phrase in the rallentando rhythm and then join in the fermata with the upper voice; the pickup note is in the original tempo.

EXCERPT 7-9

(c) *Coppélia,* piano reduction.

(Continued)

EXCERPT 7-9

(c) *Coppélia,* piano reduction (continued).

EXCERPT 7-10

(a) Franz Joseph Haydn, Symphony No. 104 *(London)*, first movement.

(Continued)

EXCERPT 7-10
(a) Symphony No. 104 (continued).

[32]
1
A
2
3
B
4
ff
ff
ff
ff

1
A
2
3
B
4

[40]
1
A
2
3
B
4
sf
sf
sf
sf
sf
sf
sf
sf
sf

EXCERPT 7-10

(b) Symphony No. 104, transposed parts.

Voice 1, B♭ transposition

Adagio

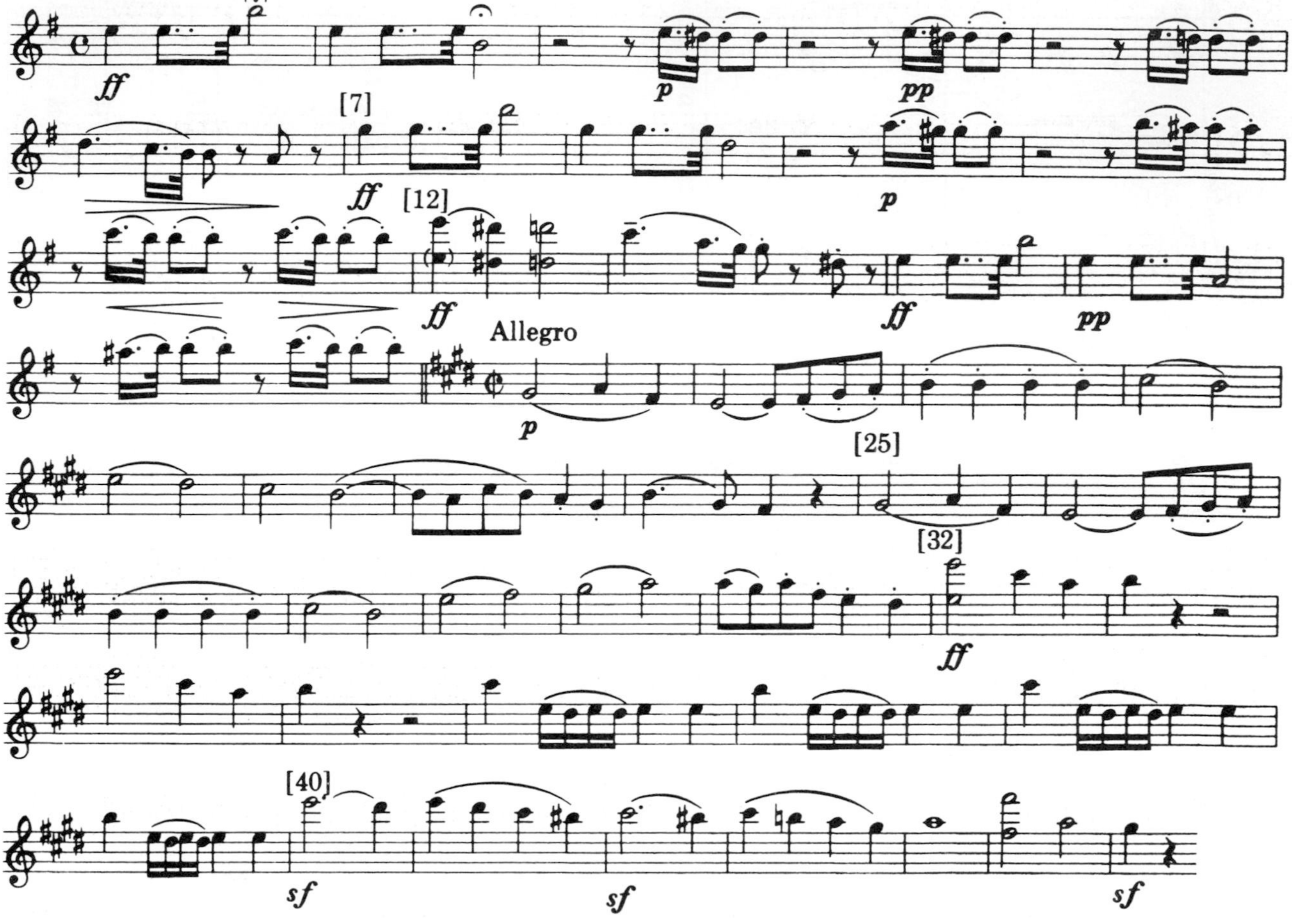

ff
p
pp
[7]
ff
p
[12]
ff
ff
pp
Allegro
p
[25]
[32]
ff
[40]
sf
sf
sf

Voice 2, B♭ transposition (div.)

Adagio

ff
p
[7]
ff
p
[12]
div.
ff
ff
pp
Allegro
p

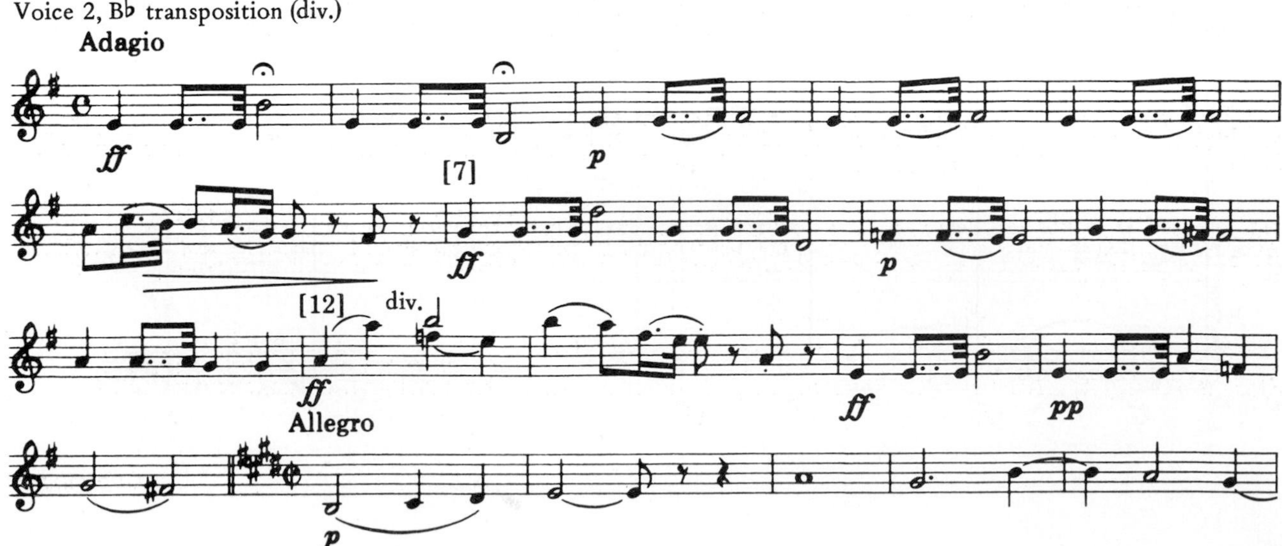

Voice 2, E♭ transposition (div.)

Adagio

ff p

[7]

ff p

div.

[12]

ff ff pp

Allegro

p

[25]

[32]

ff

[40]

sf sf sf

(Continued)

EXCERPT 7-10
(b) Symphony No. 104, transposed parts (continued).

In Schubert's Mass (Excerpt 7-11), do the following. (1) Practice release into silence; continue in tempo. (2) Practice *continuation* release into next beat.

EXCERPT 7-11

Franz Schubert, Mass in F *(Deutsche Messe)* ("German Mass"), "Introit" and "After the Transubstantiation." For four-part chorus of mixed voices with organ (or piano) accompaniment; English translation and arrangement by John Dressler.

(Continued)

EXCERPT 7-11
Mass in F (continued).

After the Transubstantiation

(can also be used as "The Lord's Prayer")

(Continued)

EXCERPT 7-11
Mass in F (continued).

mf
f
Leib, — mein Blut. Nehmt hin und den - ket mei - ner Lie - be, wenn
Gna - den-reich. Und treu - es Tun, — nach Dei - nem Wil - len mach
bod - y and blood. Take, eat and think — a - bout — my great love when-
Thou — hast giv'n. Thy will be done, — teach us — o - be-dience, that
sin, — that we may see Thy king - dom come, — O Fa - ther, from
Leib, — mein Blut. Nehmt hin und den - ket mei - ner Lie - be, wenn
Gna - den-reich. Und treu - es Tun, — nach Dei - nem Wil - len mach
bod - y and blood. Take, eat and think — a - bout — my great love when-
Thou — hast giv'n. Thy will be done, — teach us — o - be-dience, that
sin, — that we may see Thy king - dom come, — O Fa - ther, from
op - fernd ihr — ein glei - ches tut.
uns — die Er - de him - mel - gleich.
ev - er you do it, for God is good".
we — on earth may be in heav'n.
now — to all — e - ter - ni - ty
op - fernd ihr — ein glei - ches tut.
uns — die Er - de him - mel - gleich.
ev - er you do it, for God is good".
we — on earth may be in heav'n.
now — to all — e - ter - ni - ty.

EXCERPTS FOR CHAPTER 8

In the Kyrie from Persichetti's *Mass* (Excerpt 8-1), create patterns based on rhythmic groupings and the shape and flow of the melodic line.

EXCERPT 8-1
Vincent Persichetti, *Mass,* Op. 84, Kyrie.

e - lé - i - son. Ký - - - - ri - e
- e e - - - - lé - i - son. Ký - - ri - e
e - lé - i - son. Ký - - - - ri - e
- e e - - - - lé - i - son. Ký - - ri - e
rit.
A
a tempo
f sub.
mf
f
e - lé - i - son. Chri - ste e - lé - i - son. Chri -
e - - lé - i - son. Chri - ste e - lé - i - son.
e - lé - i - son. Chri - ste e - lé - i - son.
e - - lé - i - son. Chri - ste e - lé - i - son.
Meno mosso (♩ = 48)
mf
mp
- - - ste e - lé - i - son. Chri - ste e - lé - i - son.
Chri - - ste e - lé - i - son. Chri - ste e - lé - i - son.
Chri - - ste e - lé - i - son. Chri - ste e - lé - i - son.
Chri - - ste e - lé - i - son. Chri - ste e - lé - i - son.

The "Promenade" theme from *Pictures at an Exhibition* by Modest Mussorgsky (Excerpt 8-2) was composed for piano in 1874 and later scored for orchestra by both Maurice Ravel and Leopold Stokowski.

The suite opens with the "Promenade" and presents this material three other times, each in a varied form. The "Promenade" is programmatic in nature, as are all the pieces, suggesting the uneven gait of a person in an art gallery, strolling slowly from painting to painting.

The five-beat patterns should be derived from the six-beat patterns that they precede or follow. The $\frac{6}{4}$ measures are in compound meter—in three-beat groups rather than two-beat groups. The $\frac{3}{2}$ meter in measure 14 indicates that other six-beat measures would also have been marked in $\frac{3}{2}$ meter if two-beat groupings were intended. Therefore, the opening measures can be conducted with a six-beat pattern, shortened for the $\frac{5}{4}$ measures. The larger interval between the second and third beats (a perfect fourth) creates a melodic emphasis on the third beat, which may suggest shortening the first half of the six-beat pattern.

EXCERPT 8-2

(a) Modest Mussorgsky, *Pictures at an Exhibition,* "Promenade."

Allegro giusto, nel modo russico; senza allegrezza, ma poco sostenuto ♩ = 104

5
sostenuto
mf
9
cresc.
mf sostenuto
(Continued)

EXCERPT 8-2
(a) "Promenade" (continued).

EXCERPT 8-2
(b) "Promenade," transposed parts.

Voice 2, B♭ transposition(div.)
5
9 sostenuto
cresc.
13

Voice 3, B♭ transposition
5
9 sostenuto
cresc.
13

Voice 3, E♭ transposition
5
9 sostenuto
cresc.
13

In Berger's "Harvester's Song" (Excerpt 8-3), an altered three-beat pattern can be used for the $\frac{7}{4}$ measures. The third beat will be extended in all measures except the third, where the second beat should be extended, placing the metric stress on *me* rather than on *for.* The second beat of a two-beat pattern is extended for the $\frac{5}{4}$ measures.

EXCERPT 8-3

Jean Berger, *Six Madrigals,* "Harvester's Song."

[10]
Lo, here we come a - sow - ing, a - sow - ing, And sow sweet fruits of love;
Lo, here we come a - sow - ing, a - sow - ing, And sow sweet fruits of love;
Lo, here we come a - sow - ing, a - sow - ing, And sow sweet fruits of love;
Lo, here we come a - sow - ing, a - sow - ing, And sow sweet fruits of love;
[10]
[15]
In your sweet hearts well may it prove!
In your sweet hearts well may it prove!
In your sweet hearts well may it prove!
In your sweet hearts well may it prove!
[15]

In Excerpt 8-4, from Bernstein's *Mass,* the grouping of beats in asymmetrical measures is shown by dashed bar lines, which may indicate that consecutive patterns should be used. Altered six-beat patterns are also possible.

EXCERPT 8-4
Leonard Bernstein, *Mass,* "Almighty Father."

dolce
15
And fill with grace
Who shall de - fend us all. And fill with grace
Who shall de - fend us all. And fill with grace
div. dolce unis.
Who shall de - fend us all. And fill with grace
ppp
All who dwell in this place. A - men.
All who dwell in this place. A - men.
All who dwell in this place. A - men.
div.
All who dwell in this place. A - men.

Makris's *Aegean Festival* Overture (Excerpt 8-5) is an instrumental setting of melodies with seven-beat and eleven-beat patterns typical of Greek folk music. Note that the timpani part may be played on any bass-clef instrument; the class may tap the snare drum part; and if solo voice 3 is played on an E-flat instrument, it will sound one octave higher.

EXCERPT 8-5

(a) Andreas Makris, *Aegean Festival* Overture, band arrangement by Al Bader.

p (may be played or sung 8va)
poco cresc.
poco cresc.
poco cresc.
poco cresc.
[24]
mf (loco)
p
p
p
mf
p
mf
p
p
p
mf
pp
pp
pp
pp

(Continued)

EXCERPT 8-5

(a) *Aegean Festival* Overture (continued).

EXCERPT 8-5
(b) *Aegean Festival* Overture, transposed parts.

(Continued)

EXCERPT 8-5

(b) *Aegean Festival* Overture, transposed parts (continued).

Voice 3, E♭ transposition

In Grainger's "Rufford Park Poachers" (Excerpt 8-6 on the opposite page), at the tempo indicated, the most practical approach is to conduct the $\frac{5}{8}$ measures with two uneven beats, using the rebound of beat 1 for a light subdivision and a light lift on the last eighth of the measure for a division of the second beat, as in the illustration at the left below. You may also wish to show only the two main beats, as shown in the illustration at the right.

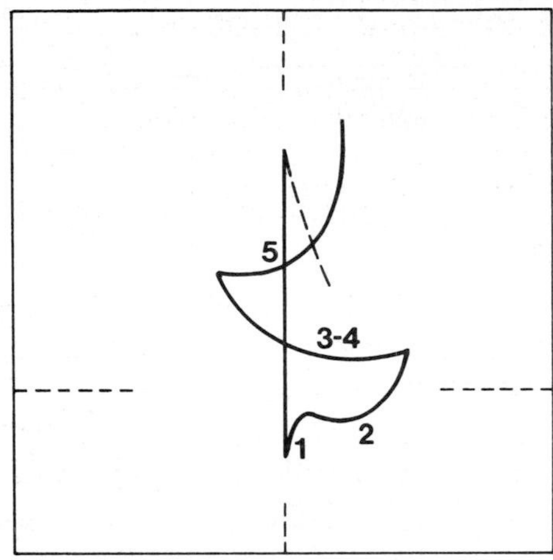

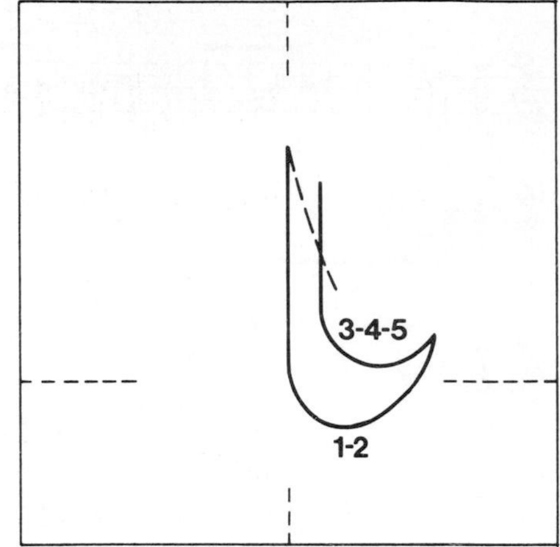

Use a *small* pattern, with much of the motion in the wrist. An overly large pattern will detract from the expressiveness and the precision, giving this a frantic mood. Concentrate on the lyricism and dynamic shapes.

The oboe and bassoon follow the upper part in canon at a distance of one beat. Cue each main entrance of the lower part, but let it follow on its own. The performers must assume much of the responsibility for imitating the dynamics and phrasing of the first part. Showing these indications for both parts is nearly impossible, and attempts to do so detract from the beautiful simplicity of the piece.

It is most helpful to rehearse the first and second parts separately, then the third and fourth parts alone, to fix the melodic and rhythmic flow in your mind before attempting the close canonic performance of four voices plus the drone fifth part.

This excerpt requires two pianos if wind instruments are not available, with piano A playing lines 1 and 2, and piano B playing lines 3 and 4.

EXCERPT 8-6

Percy Grainger, *Lincolnshire Posy,* "Rufford Park Poachers."

EXCERPT 8-7

Carl Orff, *Carmina burana, Uf dem Anger* ("On the Green"). Option: Begin at measure 5.

EXCERPTS FOR CHAPTER 9

In Excerpt 9-1, *Au Clair de la lune,* at numbers 1, 2, and 3 (and other measures of long note values), try sustaining gestures based on the alto, tenor, or bass voice. The arranger has appended the following comment: "This song will be most effective sung without accompaniment. If the chorus is able to do this, use the piano in performance to play only the passages in brackets (⌐―――――   ―――――¬), when the chorus is silent."

EXCERPT 9-1
Jean-Baptiste Lully, *Au Clair de la lune* ("Lo, there in the moonlight"), arranged by Leonard Stone.

Au Clair De La Lune

(Pierrot)

Music by Jean Baptiste Lully (1632-1687)
arr. by LEONARD STONE

Moderately

Soprano

Alto

Tenor

Bass

Moderately

mf

Piano

(Continued)

EXCERPT 9-1

Au Clair de la lune (continued).

3
mp
Je n'ai plus de feu. Ou-vre-moi ta por - te, Pour l'a-mour de
Nor have I a fire. By the Lord, do let me In thy house, good
Je n'ai plus de feu. Ou-vre-moi ta por - te, Pour l'a-mour de
Nor have I a fire. By the Lord, do let me In thy house, good
Je n'ai plus de feu. Ou-vre-moi ta por - te, Pour l'a-mour de
Nor have I a fire. By the Lord, do let me In thy house, good
Je n'ai plus de feu. Ou-vre-moi ta por - te, Pour l'a-mour de
Nor have I a fire. By the Lord, do let me In thy house, good

4
Dieu."
Sire."
Dieu."
Sire."
Dieu."
Sire."
Dieu."
Sire."
mf

In Excerpt 9-2, by Rossini, the introduction (opening andante) is conducted in an eight-beat pattern in which *sustaining gestures* are used. Only those subdivisions necessary to provide clarity of rhythmic subdivision should be used; otherwise, sustaining gestures tending toward four-beat patterns or gestures encapsulating silences and rests should be attempted to reduce the actual eighth-note pulses that are physically beaten or indicated.

EXCERPT 9-2

Gioacchino Rossini, *Il Barbiere di Siviglia* ("The Barber of Seville"), Overture.

(Continued)

EXCERPT 9-2
Il Barbiere di Siviglia (continued).

[p]
[p]
4
pp
pp

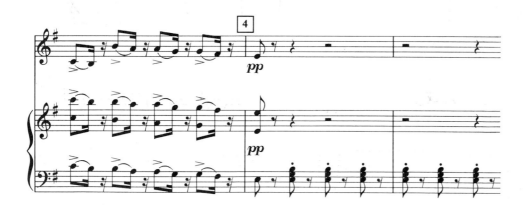

EXCERPT 9-3

(a) Franz Joseph Haydn, Symphony No. 97, first movement.

Vivace
[20]
1
A
2
3
B
4
ff
div.
p
(p)
[30]
f
(Continued)

EXCERPT 9-3

(a) Symphony No. 97 (continued).

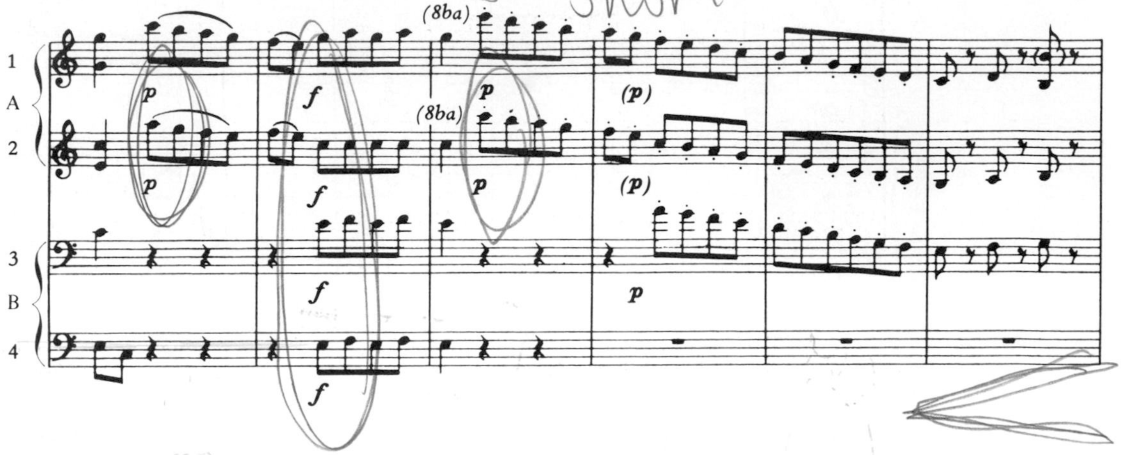

(8ba)

(8ba)

[40]

(8va ad lib.)

[60]
[B]

EXCERPT 9-3
(b) Symphony No. 97, transposed parts.

(Continued)

EXCERPT 9-3

(b) Symphony No. 97, transposed parts (continued).

Voice 3, E♭ transposition
Adagio
sim.
fp
f p
[10]
f p
p
Vivace
dim.
ff
[20]
[30]
p
(p)
f
[A]
f
p
f
[50]
div.
[60]
(8ba)
sf
[B]

EXCERPT 9-4
Percy Grainger, *Lincolnshire Posy,* "Harkstow Grange."

It is preferable to use piano four hands, or—even better—two pianos, to perform Excerpt 9-4, "Harkstow Grange." Analyze for: (1) form; (2) harmonic progression for each variation; (3) interpretative approach, melodic tension and release, climax, and ending; (4) conducting problems involving style, dynamics, crescendos and decrescendos, and tempos, rallentandos, sustaining gestures, and pattern modification.

EXCERPT 9-5

(a) Gustav Holst, *The Planets,* "Mars," score. Original is a major second higher.

[25]
1
2
3
4
5
p
mf
cresc.
[34]
f
(Continued)

EXCERPT 9-5
(a) "Mars" (continued).

[58]
1
2
3
4
5
ff
[68/71]
3
6

EXCERPT 9-5
(b) "Mars," transposed parts.

Voice 2, B♭ transposition
Allegro
7
[8]
4
p
mf
[17]
6
p cresc.
[25]
mf
mf
f
mf
f
f
[34]
cresc.
ff
[40]
fff
[50]
[58]
ff
[68/71]

(Continued)

EXCERPT 9-5
(b) "Mars," transposed parts (continued).

Voice 4, E♭ transposition

EXCERPT 9-6

(a) Leonard Bernstein, *Candide,* Overture.

(Continued)

EXCERPT 9-6
(a) *Candide,* Overture (continued).

EXCERPT 9-6
(b) *Candide* Overture, transposed parts.

Voice 2, B♭ transposition

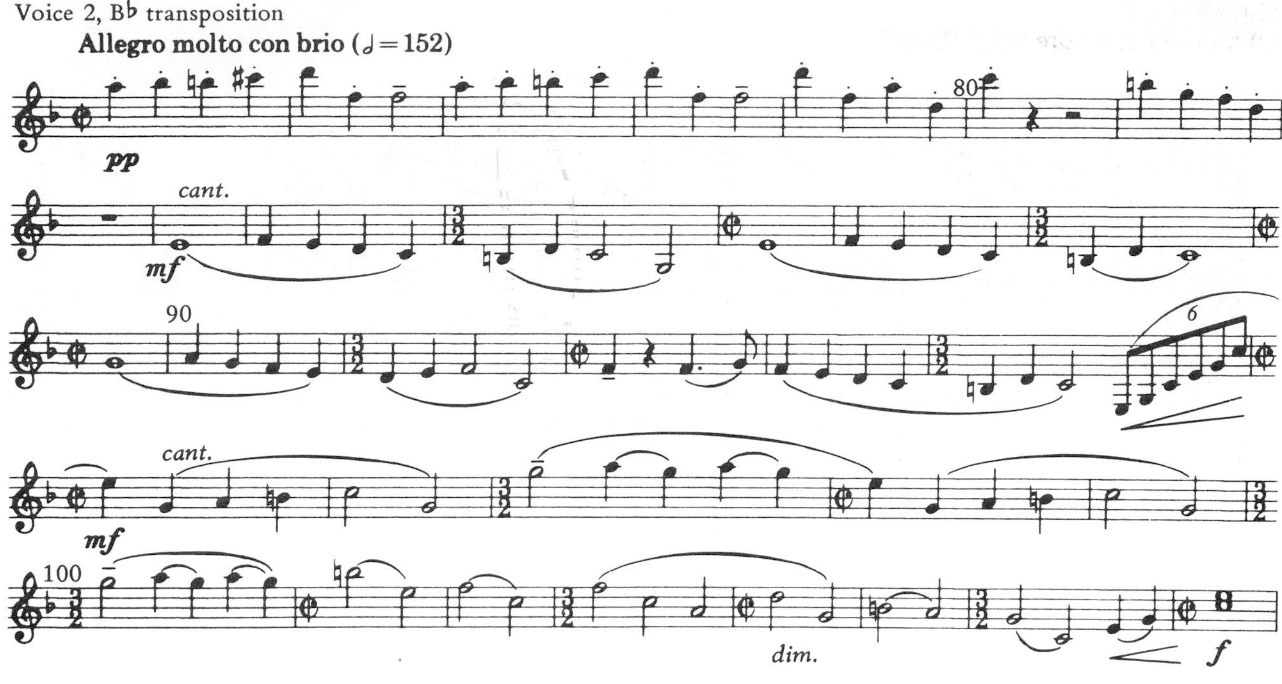

Voice 2, E♭ transposition

EXCERPT 9-6

(c) *Candide* Overture, piano reduction.

EXCERPTS FOR CHAPTER 11

In "Behold, I tell you a mystery" (Excerpt 11-1*a*), the accompaniment is in sustained or *accompagnato* style, and played at the keyboard.

EXCERPT 11-1

(a) George Frideric Handel, *Messiah,* "Behold, I tell you a mystery," recitative for bass.

EXCERPT 11-1

(b) George Frideric Handel, *Messiah,* "The trumpet shall sound," air for bass.

[46]
Bass
the trum-pet shall sound,
1
2
3
4
f
[52]
and the dead shall be raised,
be raised in-cor-
p
[55]
rup-ti-ble
be raised in-cor-rup-ti-ble
and

(Continued)

EXCERPT 11-1
(b) "The trumpet shall sound," air for bass (continued).

EXCERPT 11-1
(c) "The trumpet shall sound," keyboard with solo bass part.

(Continued)

EXCERPT 11-1
(c) "The trumpet shall sound," keyboard with solo bass part (continued).

EXCERPT 11-1
(d) "The trumpet shall sound," transposed parts.

If your conducting class does not include a flutist, another instrument can play the solo line in Excerpt 11-2. Make an ensemble by assigning members of the class to play specific parts from the score. Use a piano for some or all of the accompaniment if necessary.

EXCERPT 11-2

(a) Wolfgang Amadeus Mozart, Concerto for Flute and Orchestra in D Major, K. 314, second movement.

10
Fl. pr.
Vl.
cresc.
f
p
Vla.
Vc. e Cb.

Fl. pr.
tr
Vl.

20
Fl. pr.
tr
Vl.
f
p
Vla.
Vc. e Cb.

(Continued)

EXCERPT 11-2

(a) Concerto for Flute and Orchestra in D Major (continued).

Ob.
Cor. (G)
Fl. pr.
Vl.
Vla.
Vc. e Cb.
tr
f
p
zu 2
cresc.

EXCERPT 11-2

(b) Flute Concerto in D Major, keyboard with solo flute part.

(Continued)

EXCERPT 11-2
(b) Flute Concerto in D Major, keyboard (continued).

Excerpt 11-3 on the opposite page is in *secco* (dry) style, indicating that most of the text is sung without underlying accompaniment. The tempos and rhythms are interpreted with considerable freedom in order to make them sound like the natural irregularities of speech and to bring out the meaning of the text. The conductor must "think" the recitative along with the vocalist and interject the chords quickly in relation to the text, regardless of rhythmic discrepancies with the score.

EXCERPT 11-3
Wolfgang Amadeus Mozart, *Die Zauberflöte* ("The Magic Flute"), recitative.

Excerpt 11-4, the opening measures of *Scheherazade,* includes examples of grand pause (GP), fermatas, a quick (𝅘𝅥𝅮 𝅝) predownbeat entrance, a violin solo with accompanying chords in recitative style, and a flowing $\frac{6}{4}$ (in two) melodic section. A feeling of rubato should pervade throughout measures 1–17. The fermatas should result in length more from a feeling of musical flow than from actual metronomic beating or counting.

EXCERPT 11-4
Nikolai Rimsky-Korsakov, *Scheherazade,* opening.

Cadenza
ten.
Allegro non troppo (♩. = 56)
mf
mf
mf
tr
Ped.
Ped.
Ped.
Ped.
sf
p
sf marc.
p
pp
tr
Ped. sempre
mf
mf marc.
pp

EXCERPT 11-5
Traditional spiritual, "Sometimes I Feel Like a Motherless Child," arranged by Donald Hunsberger.

(Continued)

EXCERPT 11-5
"Sometimes I Feel Like a Motherless Child" (continued).

EXCERPTS FOR CHAPTER 12

For Étude, by Donald Hunsberger (Excerpt 12-1 on the following pages), note the following:

1 After studying the score, mark in the necessary primary cues for the right hand (RH) and secondary cues for the left hand (LH). Mark entrances and line up releases for accurate gestures.

2 Watch the contrast in dynamics and give left-hand support when necessary.

3 The thirty-second-note passages in measure 4 should be performed as rapidly as possible. The overall effect is more important than the accuracy of each part.

4 Measure 5 begins the ostinato background figures; remember that voice 1 begins each repetition of the figure forte, followed by a decrescendo.

5 The ♩ = 120 tempo of voice 5 coincides exactly with the 6-second timing of the upper voices in measure 6. The dotted lines in measures 6 and 7 line up the aleatoric and the written voices.

6 Pace the ending to allow all voices to die away slowly, leaving several seconds of silence before the final sforzando "falloff."

EXCERPT 12-1
Donald Hunsberger, Étude.

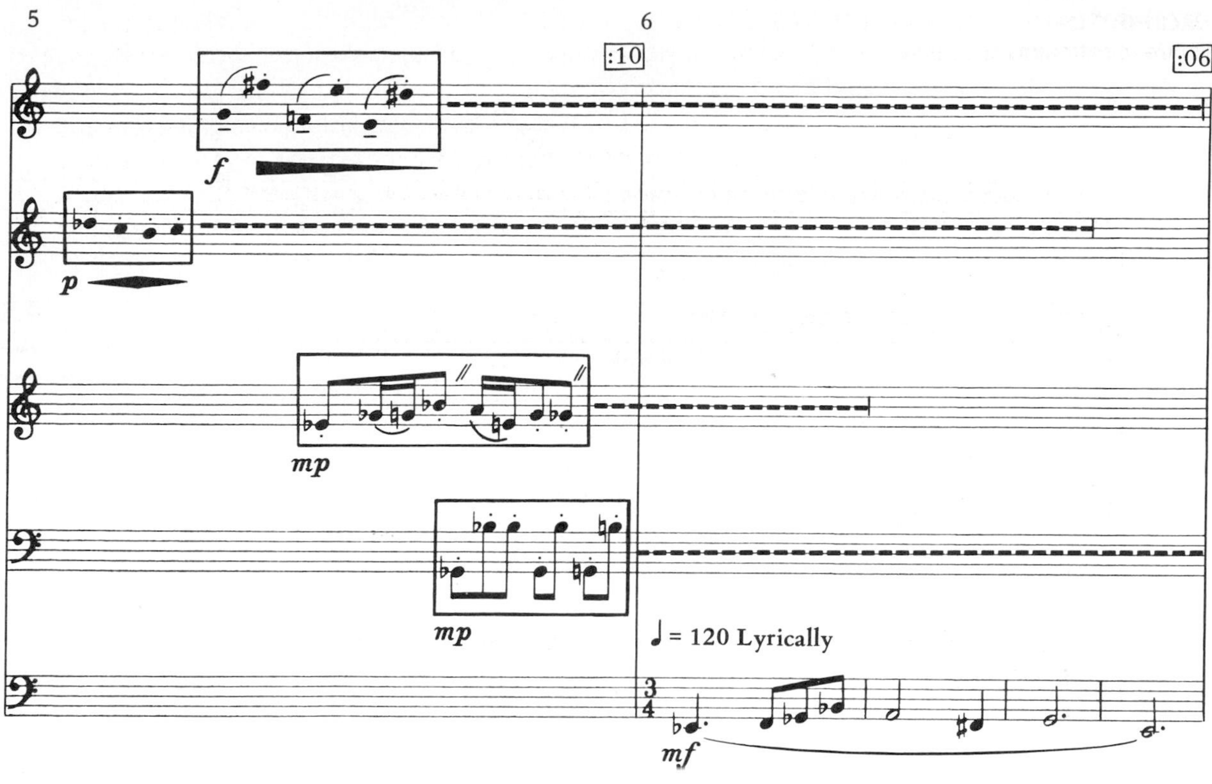

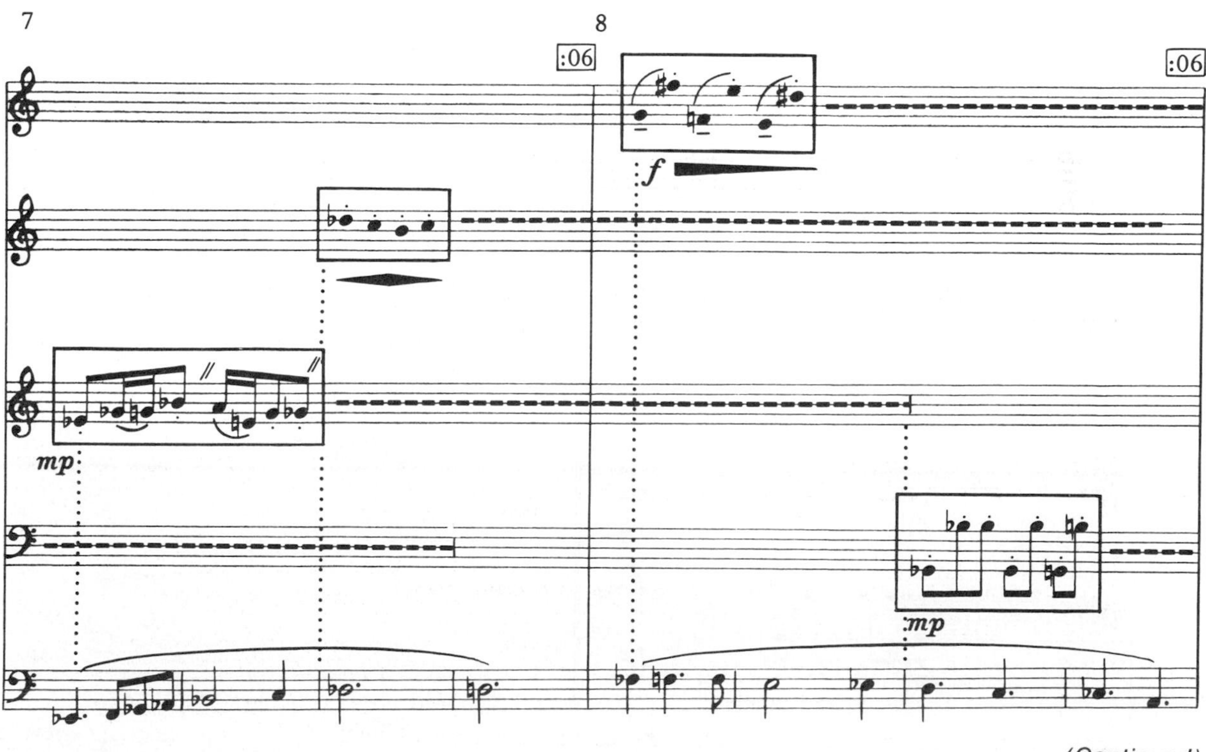

(Continued)

EXCERPT 12-1
Étude (continued).

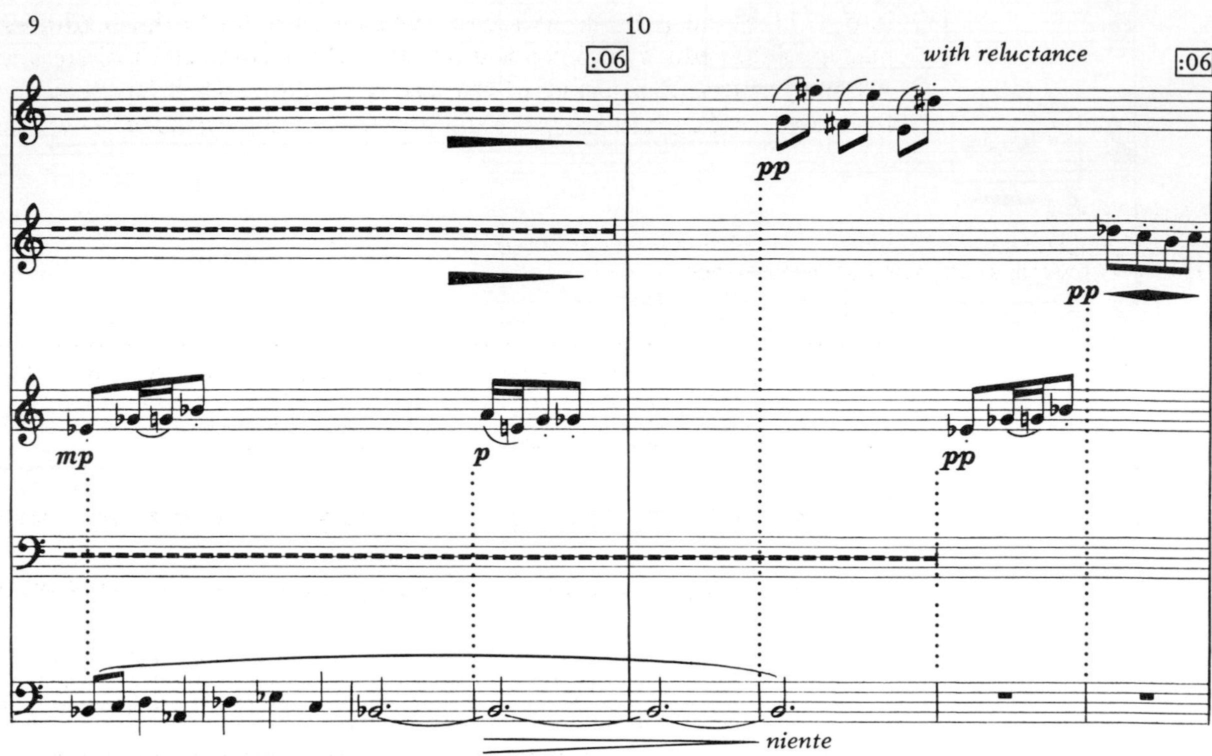

"Lord Melbourne (War Song)" from Grainger's *Lincolnshire Posy* (Excerpt 12-2) is conducted with a series of downbeats; certain areas (1, 2, 3) are grouped into a three-beat pattern. As seen in Grainger's notes to the conductor, the pacing of the individual downbeat pulses is at the conductor's discretion. Try varying rhythms and pacing of the passages. (Although it has been in print for more than 50 years, this piece still provides a unique conducting challenge.)

EXCERPT 12-2
Percy Grainger, *Lincolnshire Posy,* "Lord Melbourne (War Song),"
with the composer's own notes on performance.

N.B. In the passages marked "Free Time" (between the sign ◎ and the next bar-line) the bandleader should slightly vary his beat-lengths with that rhythmic elasticity so characteristic of many English folksingers and especially characteristic of George Wray, the singer of this song. Thus the opening phrase may be taken

arrangement of slightly varying beat-lengths. The bandleader should give free rein to his rhythmic fancy, just as folk-singers do. Each note with an arrow above it may be beaten with a down beat. Regular beat-lengths and conventional beat-gestures are taken up wherever there are bar-lines and time signatures.

For Excerpt 12-3, Hemberg's "Signpost I," observe the following performance notes:

1 Use the basic $\frac{4}{4}$ (♩ = 60) conducting pattern.
2 The , indicates a slight separation at the end of the measure with a closing of the vowel.
3 The figure [figure] in measure 7 indicates that the grace notes lead into a tone cluster ranging approximately from F^1 to E^2.
4 In measure 8, the word *hast* is spoken—forte *e ruvido* (roughly).
5 Beginning in measure 9, the tone band is symbolic of the shape of the vocalizations beginning with an *m* and passing into an *o*. The very thin line (over the first *o)* indicates the place where the outer voices converge *and* cross; the inner cluster voices remain within the outer voices.
6 In measure 15, the "teleprinter" effect is achieved by moving four times faster than the ♩ = 60 pulse, or in sixteenth-note pulses. This should be chanted, marcato. Divide the singers and pass the chant over to the sopranos and altos in measure 21.
7 The glissandos in measures 28 and 30 should be spread over four beats.

EXCERPT 12-3
Eskil Hemberg, *Signposts,* "Signpost I" (Psalm 60:2).

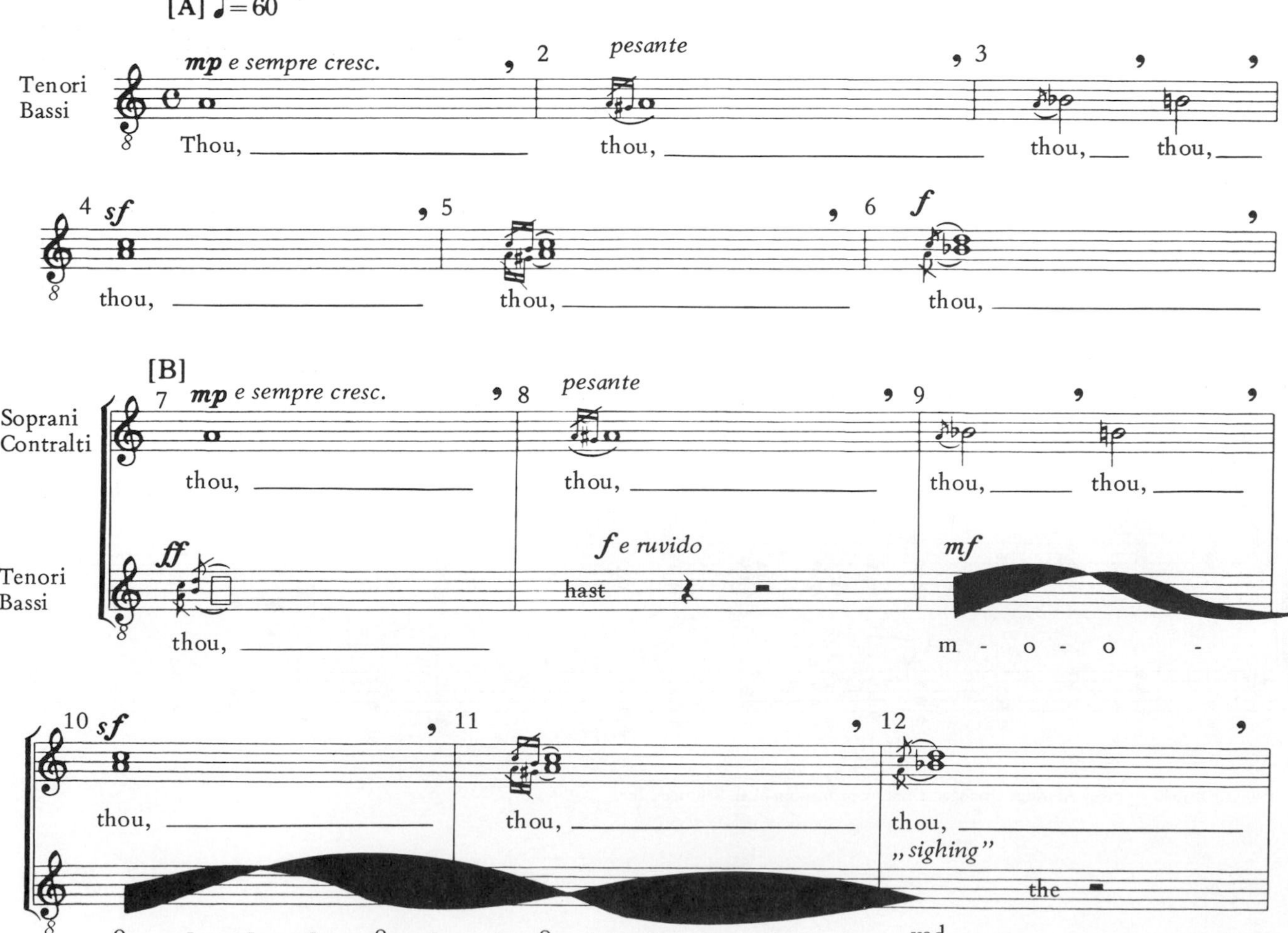

[C]
13
thou
p e dolce
land
14 f e ruvido
hast
„whispering"
and
15
mf
mo - o -
like a teleprinter
f e marcato
di - vi - ded
di - vi - ded it
di - vi -
16
17
18
„sighing"
the
o - o - o - o - o - ved
di - vi - ded it
di - vi - ded it di - vi - ded
vi - ded it di - vi - ded it di - vi - ded it di -
it di - vi - ded it di - vi - ded it di - vi - ded
di - vi - ded it di - vi - ded it di - vi - ded it
- ded it di - vi - ded it di - vi - ded it di - vi -
di - vi - ded, di - vi - ded it di -
[D]
19
p e dolce
land
„supplicating"
20
„whispering"
and
f e marcato
21
di - vi - ded
di - vi - ded it
di - vi - ded
di - vi -
di -
heal the sores there - of
heal the sores there - of, heal the so - ores heal
22
23
24
it di - vi - ded - it
di - vi - ded it di - vi - ded it di - vi - ded it
it di - vi - ded it di - vi - ded it
vi - ded, di - vi - ded it
di - vi - ded it
heal, heal, heal! For it

(Continued)

EXCERPT 12-3
"Signpost I" (continued).

Thou has moved the land, and divided it;
heal the sores thereof, for it shaketh.

Schwantner's *and the mountains rising nowhere* (Excerpt 12-4 on the opposite page) is an example of proportional notation. It uses clock time in seconds to establish the spatial rhythmic flow from the beginning to [2], where a four-beat pattern (♪ = 80) is used. Each event within the overall time span of 35 seconds receives a separate RH or LH entrance cue.

Note that the 35-second time frame is divided into sections which are introduced by right-hand motions. The third section (4 seconds of piano triplet and triangles) may be subdivided with a traditional three pattern, for ensemble accuracy. Keep accurate time with a stop watch or by counting to yourself.

EXCERPT 12-4
Joseph Schwantner, *and the mountains rising nowhere.*

to Carol Adler

and the mountains rising nowhere

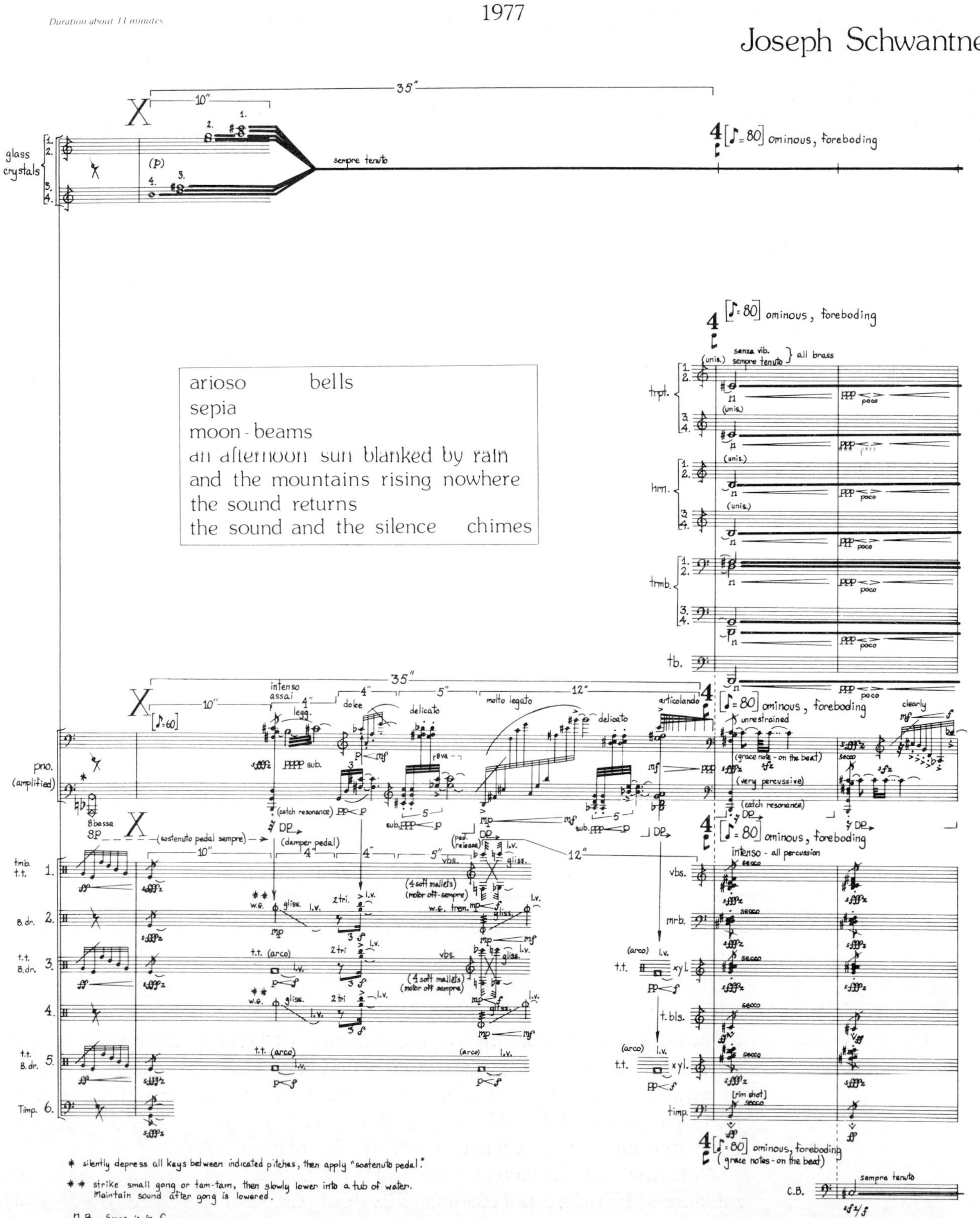

Minimalist composition, such as Excerpt 12-5, involves pulsed, repetitive textures in repeated, hypnotic patterns. These patterns are frequently modal in nature and shift slowly to create slight changes in texture and mood.

EXCERPT 12-5
John Adams, *Grand Pianola Music.*

(Continued)

EXCERPT 12-5
Grand Pianola Music (continued).

EXCERPT 12-6
Steve Reich, Octet.

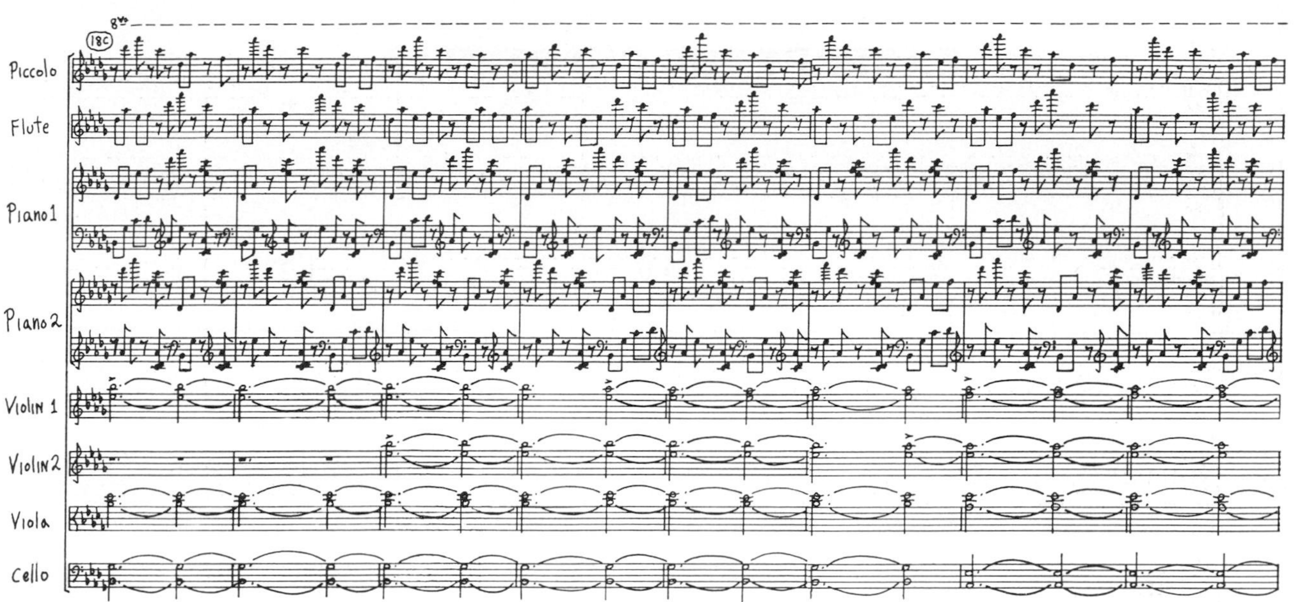

EXCERPT FOR CHAPTER 13

Excerpt 13-1 illustrates two elements of conducting musical theater: music under dialogue, and a soloist with chorus. In this example, the finale to Act I of Rodgers and Hammerstein's *Carousel,* the townspeople (the chorus) are going to an island for a picnic. Billy has learned that his girl, Julie, is to have a baby, and to get money for her, he decides to join Jigger and his friends in robbing the owner of the local factory. The townspeople are in the background while the dialogue over music leads into a rousing rendition of "June Is Busting Out All Over."

Members of the class should perform the speaking parts for each of the following characters:

Nettie
First Man
Julie
Second Man
Billy
Jigger

Conduct the music with piano only (as in an actual show rehearsal) or assign instruments to play from the score. The rest of the class can sing the final chorus. You may practice additional cuing or pacing if the chorus waits outside the classroom and is brought "onstage" in time to sing "June."

The music must be coordinated with the dialogue so that it leads into "June Is Busting Out All Over" at exactly the right time; it should neither rush the dialogue nor create a delay between the end of the dialogue and the beginning of the chorus refrain. There are several fermatas in the music that help coordinate at specific points in order to avoid a large discrepancy at the end. Study the pacing of the dialogue in order to let the music flow into the song with maximum musical and dramatic impact.

EXCERPT 13-1

Richard Rodgers and Oscar Hammerstein, *Carousel,* Act I, finale.

Cue: Nettie enters

Nettie: Hey, you roustabouts! Time to get goin'! Come and help us carry everythin' on the boats. 1st Man: All right, Nettie, we're comin'!

2nd Man: Don't need to hev a fit about it. Nettie: Hey, Billy! What's this Julie says about you not goin' to the clambake? Billy: Clambake? Mebbe I will go—after all! There's Jigger! I got to talk to him! Hey Jigger!

Come here—quick! Nettie: I'll tell Julie you're comin'. She'll be tickled pink. *(She exits.)* *Jigger (comes on)* Billy: Jigger! I changed my mind! You know—about goin' to the clambake and—

I'll do everythin' like you said. Gotta get money on account of the baby—see?

(Continued)

EXCERPT 13-1
Carousel (continued).

Jigger: Sure the baby! Did you get a knife? Billy: Knife? Jigger: I only got a pocket knife. If he shows fight we'll need a real one.
pp
8
Billy: But I ain't got— Jigger: Go inside and take the kitchen knife. Billy: Somebody might see me— Jigger: Take it so they don't see you!
Julie: (entering) Billy is it true?
pp
8
Are you comin' to the clambake? Billy: I think so. Yes— Julie: We'll have a barrel of fun. I'll show you all over the island. Know every inch of it. Been goin' to picnics there
8
since I been a little girl. Jigger: Billy! Billy! Y' better go and get that— Julie: Get what, Billy? Billy: Why—
(Chorus enters)
Jigger: The shawl. Billy said you oughter have a shawl. Gets
8
cold at nights, Fog comes up—ain't that what you said? Billy: Y-yes. I better go and get it—the shawl.
Julie: Now that was real thoughful, Billy! Billy: I'll go and get it! Nettie: C'mon all!
8

Brightly
Chorus:
June is bust - in' out all o - ver
The
mf

Nettie:
flow - ers are bust - in' from their seed.
And the

pleas - ant life of Ri - ley, That is spok - en of so

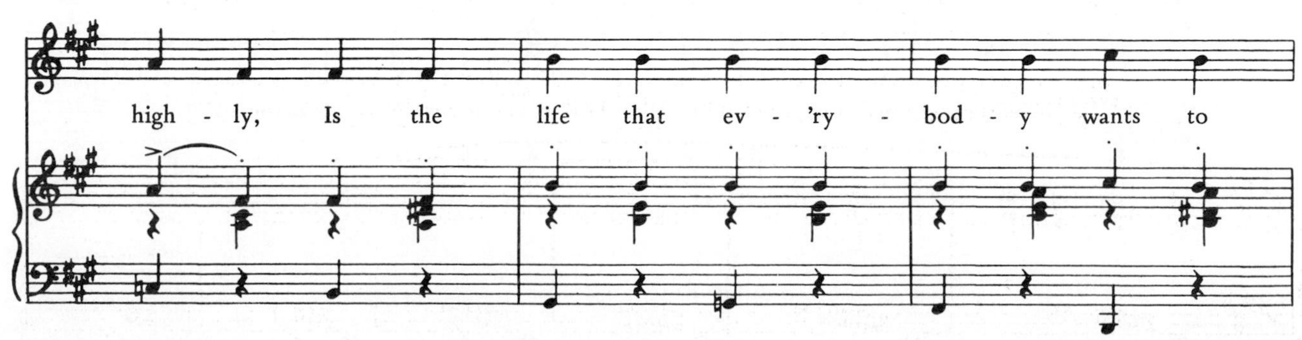
high - ly, Is the life that ev - 'ry - bod - y wants to

(Continued)

EXCERPT 13-1
Carousel (continued).

Be-cause it's June!
dim.
mf
3
7
dim. sempre
sff

EXCERPTS FOR CHAPTER 14

For Wright's *Conduction Blues* (Excerpt 14-1 on the following pages), observe the following notes by the composer:

1 Triple feel on all ♪'s. Avoid stiff rhythmic interpretation.

2 The figure ♪♩ ♪ in bars [A] 3, [A] 7 is long, short, long, and the second note must not be rushed. Director should demonstrate correct rhythm.

3 The final *t*'s on vocal syllables are the equivalent of a tongue stop for wind instruments, which is a unique technique in jazz, since it is forbidden in traditional concert music. In this case they should be emphasized.

EXCERPT 14-1
(a) Rayburn Wright, *Conduction Blues.*

(Continued)

EXCERPT 14-1

(a) *Conduction Blues* (continued).

EXCERPT 14-1
(b) *Conduction Blues,* transposed parts.

EXCERPT 14-2
(a) Manny Albam, *Pennies for Evan.*

EXCERPT 14-2

(b) *Pennies for Evan,* transposed part.

SECTION FOUR

APPENDIXES

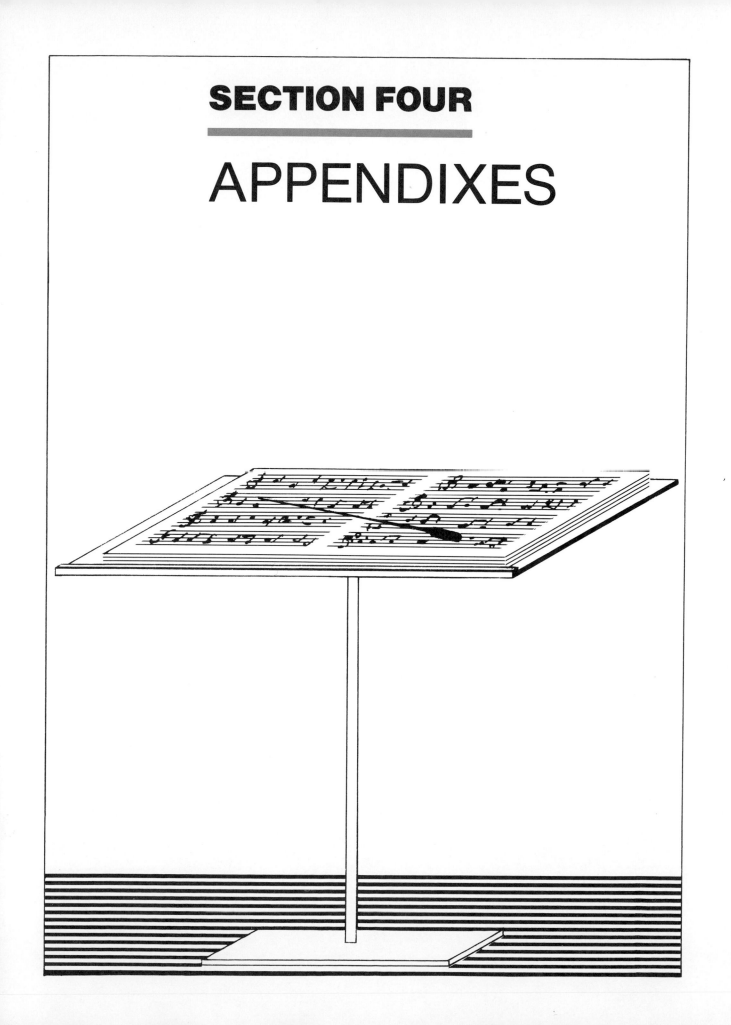

APPENDIX 1

THE CONDUCTING COURSE

COURSE DESCRIPTION AND SYLLABUS

Description

The first semester of this conducting course covers fundamentals such as beat patterns, baton technique, transposition, clef reading, score reading, cuing, subdivisions, fermatas, and releases. The class will function as an ensemble, and each student will conduct assignments approximately once each week, or as frequently as possible as the assignments become longer near the end of the semester.

Objectives

By the end of the first semester, you should be able to conduct short excerpts of standard ensemble repertoire, giving clear entrances, cues, beat patterns, releases, interpretative indications, and whatever else may be required for a good performance. You must have a thorough knowledge of the score, make a detailed diagnosis of the performance, and use effective rehearsal methods to make improvements.

Procedures

During the first few classes, much of the time will be spent conducting in unison. After that, students will take turns conducting the class. The order of the class list will be followed so that no one misses a chance to conduct. Be prepared to conduct *any* of the assigned material.

Take over the class when it is your turn. Make any changes in the ensemble or give other instructions as quickly and clearly as possible. Rehearsal time is always precious! Get as much done as you can during the allotted time.

Many of the classes might be videotaped, and you will be able to learn a great deal about your conducting by studying the tape. Instructions will be given concerning when you can view the tape outside of class. Viewing the tape may be an assignment and will be a factor in the final grade.

You must study and practice every day. Study the scores until you can sing every part. Analyze the phrases and the overall structure. Develop a convincing interpretation.

Practice singing and conducting *in front of a mirror.* At first, this may shatter some illusions about yourself, but that will soon pass and this practice will be a great help.

As a conducting student, you will become much more aware of what other conductors are doing—the details of their technique, how they interpret, and how they rehearse. Study every conductor you see as carefully as possible and try to learn as much as you can.

EVALUATION

Letter grades may *not* be given for the first few times that you conduct the class. After that, you will receive a grade each time that you conduct. You may be given brief oral comments, or the instructor may make written comments. Make a careful note of these comments so that you can use them to practice effectively.

The instructor may fill out evaluation forms for some of your performances. Use them as checklists as you practice. Notice that the physical or visual aspects of conducting are not the only important factors. You must also demonstrate (1) a good grasp of the score, (2) ability to diagnose the performance and make corrections, and (3) ability to make the ensemble play at its best.

Written assignments and tests may be given on transpositions, analysis, terms, and so forth.

A final examination will be scheduled, which will consist of conducting excerpts, assigned in advance, with a small ensemble. The final exam will have twice the value of a regular assignment. The final grade will be determined by averaging all the grades. The instructor may decide to raise the final grade a half level if the exam and assignments during the last weeks are generally higher than the overall average of the grades. The final grade may be lowered a full level or more if the student (1) does not perform in the ensemble, (2) does not cooperate for other student conductors by following instructions and playing well, and (3) misses classes.

Attending class is essential, because it is unfair for a student to conduct the class and then be absent while others are conducting. Any absence should be approved by the instructor, in advance if possible—and you should then provide a competent substitute to perform in class. More than one absence—whether excused or not—may result in forfeiting an opportunity to conduct and therefore can lower a grade.

APPENDIX 2

DAILY EXERCISES FOR WARM-UP AND REVIEW

Practice the following exercises in front of a mirror every day to maintain and improve technique. If it is not possible to practice all the exercises every day, try to do at least half of them on one day and the others on the following day. Practice with both the right and the left hand wherever possible.

1. Give preparatory gestures for each beat in a four-beat pattern, varying tempo, dynamic level, and style of articulation.
2. Practice beat patterns, gradually changing from very staccato to very legato.
3. Practice patterns with crescendo and diminuendo, varying from a small wrist motion to a full sweep with the arm.
4. Practice three styles of subdivision: (a) rebound, (b) continuation, and (c) rebound-continuation.
5. Conduct slow, legato patterns, showing the ictuses by (a) various sizes of click motion, (b) stopping the travel, and (c) changing both speed and direction of travel.
6. Develop a feeling of resistance in the travel by singing and conducting slow melodies, such as the theme from Wagner's "Elsa's Procession to the Cathedral" (Excerpt 2-2 in Section Three).
7. Conduct beat patterns with the right hand and give dynamic indications with the left hand.
8. Sing and conduct the first two measures of a simple melody such as *Frère Jacques.* Repeat the melody, changing the location of each of the following to a different beat of the second measure:

   a. Accent
   b. Right-hand cue
   c. Left-hand cue
   d. Head cue
   e. Fermata with no caesura
   f. Fermata with short caesura
   g. Fermata with long caesura

9 Sing and conduct several familiar melodies, using sustaining gestures or other pattern alterations.

10 Conduct several asymmetrical meters, using as many different patterns as you can. When using altered patterns (instead of combined), alternate between the asymmetrical pattern and the symmetrical pattern from which it was derived.

APPENDIX 3

SEATING CHARTS

ORCHESTRAS

For the traditional concert set, as shown in the illustration below, all string instruments are placed forward on the stage, for optimum projection of sound. The principal string performers form an "inner circle" around the podium, a seating that enhances visual and aural communication for solo, duo, and other special passages. Woodwinds are grouped

Clarinets	Bassoons
Flutes	Oboes

with principal performers side by side and in close proximity. Brasses face forward and play through the orchestra; the conductor can control balance and volume. Percussion is grouped along one side of the orchestra, but frequently it will be placed across the rear of the set.

TRADITIONAL CONCERT SET

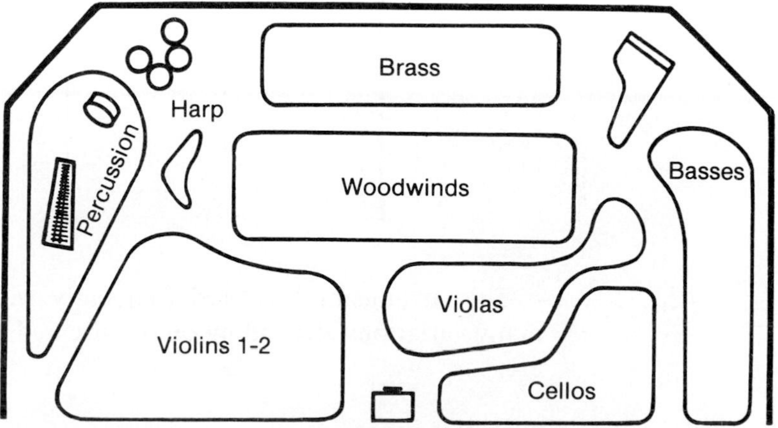

Variations of this traditional set include the baroque arrangement in which the first and second violins face each other on opposite sides of the podium.

The chart below shows a pit-style set with strings together. In a real orchestra pit, however, the set would be much "flatter" and deployed horizontally. The arrangement shown here is similar to the seating plan devised by Leopold Stokowski and based on the acoustic effect of having all the strings facing forward (with the basses and cellos on risers), so that all the f-holes face the audience instead of the side or rear walls. The woodwinds and brass again are grouped together for maximum control of ensemble and volume. Keyboard, harp, and percussion are also together.

PIT-STYLE SET, STRINGS TOGETHER

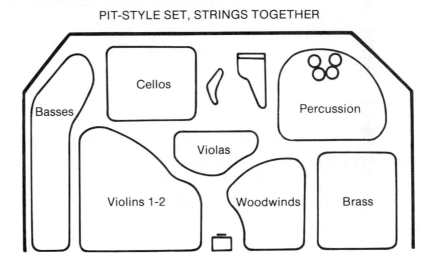

Cellos
Basses
Percussion
Violas
Violins 1-2
Woodwinds
Brass

CHORUSES

The illustration below shows the traditional SATB chorus seating.

TRADITIONAL SATB CHORUS SEATING

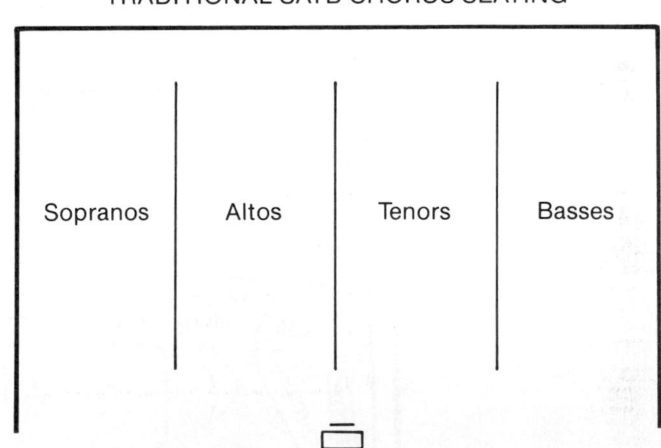

This arrangement is used frequently with large massed choruses. It has many variations, depending on the size and strength of each section; examples are:

1 STBA

2 ASTB

3 TB
SA

The chorus is placed on risers to maximize sound projection and visual communication with the conductor.

The next chart shows a chorale-style arrangement.

CHORALE-STYLE SEATING

S A T B S A T B S A T B S A T B

S A T B S A T B S A T B S A T B

S A T B S A T B S A T B S A T B

S A T B S A T B S A T B S A T B

While chorales of smaller size (twenty to eighty) may employ this traditional seating arrangement, many conductors group the singers by SATB quartets or in octets (SS AA TT BB). Size calls for considerable flexibility in creating seating plans based on the compositional demands of the music itself.

WIND BANDS

Below is a seating chart for a traditional concert wind band.

TRADITIONAL CONCERT BAND

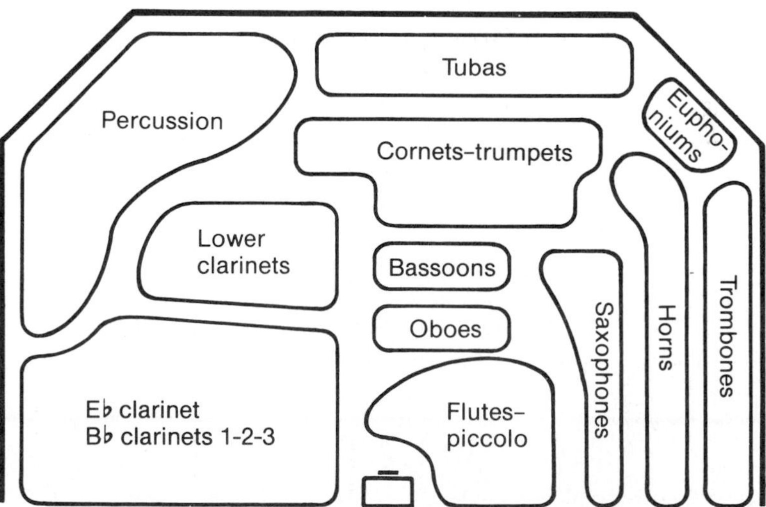

There are numerous variations of this traditional arrangment. Many conductors prefer to group the brasses together; others place the saxophones in the area occupied here by the cornets and trumpets; still others locate all woodwind bass instruments (bass clarinet, contrabass clarinet, baritone saxophone) close to the tubas for firm harmonic support. Some place the percussion across the rear of the set. The one constant factor appears to be the location of the clarinets—primarily with the solo B-flat clarinet chair in the position of the orchestral concertmaster, a practice based on the traditional concept of clarinet-violin transcriptions of orchestral repertoire.

Another arrangement for wind ensemble is the following.

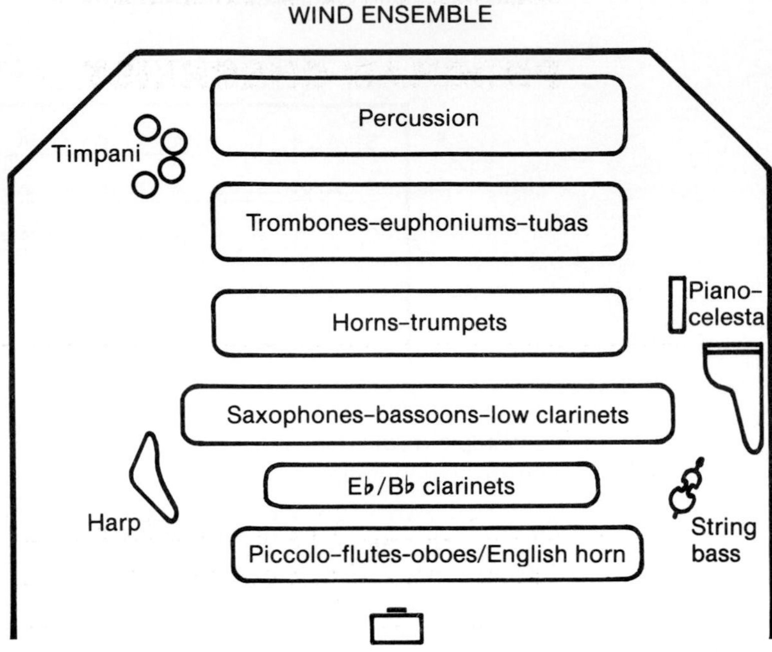

The concept of flexible personnel rotation in a wind ensemble involves varied seating patterns for individual compositions. The one shown here would be used for a work in English military band instrumentation, such as a typical composition by Holst or Jacob. The seating is much akin to the orchestral winds, with all principal performers sitting in the center of each row. The important point is that when different works have different instrumental requirements, it is not necessary to use the same seating arrangement from composition to composition.

APPENDIX 4

PROGRAM CHECKLIST

Date: ________ Title or special feature: ________________________________
Characteristics of potential audience: ________________________________

____

PROGRAM

Use the space between titles to estimate transition time, noting stage changes, personnel leaving and reentering stage, etc. Include time between movements and sections in timing pieces.

1 Title ____

Time ___ Tempo ___ Dynamics ___ Key ___ Style ___ Other ___

Transition ____

2 Title ____

Time ___ Tempo ___ Dynamics ___ Key ___ Style ___ Other ___

Transition ____

3 Title ____

Time ___ Tempo ___ Dynamics ___ Key ___ Style ___ Other ___

Transition ____

4 Title ____

Time ___ Tempo ___ Dynamics ___ Key ___ Style ___ Other ___

Transition ____

5 Title ________________________________

Time ___ Tempo ___ Dynamics ___ Key ___ Style ___ Other ___

Transition ________________________________

6 Title ________________________________

Time ___ Tempo ___ Dynamics ___ Key ___ Style ___ Other ___

Transition ________________________________

7 Title ________________________________

Time ___ Tempo ___ Dynamics ___ Key ___ Style ___ Other ___

Transition ________________________________

8 Title ________________________________

Time ___ Tempo ___ Dynamics ___ Key ___ Style ___ Other ___

Transition ________________________________

9 Title ________________________________

Time ___ Tempo ___ Dynamics ___ Key ___ Style ___ Other ___

Transition ________________________________

10 Title ________________________________

Time ___ Tempo ___ Dynamics ___ Key ___ Style ___ Other ___

Transition ________________________________

11 Title ________________________________

Time ___ Tempo ___ Dynamics ___ Key ___ Style ___ Other ___

Transition ________________________________

12 Title ________________________________

Time ___ Tempo ___ Dynamics ___ Key ___ Style ___ Other ___

Transition ________________________________

APPENDIX 5

CONCERT PREPARATION CHECKLIST

Enter dates for all of the following responsibilities in your daily calendar:

PUBLIC RELATIONS

1 *Program information.* Lead-time date ______
2 *Biography of soloist.* Lead-time date ______
3 *Newspaper feature.* Lead-time date ______
4 *Radio/television features.* Lead-time date ______
5 *Posters or fliers.* Lead-time date ______

Each of the five items above should have a minimum of 4 weeks lead time for submission of material. Prepare complete articles, human-interest stories, and special-interest items which may be used intact or reworked by the media.

6 *File of news items.* Maintain an up-to-date file of past features. Secure press packages on guest artists (photos, biographies, special-interest stories) early for your lead-time deadline.
7 *Concert coverage.* Radio and television stations are interested in covering dress rehearsals, especially those with guest artists. Work to make their visit as meaningful as possible for the best coverage.

PROGRAMS

1 Complete program information deadline: ______
2 Proofread typed program, checking for correct information on:
   a Titles of compositions and individual movements
   b Composer, dates
   c Personnel list
   d Program notes
   e Frontispiece artwork, date of concert, time, location, artists

3 Program stock should be light-colored, especially if the audience is to read a list of the movements, program notes, and so on during the concert.

4 List future programs of interest.

Proofreading is absolutely essential for accurate programs and press releases. Have two or three people other than the typist proofread the material; it is frequently difficult for a person who is familiar with the text to find mistakes, since he or she will focus more on sentences than on individual words. Reading the material backward reduces this problem.

BOX OFFICE

1 *Tickets.* Deadline for ordering: ____________________

2 *Programs.* Deadline for printing: ____________________

3 *Ushers.* Number required: __________ Deadline for requesting: __________

4 *Time of concert.* ____________________ to ____________________

5 *Police and fire notification.* ____________________

6 *Box office open for tickets and information.* ____________________

STAGE MANAGEMENT

1 Seating charts prepared: ____________________

2 Instructions to stagehands regarding setup and changes: ____________________

3 Lighting instructions: Stage lights __________ House lights __________

4 Microphones: ____________________

5 Instructions for ushers: ____________________

6 Curtain opening and closing (if any): ____________________

It is necessary to establish the lead-time deadline for each item to ascertain that all personnel connected with the concert are completing their assignments on time. The final step for the conductor is to set in-progress check times to be sure that everything is indeed on schedule.

MUSIC MATERIALS

On the opposite page is a music library's instrumental checkout form. It contains the checkout-return control for individual parts and also provides the librarian with a record of procedures for purchases, rentals, and billings.

Filed under: ______________

COMPOSER ______________ TITLE ______________ needed ___/___/___

BORROWER ______________ FILE NO. ______________

Address ______________ performance ___/___/___

______________ prepared by ______________ prep'd ___/___/___

++

RESPONSIBILITY: The borrower is personally responsible for all materials. This inventory lists exactly those parts loaned - check to see that it accurately reflects the materials you receive. Complete replacement cost will be charged for any materials not returned within ten (10) days of the performance date shown above, unless other arrangements are made with the Ensemble Librarian in advance. NO OVERDUE NOTICE WILL BE SENT.

++

___Full Score	___Flute	___Soprano Sax	___Timpani	___Violin I
___Cond Score	___Piccolo	___Alto Sax	___Percussion	___Violin II
___	___Alto Flute	___Tenor Sax	___	___
___Chorus part	___Oboe	___Baritone Sax	___Harp	___Viola
___	___English Horn	___Bass Sax	___Piano	___
___Vocal Score	___Oboe d'Amore	___Horn	___Organ	___Cello
___	___Eb Clarinet	___Cornet	___Celeste	___
___Tape	___A/Bb Clarinet	___Trumpet	___Harpsichord	___Bass
___	___Alto Clarinet	___Flügelhorn	___Cembalo	___
___Solo ______	___Bass Clarinet	___Trombone	___Continuo	___Gamba
___	___ContraB Clar	___Euphonium	___	___
___	___Bassoon	___Tuba	___	___
___	___ContraBsn	___	___	___

++

RETURNED: ______________ ret'd ___/___/___

______________ Checked by ______________ checked ___/___/___

To student accounts ___/___/___ BILL $______.______ billed ___/___/___

______________ resolved ___/___/___

++

RENTAL/PURCHASE: VENDOR ______________ ordered ___/___/___

Req/PO ______________ Condition ______________ rec'd ___/___/___

Charge to ______________ rental $______.______ ret'd ___/___/___

Missing parts ______________ shipping $______.______ total $______.______

______________ ledger $______.______ ledger ___/___/___

++

HANDLING CHARGE: Bill to ______________ $ ______.______

Address ______________ billed ___/___/___

______________ payment rec'd ___/___/___

++

APPENDIX 6

FORM FOR EVALUATING CONDUCTORS

This evaluation form is used by professional orchestras throughout the United States to evaluate conductors who are auditioning, serving as guest conductors, etc.

Printed in U.S.A. NCS Trans-Optic® MP06-77803-321

INTERNATIONAL CONFERENCE OF SYMPHONY AND OPERA MUSICIANS
CONDUCTOR EVALUATION

USE NO. 2 PENCIL ONLY

- CHOOSE ONLY ONE RESPONSE FOR EACH QUESTION
- DARKEN THE CIRCLE COMPLETELY
- ERASE CLEANLY ANY MARKS YOU WISH TO CHANGE

EXAMPLES

WRONG ① ② ③ ④ ⑤ RIGHT ① ② ③ ● ⑤

1. WHAT WAS YOUR OVERALL OPINION OF THIS CONDUCTOR?

EXCELLENT	VERY GOOD	GOOD	ABOVE AVERAGE	AVERAGE	BELOW AVERAGE	POOR	VERY POOR	UNACCEPT-ABLE
○	○	○	○	○	○	○	○	○

2. THIS CONDUCTOR:	STRONGLY AGREE	AGREE	NEUTRAL	DISAGREE	STRONGLY DISAGREE
a. . . . has a thorough knowledge of the scores conducted.	○	○	○	○	○
b. . . . is able to communicate the emotional content of the music.	○	○	○	○	○
c. . . . demonstrates excellent baton technique.	○	○	○	○	○
d. . . . chooses excellent tempi.	○	○	○	○	○
e. . . . corrects faulty intonation.	○	○	○	○	○
f. . . . corrects faulty balance among instrumental groups.	○	○	○	○	○

2. THIS CONDUCTOR:	STRONGLY AGREE	AGREE	NEUTRAL	DISAGREE	STRONGLY DISAGREE
g. . . . is a sensitive accompanist.	O	O	O	O	O
h. . . . makes efficient use of rehearsal time.	O	O	O	O	O
i. . . . makes remarks that are understandable and effective.	O	O	O	O	O
j. . . . leads rehearsals in a tactful, respectful way.	O	O	O	O	O
k. . . . achieves excellent performances.	O	O	O	O	O
l. . . . based on the above criteria, should be considered for re-engagement.	O	O	O	O	O

3. PLEASE INDICATE YOUR INSTRUMENT GROUP.

BRASS/PERCUSSION/HARP/KEYBOARD	WOODWINDS	VIOLINS I & II	VIOLA/CELLO/BASS
O	O	O	O

ANSWER BLANKS FOR OPTIONAL QUESTIONS (IF NEEDED BY YOUR ORCHESTRA)

4. ①②③④⑤ 5. ①②③④⑤ 6. ①②③④⑤ 7. ①②③④⑤ 8. ①②③④⑤

Wayne State University

WAYNE STATE UNIVERSITY
TESTING AND EVALUATION SERVICES

Enter name of conductor being evaluated.

Used by permission of the International Conference of Symphony and Opera Musicians.

APPENDIX 7

GLOSSARY

Conductors must have reference books and use them whenever necessary. The following list is not intended to replace the use of a reference library; instead, it is intended as a checklist of frequently used terms and symbols having to do with mechanics of the score, tempo, and style.

accelerando (accel.) Increase tempo.
adagio Slowly.
a due (a²) Both performers. Follows a section with only one performer on the part. a³, a⁴, etc., are also used.
affrettando (affrett.) Quicken the tempo.
agitato Excited, agitated.
allargando (allarg.) Becoming broader, slowing.
alle, alles All, every.
allegretto Moderately fast.
allegro Quick, rapid tempo.
allein Solo, alone.
allmählich Gradually.
al niente Diminish the sound to nothing.
ancora Again.
andante Moderately slow.
animando With growing animation. ***Animato, animé,*** animated.
arpeggiando (arpeg.) Roll the chord in harp style.
arrêt Stop.
a tempo Resume the original tempo.
attacca Begin the next section without pausing.
belebend With growing animation. ***Belebt,*** animated.
bestimmt Energetic.
bewegt Agitated. ***Bewegter,*** more agitated.
Blech Brass instruments.
bouché Muted French horn, using hand. Indicated by a +.
breit Broadly.
chiuso Muted French horn, using hand.
colla parte In unison with another part; for example, ***col. vln,*** with violins. Commonly used in jazz scores.
come prima Like the first time.
con With.
coro Chorus. (Not to be confused with *corno,* horn.)

da capo (DC) Return to the beginning.
dämpfer Mute. ***Mit Dämpfer,*** with mute. ***Ohne Dämpfer,*** without mute.
doppio movimento Double tempo.
en animant With increasing animation.
enchainez Continue to next section without pausing. As, *attacca.*
en dehors In front of; with emphasis; to be clearly heard through the ensemble.
erste First; for example, ***erste Mal,*** first time; ***erstes Tempo,*** first tempo.
espansione Broadening.
fiero Fiercely.
Flatterzunge Flutter tongue. Make a rapid articulation, similar in sound to a rolled *r.*
gestopft Muted French horn, using hand.
giusto Moderately.
glissando (glissez, glisser) Slide.
gradamente Gradually.
grave Slowly, solemn.
Holz Woodwinds.
immer Always; for example, ***immer in Tempo,*** always in tempo.
laissez vibrer (LV) Let vibrate, do not dampen (for harp, percussion, keyboard, etc.).
langsam Slowly.
largamente Broadly.
largo Very slowly.
lebhaft Lively.
légèrement Lightly.
lent (lentamente, lento) Slowly.
LH Left hand.
l'istesso The same (from ***lo stesso***).
l'istesso tempo The same tempo.
marcato Marked, with emphasis.
mässig Moderate.
meno Less.
mezzo Half.
MM Maelzel metronome; tempo indication; the number of beats per minute, expressed in a specific note value; e.g., MM ♩ = 72.
moderato Moderately.
modéré Moderate tempo.
modo Style.
modo ordinario In the usual manner (usually following a passage in a special style).
molto Much, very.
morendo Dying away.
mosso Movement, agitated.
moto Motion.
mouvement (mouvt.) Tempo.
muta, mutando Change; usually to indicate a change in tuning of an instrument or instruments, or a change from one instrument to another (such as flute to piccolo). Not to be confused with ***mute.***
nach After, behind.
nach gebend Becoming slower.
niente Nothing. ***A niente,*** fade away to silence.
ohne Dämpfer Without mute.
ordinario (ordinare) Return to previous method of performance (usually following instructions for a special technique).
ossia Otherwise (refers to an alternative part).
otez Remove.
parlante Sung in a speaking style.
Partitur The score.

perdendosi Gradually dying away.
petit Little.
peu A little.
piacere At the performer's pleasure.
pieno Full.
più More.
più mosso More motion; increase the tempo.
poco Little.
poco a poco Little by little.
portando la voce Vocal glissando, sliding smoothly from one note to the next.
premier mouvement (Ier mouvt.) At the original tempo. Also, ***erster Tempo, Tempo I, a tempo.***
presto Very quick tempo.
Pult Desk or stand, referring to the number of stands of performers for a part.
rallentando (rall.) Growing slower.
retenu Held back.
RH Right hand.
ritardando (ritard, rit.) Gradually slowing.
ritenuto More immediate slowing of tempo.
rubato Expressive flexibility of tempo.
ruhig Quietly, tranquil.
sans timbres Without snares (percussion).
scherzando Playfully.
schmachtend Languid, languishing.
schnell Quickly, fast.
secco, sec Dry, simple. In percussion: dampen; do not let ring.
seconda volta Second time.
segue Proceed to next section without pause. Sometimes indicates continuation of a style.
sehr Very.
sempre Always.
senza Without. ***Senza sordino,*** without mute.
sforzando, sforzato (sf, sfz) Form of attack; emphasis.
simile (sim.) In a similar manner.
smorzando (smorz.) Dying away.
sordino Mute. ***Con sordino,*** with mute. ***Senza sordino,*** without mute.
sostenuto, sostenendo Sustained.
sotto voce "Under the voice"; in a soft voice or undertone.
soutenu Sustained.
staccato Separated.
stentando, stentato (stent.) Delaying, holding back.
stesso movimento Same tempo (same as ***l'istesso tempo***).
Stimme Voice or voice part.
Stimmung Tuning.
stringendo (string.) Quickening of tempo.
subito (sub.) Immediate, suddenly.
suivez Follow. Indicates where a soloist may take liberties.
supra Above. Indicates crossing hands in piano music.
tacet, tacit Silent.
tempo primo At original tempo.
tenuto (ten.) Sustained, held back.
tranquillo Calmly, quietly.

tremolo Quick repetition of the same note; or quick repetition between different pitches, such as E and G.

très Very.

trill Rapid, usually unmeasured alternation between notes of different pitch, half-step or whole-step intervals.

troppo Too much. ***Non troppo,*** not too much.

tutti All, the entire ensemble.

vide Empty. Cut, indicated by ***vi***... at the beginning of the cut and ...***de*** at the end of the cut.

vivace (vivo) Quickly, lively.

wüthend Furiously.

Zeitmass Tempo.

zurückhaltend Ritard.

APPENDIX 8

BIBLIOGRAPHY: RECOMMENDED READINGS

CONDUCTING

Adler, Samuel. *Choral Conducting: An Anthology.* New York: Holt, Rinehart, and Winston, 1971.

Bamberger, Carl. *The Conductor's Art.* New York: McGraw-Hill, 1965.

Bowles, Michael A. *The Art of Conducting.* Garden City, N.Y.: Doubleday, 1959.

Braithwaite, Warick. *The Conductor's Art.* London: Williams and Norgute, 1952.

Davison, Archibald T. *Choral Conducting.* Cambridge, Mass.: Harvard University Press, 1940.

Decker, Harold A., and Julius Herford. *Choral Conducting Symposium.* 2d ed. Englewood Cliffs, N.J.: Prentice-Hall, 1988.

Decker, Harold A., and Colleen J. Kirk. *Choral Conducting: Focus on Communication.* Englewood Cliffs, N.J.: Prentice-Hall, 1988.

Dishinger, Christian. *A Conductor's Daily Warm-Ups.* Lebanon, Ind.: Studio PR, 1976.

Ehret, Walter. *The Choral Conductor's Handbook.* London: Augener, 1959.

Fuchs, Peter Paul. *The Psychology of Conducting.* New York: MCA Music, 1969.

Garretson, Robert. *Conducting Choral Music.* 5th ed. Boston: Allyn and Bacon, 1981.

Green, Elizabeth A. H. *The Modern Conductor.* 4th ed. Englewood Cliffs, N.J.: Prentice-Hall, 1987.

Green, Elizabeth A. H., and Nicolai Malko. *The Conductor's Score.* Englewood Cliffs, N.J.: Prentice-Hall, 1987.

Grosbayne, Benjamin. *Techniques of Modern Orchestral Conducting.* 2d ed. Cambridge, Mass.: Harvard University Press, 1973.

Haberlin, John. *Mastering Conducting Techniques.* Champaign, Ill.: Mark Foster Music, 1977.

Heffernan, Charles W. *Choral Music: Technique and Artistry.* Englewood Cliffs, N.J.: Prentice-Hall, 1982.

Jones, Archie M. *Techniques of Choral Conducting.* New York: Carl Fischer, 1948.

Kahn, Emil. *Conducting.* New York: Macmillan, 1965.

Kirk, Theron W. *Choral Tone and Technique.* Westbury, N.Y.: Pro-Art, 1956.

Labuta, Joseph. *Basic Conducting Techniques.* 2d ed. Englewood Cliffs, N.J.: Prentice-Hall, 1984.

Leinsdorf, Erich. *The Composer's Advocate.* New Haven: Yale University Press, 1981.

Long, R. Gerry. *The Conductor's Workshop.* Dubuque, Iowa: Brown, 1971.

Malko, Nicolai. *The Conductor and His Baton.* Copenhagen: Hansen, 1950.

Matthay, Tobias. *Musical Interpretation.* Westport, Conn.: Greenwood, 1977.

McElheran, Brock. *Conducting Technique.* New York: Oxford University Press, 1966.

Prausnitz, Frederik. *Score and Podium: A Complete Guide to Conducting.* New York: Norton, 1983.

Ross, Allan A. *Techniques for Beginning Conductors.* Belmont, Calif.: Wadsworth, 1976.

Rudolf, Max. *The Grammar of Conducting.* 2d ed. New York: Schirmer Books, 1980.

Saminsky, Lazanz. *Essentials of Conducting.* London: Dennis Dobson, 1958.

Simons, Harriet. *Choral Conducting: A Leadership Teaching Approach.* Champaign, Ill.: Mark Foster Music, 1978.

Thomas, Kurt. *The Choral Conductor.* Translated by Alfred Mann and William H. Reese. New York: Associated Music Publishers, 1971.

Walter, Bruno. *Of Music and Music-Making.* New York: Norton, 1961.

Scherchen, Hermann. *Handbook of Conducting.* London: Oxford University Press, 1942.

Stanton, Royal. *The Dynamic Choral Conductor.* Delaware Water Gap, Pa.: Shawnee, 1971.

OF HISTORICAL INTEREST

Berlioz, Hector. *The Orchestral Conductor.* New York: Carl Fischer, 1923.

Wagner, Richard. *On Conducting.* London: William Reeves, 1897.

MUSICAL FORM

Berry, Wallace. *Form in Music.* Englewood Cliffs, N.J.: Prentice-Hall, 1966.

Burkhart, Charles. *Anthology for Musical Analysis.* New York: Holt, Rinehart, and Winston, 1964.

Cone, Edward T. *Musical Form and Musical Performance.* New York: Norton, 1968.

Green, Douglas. *Form in Tonal Music.* New York: Holt, Rinehart, and Winston, 1965.

Leichentritt, Hugo. *Musical Form.* Cambridge, Mass.: Harvard University Press, 1951.

Stein, Erwin. *Form and Performance.* New York: Knopf, 1952.

Stein, Leon. *Anthology of Musical Forms.* Evanston, Ill.: Summy-Birchard, 1962.

INSTRUMENTS

Bartlett, Harry R., and Ronald A. Holloway. *Guide To Teaching Percussion.* Dubuque, Iowa: Brown, 1971.

Farkas, Philip. *The Art of Brass Playing.* Bloomington, Ind.: Brass Publications, 1962.

Galamian, Ivan. *Principles of Violin Playing.* Englewood Cliffs, N.J.: Prentice-Hall, 1962.

Green, Elizabeth A. H. *Orchestral Bowings and Routines.* Ann Arbor, Mich.: Campus Publishers, 1957.

Hunt, Norman. *Guide To Teaching Brass.* Dubuque, Iowa: Brown, 1968.

VOICE

Corlomi, Evelina. *Singers' Italian.* New York: G. Schirmer, 1960.

Cox, Richard G. *The Singer's Manual of German and French Diction.* New York: Schirmer Books, 1970.

Errole, Ralph. *Italian Diction for Singers.* Boulder, Colo.: Pruett, 1963.

Marshall, Madeline. *The Singer's Manual of English Diction.* New York: Schirmer Books, 1957.

Waring, Fred. *Tone Syllables.* Delaware Water Gap, Pa.: Shawnee, 1951.

ORCHESTRATION AND ARRANGING

Adler, Samuel. *The Study of Orchestration.* New York: Norton, 1982.

Bartolozzi, Bruno. *New Sounds for Woodwinds.* London: Oxford University Press, 1967.

Bennett, Robert Russell. *Instrumentally Speaking.* Melville, N.Y.: Belwin-Mills, 1975.

Berlioz, Hector. *Treatise on Instrumentation.* Revised and enlarged by Richard Strauss. Translated by Theodore Front. New York: Kalmus, 1948.

Blatter, Alfred. *Instrumentation/Orchestration.* New York: Longman, 1980.

Forsyth, Cecil. *Orchestration.* 2d ed. New York: Macmillan, 1935.

Garcia, Russell. *The Professional Arranger-Composer.* New York: Criterion Music, Book I, 1954; Book II, 1979.

Jacob, Gordon. *The Elements of Orchestration.* London: Jenkins, 1962. Reprint, Westport, Conn.: Greenwood, 1976.

Kennan, Kent. *The Technique of Orchestration.* 2d ed. Englewood Cliffs, N.J.: Prentice-Hall, 1970.

Leibowitz, René, and Jan Maguire. *Thinking For Orchestra.* New York: Schirmer Books, 1960.

Piston, Walter. *Orchestration.* New York: Norton, 1955.

Read, Gardner. *Style and Orchestration.* New York: Schirmer Books, 1979.

Rimsky-Korsakov, Nicolai. *Principles of Orchestration.* New York: Kalmus, 1954. (First published 1912.)

Wagner, Joseph. *Orchestration.* New York: McGraw-Hill, 1959.

MUSIC LIBRARIES

Byrne, Frank A., Jr. *A Practical Guide to the Music Library.* Cleveland, Ohio: Ludwig Music, 1987.

SCORE READING

Fiske, Roger. *Score Reading.* 3 vols. London: Oxford University Press, 1958.

Grunow, Richard F., and James O. Froseth. *MLR Instrumental Score Reading Program.* Chicago: G.I.A. Publications, 1979.

Jacob, Gordon. *How to Read a Score.* London: Boosey and Hawkes, 1944.

Melcher, Robert A., and Willard F. Warch. *Music for Score Reading.* Englewood Cliffs, N.J.: Prentice-Hall, 1971.

Morris, R. O., and Howard Ferguson. *Preparatory Exercises in Score Reading.* London: Oxford University Press, 1931.

TWENTIETH-CENTURY COMPOSITION

Cope, David. *New Music Composition.* New York: Schirmer Books, 1977.

Dallin, Leon. *Techniques of Twentieth-Century Composition.* 3d ed. Dubuque, Iowa: Brown, 1974.

Perle, George. *Serial Composition and Atonality.* 4th ed. Berkeley: University of California Press, 1977.

Timm, Everett L. *The Woodwinds: Performance and Instructional Techniques.* Boston: Allyn and Bacon, 1964.

Westphal, Frederick W. *Guide to Teaching Woodwinds.* Dubuque, Iowa: Brown, 1962.

Winter, James Hamilton. *The Brass Instruments: Performance and Instructional Techniques.* Boston: Allyn and Bacon, 1964.

MUSICAL THEATER AND OPERA

Engel, Lehman. *Planning and Producing the Musical Show.* New York: Crown, 1966.

Rich, Maria, ed. *Directory of Sets and Costumes for Rent, Opera Companies and Other Sources.* New York: Central Opera Service Bulletin, 1970.

Simon's Directory of Theatrical Materials, Services and Information. New York: Package Publicity Services, 1970.

JAZZ ENSEMBLES

Dobbins, Bill. *The Contemporary Jazz Pianist.* Jamestown, R.I.: GAMT Music, 1978.

Ferguson, Tom, and Sandy Feldstein. *The Jazz-Rock Ensemble: A Conductor's and Teacher's Guide.* Port Washington, N.Y.: Alfred, 1976.

Haerle, Dan. *The Jazz Language: A Theory Text.* Lebanon, Ind.: Studio 224, 1980.

Lawn, Richard. *The Jazz Ensemble Director's Manual.* Oskaloosa, Iowa: Barnhouse, 1981.

Shaw, Kirby. *Vocal Jazz Style.* Milwaukee, Wis.: Hal Leonard, 1976.

Wright, Rayburn. *Inside the Score.* Delevan, N.Y.: Kendor, 1982.

APPENDIX 9

REFERENCES

Apel, Willi. *Harvard Dictionary of Music.* 2d ed. Cambridge, Mass.: Harvard University Press, 1969.

Davidson, James. *Dictionary of Protestant Church Music.* Metuchen, N.J.: Scarecrow, 1975.

Donington, Robert. *A Performance Guide to Baroque Music.* London: Faber and Faber, 1978.

Evans, Peter. *The Music of Benjamin Britten.* Minneapolis: University of Minnesota Press, 1979.

Hartog, Howard. *European Music in the Twentieth Century.* London: Routledge and Paul, 1957.

Hawkins, Margaret B. *An Annotated Inventory of Distinctive Choral Literature for Performance at the High School Level.* ACDA monograph, 1976.

Heyer, Anna Harriet. *Historical Sets, Collected Editions, and Monuments of Music: A Guide to Their Contents.* Chicago, Ill.: American Library Association, 1969.

Ingram, Madeline D., and William C. Rice. *Vocal Techniques for Children and Youth.* Nashville, Tenn.: Abingdon, 1962.

Jacobs, Ruth Krehbiel. *Philosophy in a New Key.* Cambridge, Mass.: Harvard University Press, 1974.

Jacobs, Ruth Krehbiel. *The Successful Children's Choir.* Chicago, Ill.: FitzSimons, 1984.

Laster, J., comp. *Catalogue of Choral Music Arranged in Biblical Order.* Metuchen, N.J.: Scarecrow, 1981.

May, James D. *Avant-Garde Choral Music: An Annotated Selected Bibliography.* Metuchen, N.J.: Scarecrow, 1977.

Nordone, Thomas R., James H. Nye, and Mark Resnick. *Choral Music in Print.* Vol. 1, *Sacred Music;* Vol. 2, *Secular Music.* Philadelphia, Pa.: Musicdata, 1974–1982. (Supplements: 1976, 1981, 1982.)

Roberts, Kenneth C. *A Checklist of Twentieth Century Choral Music for Male Voices.* Detroit, Mich.: Information Coordinators, 1970.

Sadie, Stanley, ed. *New Grove Dictionary of Music and Musicians.* London: Macmillan, 1980.

Smither, Howard E. *History of Oratorio.* 2 vols. Chapel Hill, N.C.: University of North Carolina Press, 1977.

Steinitz, Paul. *Bach's Passions: Masterworks of Choral Music.* Peter Dodd, general ed. London: Paul Elek, 1979.

Terry, Charles Sanford. *Bach's Orchestra.* London: Oxford University Press, 1932.
Terry, Charles Sanford. *J. S. Bach Cantata Texts, Sacred and Secular.* London: Constable, 1926.
Tortolano, William. *Original Music for Men's Voices: A Selected Bibliography.* Metuchen, N.J.: Scarecrow, 1981.
Tufts, Nancy Poore. *The Children's Choir.* Vol. 2. Philadelphia, Pa.: Fortress, 1965.
Ulrich, Homer. *A Survey of Choral Music. The Harcourt History of Musical Forms.* New York: Harcourt Brace Jovanovich, 1973.
Vinquist, Mary, and Neal Zaslaw. *Performance Practice: A Bibliography.* New York: Norton, 1971.
Vinton, John. *Dictionary of Contemporary Music.* New York: Dutton, 1974.
White, J. P. *Twentieth Century Choral Music.* Metuchen, N.J.: Scarecrow, 1984.

INDEXES

INDEX OF COMPOSERS

SUBJECT INDEX